Bridges
to
Freedom

CREATING CHANGE THROUGH SCIENCE AND CHRISTIAN SPIRITUALITY

Don Straub, M.A, CCC

LifeRich PUBLISHING®

LifeRich Publishing is a registered trademark of The Reader's Digest Association, Inc.

LifeRich Publishing books may be ordered through booksellers or by contacting:

LifeRich Publishing
1663 Liberty Drive
Bloomington, IN 47403
www.liferichpublishing.com
1 (888) 238-8637

Picture taken by: Cyndee Banister

ISBN: 978-1-4897-2995-8 (sc)
ISBN: 978-1-4897-2996-5 (hc)
ISBN: 978-1-4897-2998-9 (e)

Library of Congress Control Number: 2020913157

Print information available on the last page.

LifeRich Publishing rev. date: 07/27/2020

Jesus replied, "I tell you the truth,
everyone who sins is a slave of sin."
John 8:34

"And you will know the truth,
and the truth will set you free."
John 8:32

Contents

About the Author

Don Straub writes from the perspective of a clinical counselor who daily helps people with common emotional and relationship problems. Many people, however, are afraid of counseling. As a result, they suffer needlessly or wait too long before they seek help. Don's counseling draws on a lifetime of experiences. He has been a teacher of elementary through secondary grades, a school principal, a pastor, and now a clinical counselor. He has a master's level education in both education and professional counseling, taken through Christian universities. Don has traveled the world and worked in several cultures, including more than two years in Africa. He shares stories of trials and heartbreak he has endured as well as miracles he has witnessed. He believes that his goal as a counselor is to help people help themselves by providing them with the tools that are described in his book, *Bridges to Freedom*.

Dedication

I dedicate this book to the four people
who call me Dad;

two step sons;

the eleven
who call me Grandpa, Papa, Gee Pa, or Grampy;

my wife Juanita,
who was the first person to read each chapter,
encouraged me to keep going,
and created the illustrations for my book, including the cover;

my friend Doug,
who was the second person to read each chapter,
and gave me constructive feedback;

and the hundreds of clients
who I have had the privilege to serve.

Foreword

In a world where freedom is sought after, Don practically balances the psychological and spiritual components that lead us all toward change. He addresses relevant topics, calling the reader toward making changes in their lives all while backing up the change process with professional experience, personal stories, and research. A great read for both practitioners and anyone wanting to find freedom.

Bradley Bender, MDIV, MAC, CCC - Counselor/Pastor of Trinity Church Kelowna, BC

Bridges to Freedom is a user-friendly manual to becoming the happy and whole person you want to be. Experienced mental health therapist and author, Don Straub, writes with confidence and humility, sharing what he has discovered from both his achievements and his disasters over a lengthy and wide-ranging career dedicated to serving God and helping others. Having earlier been successful as a high school biology teacher and as a pastor, Straub is completely at home with science and Biblical spirituality. He shares practical psychotherapeutic principles and methods that flow from both of these powerful sources. Don't just read this book. Use it as a basic guide for what to do next as you grow into the person you are meant to be.

Bruce B. Boyd, DMin (Doctor of Ministry with an emphasis on conflict transformation, professor emeritus of Religious Studies at Burman University, retired Certified Christian Conciliator and pastor)

"Don Straub knows himself, knows psychology, knows human experience, and most of all, he knows God. This is the best of all the Christian psychotherapeutic books I have read. Straub uniquely blends his knowledge base with experience as a true Christian counselor. I have known Don for nearly 50 years as a genuine person. You can trust his knowledge and his insight into psychology, counseling, spirituality, and life generally. If you want to develop or maintain an integrated personality, this book read carefully, thoughtfully, and perhaps slowly, will strengthen your purpose and meaning in life."

D. Douglas Devnich Ed. D. (Doctor of Education, retired pastor, church administrator, hospital chaplain)

"What a much needed resource! As an educator, psychotherapist, teacher, principal, parent, and pastor, Don knows people. His depth pf understanding complex situations is showcased, and this book will help anyone who is seeking guidance to overcome life's challenges. If you are yearning for freedom from emotional hurt, you must read this book!"

James LaLonde (Psychotherapist, Manager of Recovery and Addictions)

Preface

After returning from Africa with four small motherless children, people started asking me when I was going to write a book about my experiences. I am a retired teacher and pastor. After early retirement, I obtained a Master of Arts in Professional Counseling. I began to do a lot of workshops: "Marriage," "Depression and Anxiety," "Assertiveness," and my favorite, "Bridges to Freedom." Attendees kept asking me when I was going to write a book. I have never had a desire to write a book. The fact is that I was afraid to write a book. It seemed like a daunting, time-consuming project.

One night, I had a dream, woke up, and decided to write a book. Before I'd even gotten out of bed, I had the title— *Bridges to Freedom: Creating Change through Science and Christian Spirituality.* In addition to my workshop, my private practice in counseling is also called Bridges to Freedom.

I discovered that the book just entailed writing the information that I share in my workshops and with my private clients every day of my daily work life. I was also able to weave in parts of my life story. The level of Christian teaching in this book is elementary in nature, and I have kept the level of the science of psychology to what I use when counseling clients, though I have been told by some trusted professionals who've read this book that it is a useful resource for Christian counselors as well.

Over the past ten years, I have read more than a hundred books in the field of psychology, many of them written by Christian authors. Each book covers one specific topic in depth. My own library has multiple books on each topic. All of these books have provided many insights that I share with my clients. In this book, I share these insights, each one forming one of the bridges to freedom. I hope that by touching on several insights, readers will enjoy a better life in many dimensions. My clients are sincere people who are seeking self-understanding or attempting to find meaning in life. If you would like to dig deeper, I have included a list of my favorite books on each bridge to freedom at the end of the book.

Introduction - The Big Picture

This book interweaves three aspects:

1. A Christian spiritual perspective of human thinking, emotion, and behavior based on Scripture.
2. A scientific perspective on human thinking, emotion, and behavior based on scientific research.
3. My life story.

My life story is not told in chronological order. I share parts of my life as it fits with the topics covered. My topics follow an order designed to unfold in a way that helps the reader's understanding grow progressively. Each topic provides insights needed to help understand the topics that follow.

Because my life story is told by going back and forth in time, it might get confusing to the reader at times. I talk about each of my three wives by name, Nellie, Penny, and Juanita. I talk about life in Africa and life in Canada before and after Africa. I mention stories from two other trips I made to visit Africa as well. Following is an outline of my life in chronological order, which provides the big picture:

Part One

*1951 to 1973

*My birth through graduation from college

*Born and raised in Canada, but completed my bachelor's degree in science and religious studies in the US

Part Two

*1973 to 1982

*Married to Nellie in 1973, son Kerry born in 1975, son Kris born and adopted in 1977, daughter Leanne born in 1978, and daughter Jody born in 1979

*Taught elementary school in a small multi-grade school, 1973 to 1974

*Taught junior high school, 1974 to 1978; completed a Fifth Year Diploma (the equivalent of a master's level degree) in education and psychology in 1978

*Taught senior high school science and religion, 1978 to 1980

*Traveled in the Netherlands, Belgium, Switzerland, Kenya, Tanzania, Burundi, and Rwanda

*Taught senior high school science in Africa, 1980 to 1982; wife, Nellie, passed away and was buried in Africa; my four children and I moved back to Canada

Part Three

*1982 to 2004

*Married to Penny 1983 to 2004

*Taught junior high school, 1983 to 1989

*Made my second trip to Africa (a short visit) with a friend in 1983

*Made my third trip to Arica (a short visit) with my daughter Jody in 1999

*Taught senior high school science and religion from 1989 to 2009; principal of a K through 12 school, 2007 to 2009 (overlaps part three and part four)

*Pastor of a new church plant, 1999 to 2009 (overlaps part three and part four)

*Mission trips and travel in England, Germany, Italy, Tanzania x 2, Mexico x 3, Costa Rica x 3, Ukraine, Poland, East Germany, West Germany, and France

*Wife, Penny, passed away in 2004.

Part Four

*2005 to present

*Married to wife, Juanita, with two stepsons, 2005 to present

*Completed a Master's of Arts in Professional Counseling in 2012

*Diagnosed with cancer twice, and beat it back both times

*Mission trips and travel in Philippines, Thailand, Indonesia, Bolivia, Peru, Columbia, Panama, Costa Rica, Nicaragua, Guatemala, Mexico x 2, Italy, Greece, Israel, Egypt, Jordon, Oman, and the United Arab Emirates

*Presently working almost full time as a clinical counselor for a government-funded, live-in addictions program; I also have a private counseling practice named "Bridges to Freedom" (after the workshop I do several times a year).

The Day I Started a Riot on a College Campus

Authenticity—A Bridge to Freedom

"The godly man's life is exciting" (Proverbs 14:14b The Living Bible). The night I randomly opened my Bible and read this verse, I was lying on my back on the lawn of a Christian college in Canada. At the time, I never would've dreamed that my life as a Christian would be so exciting. Since then, I've visited more than thirty countries. I narrowly escaped a terrorist train bombing in Paris, tented with roaring lions in the Serengeti, and went tubing on the piranhas-filled Amazon River. I delivered my firstborn with my own hands at home, performed mime in a public square in Kyiv, Ukraine, and acted the part of Jesus a dozen times in an Easter passion play. I've gone swimming with a dolphin, allowing her to pull me down into the deep water, and then flying out from the surface with her. My son flew me into a remote village in Papa, Indonesia, which was once a region of headhunting cannibals. I've explored the narrow streets of Old Jerusalem, floated on the

Dead Sea, and ridden a camel around the pyramids in Egypt. I certainly haven't lived a boring life.

In my life's journey, I have experienced twenty-two years as a student. I still read and attend seminars to learn and grow. I've been a teacher of elementary grades, secondary science and religion, a school principal, an international missionary, and a pastor of a new church plant. I have been married three times—two of my wives passed away from diseases. I have been diagnosed with cancer twice, and beaten it both times. I am the father of four of my own (one adopted) children and two stepchildren of my wife, Juanita. My eleven grandchildren bring me happiness in this final chapter of my life.

My life experiences have been the best preparation for my current and probably final landing place as a counselor and psychotherapist. I have a specialty in marriage counseling through the Gottman Institute, and other specialties in treating trauma and addiction. I supervise student counselors at a master's degree level for various universities. My clients tell me heart-wrenching stories that are often X-rated for violence, sex, and coarse language. Helping people completely turn their lives around is both gratifying and challenging.

An Unexpected Phone Call

"Don, I just received a phone call from the president of a college in Canada reporting that you have started a riot on their campus. He's demanding that I get you back home immediately!"

It was the voice of the dean of Student Affairs of my college back in the US.

"But I trust you, Don, so I'm asking that you not return until you first make peace with that college."

The dean was quite familiar with what we had been up to because he'd been one of the faculty who'd sat crossed-legged on the floor of our student life building during our evening Bible studies.

My exciting life as a Christ follower began in the early 1970s when there was a revival on our college campus in the US. It was at the time of the "Jesus Freak" movement that crossed America. As a confessed Jesus freak, on weekends I was on the streets of our local city witnessing for Jesus, and handing out our underground newspaper called *Truth*. In it were testimonies and news reports about revivals breaking out on high school and college campuses.

I was a part of a small group who accepted a special invitation from my pastor in Canada. We were invited to share our testimonies at a province-wide youth rally. At that rally, a couple of staff members from a nearby Christian college asked us to come to their campus and speak to the students. No one had any idea that one evening would turn that campus on fire for God. We went overtime with our evening worship in the college chapel. Then students kept asking questions and wanted to hear more, so we took up their study time. After that, the conversation resumed outside on the lawn, far past their curfew. Students were hugging one another, confessing things like shoplifting, and making plans to return to the stores to make things right. There were tears of repentance mixed with joy and laughter, and students openly praising God. The night watchman didn't know what to do with the breaking of curfew and the mixing of genders at such an "unearthly" hour of the night! The college administration heard about what was happening. This is what prompted the unexpected phone call from the dean of my college regarding the "riot" we had started.

Our Trip to Canada

How we'd ended up in Canada and this situation was quite miraculous. Five of us started from our college, driving a Chevy Nova pulling a U-Haul trailer to accommodate our luggage and musical instruments, which included a colossal bass violin. On the way to Canada, we began to have car trouble. We had no idea what to do, but we were driving by a Christian high school that one of us had attended, so we pulled in to say hello and ask for help. Upon finding out what we were doing, they invited us to hold an assembly with the students and share our stories and music. Some of the faculty were impressed by how the students responded; one of them insisted that we use her more powerful Mustang to continue our journey north. She also insisted that we get some sleep at her place, and then leave early in the morning in order to make it to our Canadian destination on time.

We arrived at the Canadian border just as it was opening for the day, only to discover that they were not willing to let us cross into Canada. The problems were that someone had loaned us the car and the trailer had been rented in the US. They also seemed to doubt our story about why we were traveling to Canada, so we got out the musical instruments, took them inside, and sang them a couple of our songs. We impressed them enough to let us through, with the promise that we check in with them on our way back to the US with the same car, U-Haul, and musical instruments. If we failed to do so within an allotted period, there would be severe repercussions.

Riot or Revival?

Now, there we were in the middle of a riot, or revival, depending on who you talked to. And we'd been given the responsibility to repair the relationship between the two colleges. The Canadian college thought we were involved in a creative attempt to recruit students to our college in the US. We discovered that this was the reason none of the students had been allowed to attend the earlier province-wide youth rally. A couple of their staff, however, had attended. Recruiting students had never crossed our minds. We also realized that this new revival would need a bit of guidance to keep it going and help it to grow. Starting a revival is like starting an acetylene torch. To start an acetylene torch, one needs to first reduce the oxygen supply. This produces a bright yellow showy flame, which is not very useful except to warm up the head of the torch. Once warm, oxygen can then be added to bring the large flashy flame down to a small, almost invisible blue flame that can cut steel. If you add the oxygen too soon and too fast, the flame pops out, and you need to start over again.

Revivals usually start as a tremendously showy experience, but if it isn't nurtured carefully, it can quickly fade out. This leads to people questioning what happened. We felt that we needed to stay and educate the students on how to keep the revival going by having a steady, daily relationship with God.

But the borrowed car, the U-Haul trailer, and the musical instruments needed to be at the border soon. Three of our team members headed for the border and back to our college. Two of us stayed behind. We spoke in a few religion classes at some teachers' requests, and at another joint student worship. The intent was to accomplish our mission of keeping the revival from dying out. We were still called, however, to give an account of ourselves to the college disciplinary committee.

It was a late-evening meeting, and we stood in front of a large group of faculty members. Each of us gave our testimony, explaining why we had ended up at their college campus. We'd had no idea that it would have such an effect on their students. We ended the meeting by singing the traditional closing song we'd sing at our Bible studies back home. We asked them to all join hands in a big circle while we sang a song about joining hands in heaven and singing songs together. As we sang, I slowly looked into the eyes of the faculty around the circle, and I could see a mixture of frowns and smiles. We left the meeting knowing that they would then have a long debate about the student leaders' request to hold their own optional Bible studies following the mandatory daily worship time. It turned out well as they granted the request.

At the end of the week, our driver returned with his Nova to bring us back home. Before leaving, we went to the college cafeteria to pay our food bill, but the head cook told us that the college president had told him that our bill had been paid in full. After that, we stopped at the president's home to thank him. He and his wife left their dinner table and knelt in their living room to pray for us. Peace was achieved, and then we were on our way home.

After driving all night, we arrived back on our campus. I quickly discovered that my boss was angry with me for not showing up at work, and one of my teachers didn't know what to do because I'd missed his midterm exam. I had instructed one of the guys who'd returned early to communicate my situation to my boss and my teacher. He must have forgotten. The dean informed me that my name was coming up before the disciplinary committee that evening because of it. I explained the entire story to the dean, so he could relay it to the committee. The next day, when I reported to work, my boss was smiling, praised me for what happened, and gladly let me continue with my job. Likewise, my teacher congratulated me, and allowed me to write the exam at my convenience. All was well again. "The godly man's life is exciting" (Proverbs 14:14b TLB).

Hypocrisy or Authenticity

It was not my first encounter with the frailties of organized religion, nor would it be my last. For the most part, I have weathered these occurrences with the help of a parable that I first heard in the early 1970s (Venden 1994). You can insert whatever vehicle you might covet. Mine is the fully electric and potentially self-driven Tesla, which I will probably never own. I know that Tesla are not sold at dealerships, but here is the illustration anyway.

I receive a flyer in the mail stating that the local car dealer is giving away five free Tesla to the first five people who walk through their doors for a test drive the next morning. I get up at three in the morning to be sure to get into line. There I am, one of the first five people in line. My Tesla is in my hands! But then I begin to look around at who else is going to get a free Tesla. I recognize some of them, and know them to be hypocrites. The more I ruminate on these hypocrites, the angrier I become. Finally, I think, "If that's the kind of people they're going to give a free Tesla to, I don't want one!" and so I go home without one.

> Don't let the hypocrites cause you to give up on God.

It's easy to get fixated on the hypocrites in the church. And yet they have been around since the mixed multitude that left Egypt with Moses (see Exodus 12:38). They were also there in the days of Jesus (see Matthew 6:5). Hypocrites outwardly claim to be something they know they are not. To them, it is all about public appearances.

In the field of psychology, this phenomenon is known as personas, imposters, or people who wear masks. We all wear masks at times, like when we want to put our best foot forward on a first date, at a job interview, or when we go to church. But masks get too heavy to wear day after day. Imposters are people pleasers. They cannot say "no" with the same confidence as they can say "yes." They fear not living up to the expectations of others. They can be extremely driven and are often overachievers. Imposters have huge rejection fears. Imposters are always comparing themselves with others. Psychologically, it's never wise to compare yourself with others because then you will end up feeling either lower or higher than others. Almost everybody does it, but it is not healthy.

> It is never wise to compare yourself with others.

A better approach is to notice how we are different from others, and that it's okay to be unique.

God desires honesty from the heart (see Psalm 51:6). He wants authentic people who allow themselves to be vulnerable and are quick to admit their weaknesses and mistakes. Christ-followers long to share the good news about God with others. If I learned anything from pastoring a new church plant, it's that people want authenticity. Being authentic is a way to find freedom from having to pretend to be someone you are not and the pressure of trying to continually keep up appearances. Authenticity is the only way to achieve real intimacy, "into me see." Worst of all, imposters have no real intimacy with God because they refuse to be their authentic selves with God. Being our authentic selves means accepting the reality of our sinfulness and admitting our imperfections.

I have often heard Christians declare that the church is not a rest home for saints but a hospital for sinners. So why do we have this constant need to appear better than who we are? I believe it is a strong feeling of shame that drives a need to avoid judgment and rejection. I've asked hundreds of people in my therapy groups why one of the top three fears that people have is public speaking. Consistently, they point to fear of rejection or fear of judgment. I believe this is because our greatest need is acceptance, and our greatest fear is rejection. Shame is an icky feeling coming from a sense of not being good enough, smart enough, beautiful enough, strong enough, etc. It's like being naked in public because we feel exposed for who we really are.

> Our greatest need is acceptance and
> our greatest fear is rejection.

Unlike Scripture, the science of psychology differentiates between shame and guilt. I will go into this more deeply in a later chapter, but for now, think of guilt as an emotion you feel when you have truly done something wrong or hurtful. Think of shame as an emotion you feel that is attached to a negative belief you hold about yourself. Both emotions feel the same, but shame is false guilt because you actually never did anything wrong in terms of your behavior. You feel like you are unworthy, unimportant, a failure, ugly, or a loser. Christians deal with guilt and shame differently, instead of lumping them together. We deal with guilt through forgiveness and making amends. We deal with shame by telling ourselves the truth, "I am a child of God," "I am acceptable in God's eyes," or "God sees me as worthy and valuable."

This feeling of shame goes right back to the beginning of sin. Adam and Eve immediately felt guilt and shame, causing them to cover themselves with leaves and hide from God, with whom they'd had a personal relationship up to that moment (see Genesis 3:7-10). How often do Christ-followers get together and become vulnerable enough to confess their sins? "Confess your sins to each other and pray for each other so that you may be healed" (James

5:16a). Even the thought of doing this petrifies most people. Should not the church be the most accepting place on earth? And yet we have so much fear of judgment and rejection. That is the power of shame because we allow judgment and rejection to destroy our true selves.

With the knowledge that I now have about these things, I can look back on that experience in college through a new set of glasses. We had been accused of starting a riot and causing adverse reactions by a few Christian teachers and leaders. We were just inexperienced college students still in our teens and wet behind the ears. Yet God accomplished tremendous things through our simple testimonies. These were outcomes that professionals had been trying to achieve for years but never did. It probably plucked at their chords of insecurity, and generated feelings of not being good enough. This feeling of shame can bring out the worst in us, a very real and human reaction. I have since discovered it in myself as a mature professional. No one is beyond this, but it can be healed through self-awareness. You cannot heal what you do not acknowledge.

God and Church

Don't get God and church mixed up. The church is not God, and God is not the church. After seeing hypocrites in the church, many have said, "Good riddance," to the church and, in the same breath, "Goodbye, God." When I'm tempted to take that route, I focus on those around me who are reflections of God's goodness. In this case, I thought of my pastor, who trusted us to take over a weekend at his church, and trusted me to preach my first sermon at the age of eighteen. Fifty years later, this pastor is now one of my closest friends. I am also grateful for a high school faculty member who lent us her new car, trusting that we would return it in good shape. Then there were the college religion teachers who trusted us to take over entire college classes to share our faith with their students. We would never have made it without the many people who pushed cash into my pocket or my hand to cover our expenses.

Finally, I'm thankful for the college president, who was humble enough to acknowledge his mistake, pay for our food bill, and pray for us. We left our college with a tank of gas and no cash in faith that God would provide, and he did provide through authentic Christians. Don't let the hypocrites cause you to give up your relationship with God. Don't allow your own insecurities and pride to get in the way of allowing God to use whomever or whatever to accomplish what you never could. It is a paradox that until we accept ourselves just as we are, we cannot change. Who are we not to accept ourselves just as we are when God does? "But God showed his great love for us by sending Christ to die for us while we were still sinners" (Romans 5:8). "The free gift of God is eternal life through Christ Jesus our Lord" (Romans 6:23b). Don't let the hypocrites cause you to give up what is rightfully yours. Salvation is not based on what you do or don't do. It is a gift from God.

Authenticity is a bridge to freedom. Be free!

2

Sorry Enough to Quit
Grace – A Bridge to Freedom

One of the challenges we faced when we lived in Africa was a regular shortage of fuel for our car. The closest source of fuel was five to eight hours away, depending on which places had some. Usually, I could fill the tank and get home with little more than enough fuel to get back for another fill-up. This didn't allow me the ability to use the car very much in the area that we lived. For example, we were often called upon to make an emergency trip to take someone to the medical clinic at the bottom of the mountain on which we lived.

One day, I was called to a hut where a fire burned a small child so extensively I couldn't see any skin on his naked body. After his bath, the mother had placed the child by a fire to keep warm. The light cloth that she'd wrapped him in caught fire. Instantly, I knew that this boy would not live, even with the most advanced facilities we had in America. Out of respect for the family's request to help him, I laid him on a large cushion I had brought from home. His eyes were open wide, but he could not make a sound.

I was sure that he might not be able to feel any pain because his nerve endings were gone. I slowly drove him to the clinic and left him there. There are many more stories like this. Most of them, however, are about saved lives.

I came across a rare find in the city market place one day, a fifty-gallon drum for fuel. It cost me half of one month's wages, but it would be a lifesaver. I brought it home to use as a fuel storage supply, and was planning to weld a chain on it so that I could lock it up. One night, some students knocked on my door to report that a suspicious-looking stranger had been hanging around my house. Immediately, I thought of the steel drum. I rushed to the back door, and, sure enough, it was gone. Even though it was empty, it was still quite heavy. I surmised he couldn't have gone far.

Someone sounded the emergency assembly alarm (a steel bar hitting a hanging wheel rim) on campus. Within minutes, we had more than a hundred students combing the surrounding densely treed paths branching out from our house. I was with a group who received information about a man carrying a blue drum on his head. It seemed that we were hot on his trail. It was dark by now, and began to rain heavily. We kept pursuing him for hours, until we finally came to a house where they thought the suspect lived. The students arrested him and brought him immediately back to the school for questioning. These were only high school students, but they do things differently in that part of the world.

After a lengthy interrogation, it became apparent that he was innocent. I felt so bad for dragging this man away from his home that I gave him one of my best shirts as a peace offering, and we released him around three in the morning.

Early the next day, I began walking up the same path we'd been on the previous evening. Someone told me that they'd seen a man named Sibonde carrying a blue drum, so I started asking people if they knew someone by that name. Some of the people that did also reported seeing him carrying a blue steel drum the night before. He was quite well known, so I quickly found his house. He wasn't at home, but next door I met someone who knew his place of work. Sibonde was a manufacturer of *asali amiyah* (sugar cane syrup). I suddenly envisioned my drum, the top sawed off, placed over a fire with boiling sugar cane syrup in it. I would not be able to use it for car fuel.

As we came near Sibonde's place of work, my guide recognized him coming toward us. We stopped, and I asked him a few questions regarding where he was the evening before. He claimed to be at his father's house, pointing in a direction opposite to my house. He seemed extremely nervous and, therefore, guilty. We immediately went to the school. A group of students went to arrest Sibonde and brought him back for trial.

The students used the headmaster's office, and the questioning began. Sibonde contradicted himself several times by changing the story he had told me on the trail. He claimed that he didn't understand my Swahili, but the guide who was with me confirmed that my Swahili had been clear. A couple of hours into the trial, one of the teachers came in to retrieve something from the office filing cabinet. He overheard the conversation, turned to look at Sibonde, and said, "I saw you on the football field last night, and you asked me for directions to the white man's house." It was just minutes before the theft. It was quite apparent that Sibonde was guilty, but he would still not confess.

We took a break at noon, locking Sibonde up in one of the school buildings. After the break, as I was returning to the campus, one of the teachers came to me with a suggestion.

"We know he is guilty. If he doesn't confess and return the drum, we could turn him over to the local courts. The local authorities would beat him, and torture him by sticking needles in his body until he confesses." I felt sick to my stomach. I sat down in despair by the side of the road and considered dropping the charges altogether.

"But," the teacher continued, "we have a better plan. We could get a group of students, surround him with sticks, and threaten to beat him if he doesn't confess. That would save the trouble of taking him to the village." I felt even sicker and struggled with what to do now.

"I've got another idea," I said. "Let me take Sibonde home to meet my family and talk with him. We could explain why we need the drum. Maybe then he'll confess."

They thought I was crazy, but they agreed to go along with it if I allowed a few bodyguards to come as well.

They took Sibonde up to my house with one bodyguard on each side, holding tightly to his arms. Just as we were about to go up the steps of my front porch, he froze and refused to go farther. He claimed that he was afraid we had a gun in the house, and this was a trick to kill him. We finally convinced him we had no gun, and we just wanted to talk.

Once inside, I introduced Sibonde to my wife, Nellie, and my four children, ages two to seven. I then asked my hired helper to stay in the kitchen and keep an eye out for my kids while they played in the backyard. I also asked her to pray while Nellie and I talked to Sibonde in the living room. We told Sibonde why we'd come to Africa. We explained why we needed the drum for the fuel, so we could take people to the medical clinic in emergencies.

Sibonde sat silent and didn't seem to be affected by any of what was said, so Nellie went into the bedroom to get the "gun." She brought back a Swahili Bible. She turned to a passage, handed it to Sibonde, and asked him to read it out loud. "If we say we have no sin, we are only fooling ourselves and refusing to accept the truth. But if we confess our sins, he is faithful and just and will forgive us and cleanse us from every wrong" (1 John 1:8-9).

Sibonde lowered his head and began to cry. Then he told us about how he'd been raised by his grandmother to believe in Jesus, and how he'd left his Christian faith. Then he admitted to taking our drum, and that he was very sorry. He said he wanted to return the drum but was afraid that he would be beaten up by the students from the school. We agreed to release him, and he promised to return the drum in the middle of the night, after the students went to sleep. It was the rainy season, so when it began to rain again we knew it was going to pour for the rest of the night. We gave him an umbrella and the Swahili Bible. We told him to keep them both as a gift from us.

As soon as Sibonde left our home, the bodyguards began to scoff. "He's not sorry. You will never see him again. He'll flee the area, and that will be the end of your drum. You should have either let us take him to the authorities in the village, or let us handle it ourselves."

Nevertheless, Nellie and I felt Sibonde was genuinely sorry, and would return the drum that night. We both agreed that at this point it was no longer about the drum but Sibonde. He could keep the drum for all we cared.

Sibonde knew Jesus as a friend in his younger years. All we did was bring him back to that memory, and he felt sorry enough to admit the theft.

Often, people take a behavioral approach to Christianity. They think we must repent to become a Christian. We must come to Jesus, however, just as we are. Repentance comes after we come to Christ. In fact, repentance is an ongoing process in a Christian's walk with God.

Repentance

Coming to Christ begins with a desire or a searching for something more, something better in life. A knowledge of God and salvation follows this step, but it must be the right knowledge. A wrong knowledge or understanding of salvation usually leads to a behavioral approach in which one reasons that being a Christian is about merely doing the right things and not doing the wrong things. This tends to lead a person off track, and they may give up altogether because of a continuing failure to perform. Or if a person is successful in outward obedience, there's the real danger of living a life apart from a personal relationship with Jesus.

People who have stood up during a call at some Christian meetings may not have come to Christ at all. They may have only come to the preacher. Even if a person has stood up and spoken words like, "I stand before this audience, and I promise never to do certain things again," they may have only come to more promises. If the person is strong, this keeps them from having to come to Christ. An attitude of not needing Jesus develops because of their outward success.

If our knowledge of salvation is based on grace, however, then we realize that we are helpless apart from God. A sense of helplessness leads to surrender and a coming to God "just as I am."

A lot of people who think they have come to Christ may not have come to Christ at all, but only to themselves. A lot of people who believe they've come to Christ have come, but then later they think they haven't because the relationship didn't last. This is one of the biggest dilemmas in the Christian life. I believe there are hundreds of people who have sincerely come to Christ with a great sense of need, and then later become disenchanted because it didn't last.

I suggest a relationship with Christ doesn't last unless we know how to come to him every day. This is the challenge. After a person believes in Christ, they shouldn't think that they really didn't mean it or that their baptism wasn't real. The problem may have been that they didn't know how to stay there—that's all! How to experience this coming to Christ every day is what we need to know.

Repentance is a Gift from God

One thing that happens after a person comes to Christ is repentance. Repentance is doing a U-turn, and going in the opposite direction with your life. Repentance is not something we do to get to Christ. Repentance is a gift—given to us by Christ after we come to him. And yet think of how many Christians have the idea that we repent and forsake our sins to come to Christ. We have them in the wrong order. I can't repent until I have first come to Christ just as I am. I want you to have a clear understanding of what repentance is all about.

Paul talks about two kinds of repentance in 2 Corinthians 7:10 (New International Version): "Godly sorrow brings repentance that leads to salvation and leaves no regret, but worldly sorrow brings death." The sorrow of the world is the sorrow of the behaviorist who is operating purely in the realm of the externals—the dos and the don'ts. When people with worldly sorrow discover that they have done something wrong, they have all kinds of fears: fear of judgment, fear of losing a reputation or a job, fear of condemnation, censorship, or rejection.

Godly sorrow is the sorrow of the person who has a relationship with God—the one who knows a meaningful, dynamic, daily walk with Christ. There is as much difference between the two as night is from the day. One is the sorrow that I have broken the law. The other is the sorrow that I've broken someone's heart. Don't forget this point.

If I am sorry for my sins because I'm afraid I'm not going to make it to heaven, I'm going to get kicked out of school, go to jail, or any other human reason, that is not sorrow, it's fear. But when I'm sorry because I have disappointed my best friend and let that person down, that leads to true repentance. That is real sorrow.

When Jesus becomes your best friend because of your daily communication with him through his Word and prayer, repentance comes naturally and daily. When the enemy succeeds in causing you to do something that you know has brought disappointment to the heart of Christ, it breaks your heart. When you realize that he accepts you back immediately again, without asking any questions, it makes you want to change.

I often ask, "Why do people keep doing the same thing over and over, when it comes to behavior that they don't want to do?" Blank stares always follow this question. No one seems to know the answer, so I share what I have observed over the years through my experience of counseling people with addictions. When I've done something particularly wrong, I feel bad, so now I believe that I need to be punished. Most people have grown up with this idea. Alright, who is going to punish me? Well, I may be the only one who knew I did something wrong. The best way to punish myself is to do it again, so I will feel worse. Now I feel worse, and so to punish myself some more, I do it again. Now I feel even worse. And this becomes the cycle of addiction. At this point, people are nodding their heads like that is exactly how it feels. This puts into words what they have felt all along but couldn't explain.

The devil is behind this. It is the devil who condemns. "Who then will condemn us? Will Christ Jesus? No, for he is the one who died for us and was raised to life for us. Can anything separate us from Christ's love?" (Romans 8:34-35). "For God so loved the world that he gave his only Son so that everyone who believes in him will not perish but have eternal life. God did not send his Son into the world to condemn it, but to save it" (John 3:16-17). Who is it then that condemns? It is not God.

Grace

They brought her to Jesus, hoping to somehow trap him into saying something heretical. I believe that they set the whole thing up to frame her for just this purpose. After all, where was the male partner in all of this?

"We caught this woman in the very act of sexual sin. The law says she should be stoned. What do you say, Jesus?"

Jesus knelt and wrote something in the sand. There is much speculation about what he wrote. Perhaps it was some of the prevalent sins of the crowd that brought her there. Then he provided his answer, "Let the person who has no sin cast the first stone." They all disappeared from the scene.

Jesus then turned to the woman and asked, "Where are your accusers?"

"They are gone," she replied.

"Neither do I condemn you. Go and sin no more." (A summary of John 8:1-11)

"Neither do I condemn you. Go and sin no more." The fact that Jesus didn't condemn this woman made it possible for her to go and sin no more because she didn't have to punish herself. Jesus said, "You don't need punishment; you need power, you need forgiveness, you need grace."

The fact that Jesus doesn't condemn makes change possible.

When I realize the total loving acceptance of a father of love and of Jesus, who came to reveal his character, I no longer need to keep doing the same things to punish myself because he says, "I don't condemn you."

That's where the power comes from—Christ's presence in my life, from which I learn to understand myself and how God sees me. Then this is coupled with the knowledge of what real repentance is all about. It is feeling sorry that I disappointed my best friend. That's why a personal relationship with Jesus day by day is necessary to repentance. You have no repentance without it. And repentance then becomes NOT something that I DO. If I know Jesus, repentance becomes something I can't help doing.

All this translates into human relationships as well. There have been times when I realized that I let my wife or one of my children down. Realizing this drove me to apologize and make amends.

Knowing Jesus, as with getting to know anyone, is a progressive experience. "And this is the way to have eternal life, to know you the only true God, and Jesus Christ, the one you sent to earth" (John 17:3). The word *know* in this verse has the same meaning as the word *know* in Genesis, "And Adam **knew** Eve, his wife, and she conceived, and bare Cain" (Genesis 4:1 King James Version, emphasis mine). It is a very personal, intimate knowing—intimacy—in-to-me-see.

Did you know that repentance is a gift from God? Repentance is no less a gift than our pardon, and it cannot be experienced except as it is given by Christ, just as Christ gives us forgiveness.

"God exalted him at his right hand as Leader and Savior, to give repentance to Israel and forgiveness of sins." (Acts 5:31 English Standard Version). To how many does God want to give repentance? Listen to his heart: "The Lord isn't really being slow about his promise to return, as some people think. No, he is being patient for your sake. He does not want anyone to perish, so he is giving more time for everyone to repent" (2 Peter 3:9).

> Repentance is no less a gift than forgiveness.

What must I do if I desire to be genuinely repentant? I must come to Jesus JUST AS I AM, without delay. "God's kindness is meant to lead you to repentance" (Romans 2:4b ESV). It is his goodness, his kindness in the presence of your ingratitude that breaks your heart.

When working with clients in counseling, especially with those in addiction, the client must feel safe and accepted by the counselor and the staff in the treatment facility. In my work at a live-in addiction treatment program, we make this a priority. There is no judgment, no shaming, only unconditional acceptance. The research shows that a positive relationship between the client and the counselor is far more important to the final outcome than the particular type of treatment used (Meyers 2014). If a church provides an atmosphere of unconditional acceptance and non-judgment, people can grow and change. It's called grace.

The Parable of the Land Owner

Jesus often introduced a parable or story with the words, "For the kingdom of heaven is like. . ." Another way to say this is, "For the character of God is like. . ." One such parable, found in Matthew 20, is about a landowner who needed workers to harvest his vineyard. He went out very early in the morning to the local square, hoping to find enough workers. It would be common in those days to work a twelve-hour day, sunrise to sunset. The employer would go to the town square at about six o'clock in the morning to look for laborers and offer them a fair or typical day's wage.

Some people are keen to work. They are up and ready as soon as the sun comes up. In the story, the landowner was not willing to negotiate the wage. He only says, "I will pay you a fair day's wage." He then sends them out to work. Around nine in the morning, he realizes that he's going to need more workers to finish the job, so he goes back to the square to find more help. There are now more people waiting around, wanting to work. These are the ones who prefer to sleep in, have a hot breakfast, and wait until the chill is off the air before going to the square to find work. But the landowner says to them, "I'll pay you whatever is right if you work the rest of the day," and so they go to work. Maybe they heard about this landowner and knew they could trust him to pay them what was fair.

Again at noon, and again at three in the afternoon, the landowner has to find more workers. These are the ones who not only slept in and had a hot breakfast, they took time to play with the kids and do a few things around the house, probably procrastinating because they weren't that motivated to work all day. Again, he tells them that he will pay them what is fair and puts them to work.

At five in the afternoon, the landowner realizes that with the current number of workers, they're not going to get the job finished before the sun sets. He goes one more time to look for workers in the town square. He finds some milling around and says, "Why haven't you been working today?" Indeed, these people have no good reason for being this late. But they make up a lame excuse: "Because no one hired us." The landowner ignores this and tells them to come and join the others for the last hour of the day. This time, he doesn't even mention a wage at all.

At six in the afternoon, the end of the day, the landowner orders his foreman to have the workers all line up: first the ones who came at five in the afternoon, then the ones at three in the afternoon, then at noon, at nine in the morning, and finally those that came at six in the morning—last in line! The foreman begins to hand out the wages, giving the ones who worked only one hour a full day's wage. When the ones down the line hear this, they probably get excited about what they are going to get paid! But each group of workers gets the very same wage, a fair day's wage. The ones who are paid last start to grumble, and complain to the owner about how unfair this is.

The landowner answers, "Friend, I haven't been unfair! Didn't you agree to work all day for the usual wage? Take it and go. I wanted to pay this last worker the same as you. Is it against the law for me to do what I want with my money? Should you be angry because I am kind?" (Matthew 20:13-15).

God prefers friends than slaves.

The landowner represents God in this parable. The kingdom of God is like a landowner who went out to find laborers. This story is a demonstration of God's grace. Those who worked the full day endured the cold morning and the hot afternoon sun. They had sore muscles and burned skin. Those who came at five in the afternoon arrived just as the sun was going down. The cool evening breeze was now blowing. Why did they even waste their time showing up in the square at such a late hour? It was not fair. Whether you come to God in your teen years or your nineties, in the end, we all get the same gift of eternal life. It is not an earned wage. It's not fair! It's grace.

We are not slaves or even hired help in God's kingdom. God prefers friends. He is a lover and values our relationship with him.

My favorite scripture is when Jesus said, "I no longer call you servants because a master doesn't confide in his servants. Now you are my friends since I have told you everything the Father told me" (John 15:15). Some might say, "But that's Jesus. What about God?" Previous to the above text, in John 14, it says "Phillip said to Jesus, 'Lord, show us the Father, and we will be satisfied.' Jesus replied, 'Phillip, don't you even know who I am, even after all the time I have been with you? Anyone who has seen me has seen the Father! So why are you asking to see him?'" (John 14:8-9).

The Parable of the King Collecting on Debt

Once again, beginning with Matthew 18:23, Jesus said, "The Kingdom of Heaven is like a king who decided to bring his accounts up to date." This time a king represents God. This king brings in those who owe him money to collect from them. One man who is called in owes 10,000 talents. In today's currency, that would be about 20 million dollars! Who could ever pay off that debt on the spot? In fact, who could pay that debt off over time? Even if the interest rate were only three percent, that would be $600,000 per year or $50,000 per month just in interest. Let's say the king says, "Okay, no interest. Only pay me the principle owing." At a payment of $8,333 per month, it would still take two hundred years to pay back. How could any wage earner pay off $20 million in one lifetime? It would be impossible, which is why Jesus chose this excessive amount. The parable illustrates the absolute impossibility of acceptance with God through human effort. And yet, instead of asking to be forgiven the impossible debt, this man begs for extra time, promising to pay him off. How is he ever going to do that? The king, of course, knows better, but he is so moved with compassion, he forgives him the entire debt! Now that is grace.

Shortly after leaving the king, this guy comes across someone who owes him $2,000. This person could not pay the $2,000 right then and there, so he pleads for time to come up with the money. But this creditor has him thrown into prison. Now how is he going to pay the $2,000 sitting in jail? To put that in perspective, this is one ten-thousandth of the debt he once owed the king and had been forgiven. To make that even more understandable, if someone forgave your debt of $10,000, it would be like finding someone afterwards who owes you $1 and making sure you collect on it.

Some very agitated people come to the king to report this man. Perhaps they'd heard about how he had been forgiven a $20 million debt by the king. The king promptly brings him back in to see him. The king reminds him of the amount he had forgiven him, and chastises him for the way he has treated someone else. Then he throws him into prison until he pays off the whole debt.

How often do we, metaphorically speaking, throw people into prison for only a one dollar debt? "I'm not ever going to speak to that person again." "He is such a complainer." "She is such a gossiper." "He is such a hypocrite." "They are so closed-minded." Perhaps a fleet of trucks could not carry all the dollars that you have not been able to forgive.

But what if someone owes you $20 million? How do you let that go? There are things that people do that no amount of money can undo or replace, sexual assault or murder of a loved one, for example. How can a person extend grace in these situations? How can God extend grace in these situations? I will say more about this in the chapter on forgiveness.

> Sin has its own built in consequences.

In Matthew 6:12, Jesus taught us to pray, "Forgive us our sins, just as we have forgiven those who have sinned against us." In other words, "God, forgive me in the same way or to the extent that I forgive others." Grace is a character trait of God, and he wants us to pass it on.

Extending grace doesn't mean there will be no consequences to the actions. There are natural consequences that will happen sooner or later. As parents, teachers, employers, and judges, we must have some boundaries in society to protect the innocent.

Raising four teenagers was quite the adventure. One day, I discovered what looked like dried marijuana in my son's closet. He'd used an iron to dry it. He thought he'd found some fresh plants, but when I took a sample into the police station for inspection, they told me it was only a harmless plant that looked like marijuana. I confronted Kris anyway, asking him why he wanted to use pot. I have never forgotten his answer.

"Well, Dad, I just figured that I could put in some time partying and enjoying life now. Later, I'll ask God to forgive me, and everything will be alright then."

For a few seconds, my mind went blank. How do I respond to this? I finally came out with, "That's right, Kris. God will always, always, always forgive you whenever you ask. Never forget that for as long as you live. If you get drunk or stoned and do something risky or foolish, resulting in the loss of a leg or an arm, God will forgive you, but will not grow the leg or arm back for you. If you get a girl pregnant, he will not make the baby disappear. There are always consequences to every action we take. Are you willing to risk these consequences?" He had nothing to say.

God doesn't have to sit up there, dreaming up consequences for sin. Sin has its own consequences. The consequences don't always come on the heels of sin, but just wait.

I am told that free-falling before pulling the cord of a parachute is quite a thrill. I've been to the 125th floor of the Burj Khalifa in Dubai. It's the tallest building in the world (at this point in time). I could have gone to the 148th floor, but the extra cost wasn't worth it to me.

Let's say that you jump off the 148th floor, and I wave at you passing by me at the 125th floor.

You might say to me, "This is awesome! What a rush! You should try it!"

I would reply, "Just wait!"

In fact, at the 100th floor, it will feel even more thrilling.

But I would reply, "I'm sure it is, but just wait!"

At the 50th floor, you would experience an even greater adrenaline rush.

But all I can say to you is, "Just wait!"

There is a natural law in action—a law that cannot be broken.

Back to Sibonde

Our hired help, Doris, was praying for Sibonde in the kitchen. Nellie and I told Sibonde of God's unconditional love and forgiveness. We even said to him that we no longer cared about our drum, but we cared about him. He could keep the drum if he thought he needed it more than we did. But he still insisted on returning it. When Sibonde left our home, we could see a new spring in his step as he hopped and skipped in the pouring rain with the Bible under his arm and the umbrella over his head. The bodyguards told us that Sibonde took us for a ride, and we would never see him or the drum again.

Of course, the real test would come now that he was a free man. Would he return the drum as he promised? Did he mean what he said in his prayer of repentance and confession?

Nellie and I didn't sleep much that night. We prayed for Sibonde. Almost every hour, I got up and looked out the back window to see if the drum was there yet. Midnight came, still not there. I returned to bed, and we prayed again; two in the morning, three in the morning—no drum. Finally, the sun came up, and still no drum. My heart sank, but I wasn't ready to give up on what I truly believed happened. I dressed and went exploring up the trail towards Sibonde's house. I'd only rounded the first bend in the path, and there in the middle of a small garden, where I couldn't miss it, was my blue drum.

The woman who owned the garden knew the story, and knew that the drum was there for me. Sibonde told her of his fear of the students and the night watchman, so her garden was as far as he would come with it.

Over the next few days, people came by to ask me if I gave Sibonde an umbrella and a Bible. He told them that the white man forgave him and had given him these things to keep. It was apparent that Sibonde had a poor reputation because no one believed him. He was now telling others about God's love. Nellie passed away shortly after this incident. I never did meet Sibonde again.

Sibonde had recalled the time when he knew Jesus as a friend. Throughout our lives, we will often have to bow down and confess our sins. Still, it is the ongoing relationship that keeps this process of repentance going. In our daily walk with Jesus, we would do well to especially reflect on the last days of Christ's life and his death for us on the cross. The cross tells us three significant truths about God and salvation. First, the cross shows that sin destroys and kills. There are always consequences. Second, the cross reveals God's amazing love and grace for us. Third, the cross shows us our worth. We are worthy and valuable to God. So much so, you cannot put a price on any human being other than the life of God himself. You are priceless! As often as possible, reflect on the cross, this demonstration of God's grace, and it will cause you to want to change. It is the goodness and grace of God that brings us to repentance.

Modeling Grace

A medical doctor is bound by an oath to treat all persons regardless of race, gender, sexual orientation, or religion. The same medical treatments work on all people. Likewise, a clinical counselor is bound by the same code of ethics. Using much of the science we have about the brain, the same therapeutic techniques can help an atheist, a Christian, a Muslim, or a Buddhist. I can help my non-Christian clients by teaching them scriptural principles—such as grace, forgiveness, confession, love, acceptance, and non-judgment—without referring to the Bible or God. In my world view, God is working on the minds and hearts (thoughts and feelings) of all people, regardless of where they are in their relationship with him. For example, God led foreign scholars far removed from Judea by distance, culture, and spiritual understanding (traditionally referred to as magi) to seek out and bring gifts to Jesus. These gifts most likely helped Mary and Joseph pay for the expenses of fleeing to Egypt.

My clients are people of all faiths, including atheists and agnostics. I believe that just as a mission statement can help a company to stay on track, so a personal mission statement can help us as individuals. I share my declaration/mission statement before assisting my clients in developing their own: "I am a passionate, caring man helping others to experience God, find their purpose, and come alive." I created this statement many years ago when I was in a therapy group as a participant. It has been my north star, guiding me ever since. After sharing it, I explain to the client that

I believe in God, and I believe that God is love. If God is love, then anytime I help someone love more or better, that person is experiencing God. It makes sense to them.

On top of that personal testimony, I do my best to make sure that up to that point, my life has shown each of them unconditional acceptance, love, and regard. Without that, my words are like spitting into the wind. As Paul declared, "If I could speak in the language of earth and angels, but didn't love others, I would be a noisy gong or a clanging cymbal" (1 Corinthians 13:1).

Love and grace must be modeled. As Christians, we are called to be salt in the world—salt that makes people thirsty for Jesus.

Living as salt in the earth makes people thirsty for Jesus.

Many years ago, my wife, Juanita, and I were participants in a four-day group therapy session. We had no idea what the session was about. We just trusted the process. Before going, we were instructed to bring something to give away as a gift. It had to be something dear to us, something difficult to part with. For weeks leading up to the session, I struggled with what to bring. I have no idea why I chose what I chose, but I said goodbye to it and wrapped it up.

As we registered for the weekend, we each drew a name from a box. The name we got was the person we were to secretly focus on, and get to know as much as we could throughout the four days. It turned out that the person I drew was very anti-Christian. He made no bones about it during the program. He eventually found out that I was a Christian pastor, but he never knew that I was his secret partner. Over the four days, I did my best to act nonchalant around this man while attempting to have casual conversations with him.

One day, he said, "I love your shirt. Where did you get it?" I explained how I'd bought it in the Philippines. This led to a further conversation about what I'd been doing in that country. I explained that I'd taken a group of teens from my church to help people with various medical needs. He then launched into his beliefs about how Christian missionaries are always trying to change people's culture. I explained to him that our goal was just the opposite. We honor and protect their culture. We respect their culture by adapting ourselves to it if it doesn't compromise our moral values. For example, our female missionaries wear dresses instead of pants or shorts so as not to offend the people in some cultures. I recalled a time when, after preaching, the chief of a village chose to become a Christian. It was not my goal, as a monogamist, to make him divorce one of his twin-eighty-year-old wives. She would never have survived alone in that culture. But we did teach single Christian men to marry only one wife. My secret partner seemed surprised and impressed with my views on this topic.

One of the very last exercises we did was the giving of our gifts. That was when I discovered that the person who I was getting to know had a gift for me, and the person who was secretly getting to know me received my gift. When this very anti-Christian man found out it was me, I had to go to him, look him in the eyes and tell him what I found attractive about him through my observations. I can't remember exactly what I said, but it included something about how I appreciated his honesty about how he experienced Christians. I like genuine, authentic people. He then presented me with a huge quartz crystal from his altar and proceeded to hug me and weep out loud. We really connected at that moment.

Next came the part when I gave my gift to the person who was secretly observing me. A woman came to me, took me by the hands, and looked into my eyes. The woman said that as she watched me, she decided that she wanted to get to know me more in the future. She believed that I would give her a picture of Jesus. Then I broke down and wept as I handed her my gift. I had wrapped up a picture of myself playing the role of Jesus in an Easter passion play. On the back of the picture was a poem titled, "A Picture of Jesus." The entire room exploded with awe and wonder at the miracle that had just happened. It was surreal and unbelievable!

> You maybe someone's only picture of Jesus.

We may be someone's only picture of Jesus because they have never been exposed to Christianity in any positive way, if at all. This is more and more true in our modern culture. What picture of God do others see in you? A large church that I attend and support, by regularly doing my "Bridges to Freedom" weekends and other workshops, has a fantastic project. It has only one agenda, showing a Syrian refugee family grace and love. The church supports them by teaching them English and meeting any needs that they have as they integrate into Canada. There is no agenda to convert them. They accept them, respect them, and honor them just as they are with their Muslim faith. No greater sermon can be preached than the picture we give of God's grace.

Grace is a bridge to freedom. Be Free!

3

We Have Two Brains

Understanding—A Bridge to Freedom

So far, I may have given the impression that change is easier than it really is. I'm sure that we've all discovered by experience that it's not that easy. Listen to what Paul experienced and see if you relate to it. "It seems to be a fact of life that when I want to do what is right, I inevitably do what is wrong. I love God's law with all my heart. But there is another law at work within me that is at war with my mind. This law wins the fight and makes me a slave to the sin that is still within me. Oh, what a miserable person I am!" (Romans 7:21-24).

Paul refers to the sinful nature of humankind as if it is a natural law at work within us. I believe it is such a thing. In the realm of science, some things fall into the category of law, such as the law of gravity.

It occurred to me one day that we could look at God's law as a scientific law like the law of gravity. A scientific law is a description of how the universe behaves. Refer to the word *law* in any good dictionary. Therefore, if you look at God's law in this manner, you can't speak about discarding the law, just as you can't do away with the law of gravity. Every time I drop an object, it's attracted to the earth at an acceleration rate that follows the mathematical law of gravity. Gravity keeps the planets in motion in such a way that they don't collide with one another. It also keeps the milk and cereal in my bowl and my feet on the ground so I can walk. Doing away with the law of gravity would result in chaos and the inevitable destruction of the universe.

Similarly, one cannot do away with the law of God if you think of it as merely a description of how the universe behaves. Stealing causes pain and suffering. A significant betrayal or repeated betrayals like this can make a person feel like life is not worth living, a living death. You cannot get rid of the law in that sense. Doing away with the law of God would result in a universe filled with chaos, pain, and suffering. "The wages of sin is death" (Romans 6:23). This is how Scripture states it. Jesus put it in more scientific terms: "You don't pick grapes from thorn bushes, or figs from thistles. A healthy tree produces good fruit, and an unhealthy tree produces bad fruit. A good tree can't produce bad fruit, and a bad tree can't produce good fruit. So, every tree that does not produce good fruit is chopped down and thrown into the fire. Yes, the way to identify a tree or a person is by the kind of fruit that is produced" (Matthew 7:17-20). "Don't be misled. Remember that you can't ignore God and get away with it. You will always reap what you sow!" (Galatians 6:7). So you cannot remove the law any more than you could remove the law of gravity from this universe because the law is simply a description of how the universe operates.

God's law is comparable to the law of gravity.

Science and Spirituality

I was privileged to receive a Master of Arts Professional Counseling Graduate with Distinction from a Christian university in the US. It was there that I had to wrestle with my own beliefs about the integration of science and spirituality. I had to submit a thorough paper on this to graduate. I have always understood that the natural world around us is another "book" that reveals God to us. "The heavens tell of the glory of God. The skies display his marvelous craftsmanship. Day to day, they continue to speak; night after night, they make him known. They speak without a sound or a word; their voice is silent in the skies, yet their message has gone out to all the earth and their words to all the world" (Psalm 19:1-4). Truth, therefore, can be found through the two books of Scripture and science. Truth is truth, regardless of the source. Of course, neither Scripture nor science is always easy to interpret.

We Are All Biased

It takes considerable effort to sort out the truth, and, even then, we are all biased in this endeavor. The reason for this bias is because of how our brains operate. The brain has what is called the reticular formation. The reticular formation is a diffuse network of nerve pathways in the brainstem that mediates the overall level of consciousness. In simple terms, the brain has a filter. Without this filter, we would go crazy from overstimulation. Through sight, hearing, touch, smell, and taste, we take in far more information every second than our conscious mind can process. The filter helps by deciding for us what to allow through and what to filter out. For example, if you step into a room that has an odor, after a time you no longer notice the smell, until someone else enters the room and points it out. It works the same for a fan blowing or a clock ticking in the background. One of my sons has a small problem with his filter. He can't enjoy a movie if people watching are eating popcorn because the sound of people eating popcorn competes with the sound of the movie.

Your filter can be quite selective at times. For example, if you get a new car, you will notice the same model everywhere because the brain has figured out that this car is important to you.

What are your first thoughts when you wake up each day? If you say to yourself, "This is going to be a terrible day," your filter will allow through more of the terrible things that happen and filter out more of the good stuff. If you say to yourself, "This is going to be a great day," your filter will allow through more of the good things that happen and filter out more of the bad.

This filter, therefore, becomes problematic when you want to remain unbiased. Your brain will filter out data that does not fit the belief system you hold, and allows in anything that supports your specific belief. Your brain not only filters things out, it interprets what it lets in by making it fit with what you already believe. We have created phrases for this, "You have selective hearing," "You only hear what you want to hear," and "You only see what you want to see." Scripture puts it like this, "They have ears but cannot hear" (Psalm 115:6a). It explains how people of different denominations or different political parties can be challenged by alternate viewpoints. Often, people cannot see what others see because it is so "clear" to them what the truth is.

This filter can be problematic when one person in a marriage begins to think negatively of their partner. Now the filter will allow in anything that supports that negative belief, and filters out any anomalies like positive words said or kind deeds done. Quite often, I hear this sort of conversation when counseling a couple:

"You never say anything nice about me."

"What? I just said something nice about you a minute ago."

"No, you didn't."

At that point, I jump in and say, "Yes, he did," or "Yes, she did."

The person didn't hear it because their brain filtered it out. When a relationship has reached this state, it's called a negative perspective. Nothing good comes out of it. The couple cannot manage conflict, build dreams together, or share meaning (Gottman 2006).

Valid Perspectives

There are other features of the brain that work alongside this to the same results. We have a few instincts when we are born, such as sucking milk, but for the most part the brain is a blank slate, an empty database. Life experiences begin to fill the mind with information. At any given moment, our brains are interpreting the situation by reaching back into our database and pulling out anything that can help interpret or understand the present. For example, if you see an object that has four legs and a flat top, you would probably think, "table." This is only because you have seen tables before, even though not this specific table. If you were to come across an unfamiliar object, you'd be stumped as to what to call it or even what to do with it. With my clients, I hold up something that almost everyone thinks is a bracelet made of black polished stones. They imagine that there is a string holding the stones together in a circle. Then I show them that there is no string by pulling the magnetized stones apart. This is how the brain works. It can only use what it has already stored in its files to interpret the present.

We refer to this phenomenon as seeing the world through our own glasses. We interpret the world through our own experiences, family of origin, education, religion, the reading we've done, the media we've watched, and the friends we've hung out with. To illustrate this with couples who can't see eye to eye about something, I place a tissue box on its end on a table situated somewhat between them. Then I ask each of them to tell the other what they see. Of course, each sees something different. Then I ask them, "Which one of you is right?" Once again, the obvious answer is, "We are both right," or as I prefer to express it, "You both have a valid perspective of the box." The box symbolizes the many issues couples, church members, or friends deal with daily. We wrestle with issues of parenting, finances, household responsibilities, worship styles, and political views. Each of us has a valid perspective because our experiences and the information we've gleaned over time have created our perspective.

How can we use this fact to work through conflict? We can achieve resolution by externalizing the problem. Instead of making each other the problem, think of the problem as an external entity, and yourselves as a team exploring it and working together to find a win-win solution. To do it any other way sets the couple up for a win-lose situation. Imagine a win-lose argument as having an arm-wrestling contest with each person trying to win, playing "I'm right!" Now visualize a win-win discussion where each partner takes the time to listen, understand, and validate the other's perspective. Only after that is achieved, can the couple brainstorm possible solutions that are acceptable to both—a win-win.

> There are always two valid perspectives
> in a marital disagreement.

John Gottman has been referred to as the country's foremost relationship expert. His books, such as *10 Lessons to Transform Your Marriage*, are well worth the investment if you want to improve your relationship. Much of what I share on relationships has been learned from John Gottman during my training. Gottman claims his research shows that, on average, two-thirds of issues that couples fight over are unsolvable (Brittle 2014). He refers to them as perpetual problems or gridlocked conflicts (Gottman 2006). They are unsolvable because of differences in personality, values, and life experiences. Two-thirds (e.g. six out of nine) is a sobering number. His solution to this dilemma is to stop fighting; stop trying to solve the unsolvable. A couple must agree to disagree, and find a way to dialogue about it with humor, living with it like one would live with a tennis elbow. You figure out a way to adapt. If you continue to fight, you will only begin to view your partner as the enemy (hence the filter again). You then sink deeper into a gridlocked situation. The filter is now set to a negative perspective, and it's downhill all the way (Gottman 2006).

> Two-thirds of marital conflicts are not solvable.

Another feature of the brain that skews our perception occurs when we become flooded with emotion. When this happens, it's called being triggered. Our heart rates rise considerably, putting us in a state called "flooded." In a flooded state, we cannot see or hear as much as when we are not flooded. We call this tunnel vision. Try looking through a cardboard tube, and you will see what I mean. I remember hearing from one of my teachers about a study where they took a group of people, got them all worked up emotionally (flooded), and then put them in front of a TV screen. Playing on the TV screen was a basketball game. Someone, dressed as a witch and carrying a witch's broom, walked right through the middle of the court during the game. Most of the people in a flooded state did not see it. If you are in a flooded state, it is useless to continue arguing. It works best to take some time out and calm down before resuming the conversation. I give a suggested method of doing this in a later chapter. If you wish to check out a similar experiment, search on YouTube for "The Monkey Business Illusion" by Daniel Simons (2010). Even though this illustration is not about being flooded, but about being super focused on one thing, it shows how our brains can completely miss seeing things that are right in front of our faces. Magic tricks are based on the fact that our filter keeps us from seeing some things. This is why magicians are more appropriately called illusionists. We are all biased.

I believe Gottman's book, *10 Lessons to Transform Your Marriage*, should be required reading for any couple wanting to be married. He provides practical methods of communication based on scientific observations done over the years. We take our vehicles for maintenance regularly. Why not do this with a marriage relationship? If you can't afford a workshop now and again, read a book on the topic together. I do a workshop called "Bridges to a Better Marriage." Often, churches pay me for travel and a stipend, but provide the workshop free to the attendees. Check out the websites of nearby churches to see what may be available.

How the Brain Works

Let's go into even more detail about the brain. What follows can be found in many psychology textbooks and self-help books available to anyone. I own many of them myself. One of my favorites is Daniel Siegel's book, *Mindsight: The New Science of Personal Transformation*. Because I counsel people from children on up to seniors, most of whom have less than a college education, I need to be able to explain things to them in understandable ways. I believe in the KISS principle— Keep It Simple, Sweetheart! My favorite unit in teaching grade twelve biology was neurobiology.

Since those days, I have learned so much more on this subject through my own reading. With the invention of the CAT and MRI scans, we know far more about the brain than what I learned in college forty-five years ago. Somethings are the complete opposite of what I'd learned.

The hindbrain (the back of your brain, including the spinal cord) is a significant part of the autonomic nervous system. The word autonomic is like the word automatic. This part of the brain does things for you without your choice. It keeps you alive. It's for survival. The hindbrain takes care of heart rate, blood pressure, the distribution of blood in the body, breathing, body temperature, and so much more. It works twenty-four-seven.

A typical example that we are all familiar with is what happens when we touch something very hot. Heat creates a nerve impulse that travels to the spine. The spine is a part of the hindbrain. It automatically sends nerve impulses to all the required muscles in the arm and hand to retract. It saves you from burning more flesh than if you had to wait for your logical mind to make the decision. Milliseconds later, the original nerve impulse arrives at your conscious brain, and you say, "Ouch!" You didn't make a conscious decision to move your hand. Your autonomic brain did it for you. Thank God for this system, even though it can get us into trouble at times.

The middle of the brain or limbic system is also a part of the autonomic system that makes decisions for you without your logical brain becoming engaged. The middle brain is where fight, flight, or freeze responses originate. It is, however, much more complicated than this. The hindbrain also becomes involved for some things like the freeze response. The middle brain has its own memory, called implicit memory. I will say more about the implicit memory later.

The outer layer of the brain is the conscious brain. This part of the brain is where you are aware of any information coming from the five senses: sight, sound, touch, smell, and taste. It is also where you have conscious control over your muscular system so you can choose to move in the various ways and speak what you wish to say.

The part of the conscious brain that is just behind the brow is the frontal lobe. Only humans have a highly developed frontal lobe. This explains why humans have a prominent forehead instead of a forehead that slopes back like a dog's. This is where we can do calculus (at least some of us can), wrestle with philosophy, morals, and make judgments based on reason.

The frontal lobe is loosely connected to the limbic system. Mindfulness exercises can improve this connection and other important connections in the brain. These exercises train the brain to focus instead of wander. Some people have practiced these techniques so much they can raise and lower their body temperature, heart rate, and blood pressure just by thinking. Mindfulness is not voodoo. It's science. A mentally healthy person may learn how to manage emotions by practicing techniques that focus the attention of the conscious brain. I give some examples of these techniques in the chapter on psychotherapy.

The autonomic brain can do things without our choice.

I tried neurofeedback with a practitioner who had a computer with the required software. A band, placed around my forehead, was hooked up to the computer. The computer was reading activity in my brain while I was watching a movie on the screen. The movie would pause suddenly, and the screen would go black except for a green bar graph on the left side. My task was to use my conscious mind to focus on the green bar and to make it extend to the red line at the top of the screen. It seemed impossible at first. I started using mindfulness techniques to focus all my attention on the bar until I got it to rise to the top, which started the movie again. I discovered that whenever I allowed my mind to wander onto something else other than the movie, the computer software could detect it, and would pause the movie again. Through practice, I improved my focus and concentration so that the movie would never pause.

Implicit Memory

Through a practice of mindfulness, we can override some of the autonomic reactions that happen without our conscious choice. Let me go back now to the middle brain and implicit memory. In a sense, we have two brains. Some neurologists divide it up into three brains, but, to keep things simple, I combine the hind and middle brain as one—the autonomic system.

The conscious brain has an explicit memory composed of facts and timelines. For example, my explicit memory recalls the specific house I lived in during elementary school. I can't remember my exact age. I can't remember what it looked like inside my house. I only remember that the kitchen was at the back. Brain research reveals that our memories are not to be entirely trusted because they do change over time. I remember a birthday party my mom had for me. I can only remember playing pin the tail on the donkey and eating chocolate cake. My mom had cut the cake into wedges, and what stands out was finding coins wrapped in wax paper buried in the cake. These facts are stored in my explicit memory.

When I think about the birthday or talk about it, I get goosebumps on my shoulders, neck, and arms. It feels good emotionally to recall this memory. These emotions and bodily sensations are coming from my implicit memory. When I make a conscious choice to recall the explicit memory (the facts), it triggers my implicit memory. I do not even have to consciously think about this story to trigger my implicit memory. For example, if I see wax paper, I get a good feeling in my body! If we experience in the present something connected to an explicit memory (sight, sound, smell, touch, or taste), we may have an implicit memory response (emotions and bodily sensations).

We all have memories that we don't want to think about. When we do, we feel uncomfortable emotions and even painful feelings in our physical bodies. This is implicit memory. The bodily sensations are often referred to as body memory. We can get good at pushing painful explicit memories down and not thinking about them.

I can no longer eat salmon because of my experiences commercial fishing with my family in Alaska. I experience seasickness even though I'm not in a boat. I have a similar feeling linked to sweet and sour sauce after I ate it when I had the stomach flu. Some songs make me tear up immediately because of a movie the song was in or an event I attended, such as a funeral. How does the song "Edelweiss" from the "Sound of Music" affect you? I immediately have a feeling of sadness.

These feelings can be so overpowering that we quickly react in a fight, flight, or freeze reaction. Often this kind of response is not helpful, and can even be harmful to ourselves and those near us. This reaction is not our conscious choice. This is the main idea I want you to understand. This reaction is not our conscious choice at that moment. It's why we don't understand ourselves at times, and we end up having to apologize for the crazy things we've said and done. This reaction is the reason we get flooded, as I mentioned before. The person we care about the most becomes a "lion" about to attack at that moment. It's not logical because it comes from the implicit or feeling brain.

Along with emotions and physical sensations, there is a third type of implicit memory—implicit beliefs. Let me use an illustration to explain it. Donny is a four-year-old boy, playing with his toy airplane like any four-year-old would do. He's racing around the house, making airplane noises with his mouth. His father comes home from work, distraught about his boss and perhaps some uncertainty about his job. He's sitting in the living room reading a newspaper, when Donny comes flying by, making his airplane sounds. His dad snaps and yells at Donny, "I've told you a million times that I need peace and quiet when I come home from work! Go to your room and shut up!" Donny bursts into tears and runs to his room, crying. He sits on his bed, and then suddenly stops crying, saying to himself, "Hey, this is my dad's stuff. He probably had a hard day at work, and he's just taking it out on me, the innocent child." Nope! Donny is only four and doesn't think this way. Donny is egocentric. In Donny's mind, everything is about him. Some may call it the selfish, sinful nature, but this is how we survive as babies and very young children. Babies cry to let the world know that they're in trouble, hungry, have a wet diaper, or a pinched finger. They cry out for attention to get their needs met. It can't be a sin to cry for attention at such a young age.

Because of his egocentricity, Donny sits on his bed, feeling hurt. He also feels stupid because he doesn't remember his dad saying this before. Not only that, Donny feels he made his dad angry, and therefore he feels like he is a bad person. My emphasis here is on feeling thoughts, not cognitive thoughts—feeling stupid, feeling guilty (even when I am not), and feeling like a bad person. In psychology, these are called automatic thoughts or implicit beliefs. They are also a part of something called emotional reasoning.

From age zero to two, our brain waves are in the lowest frequency—delta. This is the wavelength adults have when sleeping, but the baby is in delta both asleep and awake. From two to six, our brain waves are in a bit higher frequency—theta. This is the wavelength adults have when they are just falling asleep or when they are being hypnotized. Our brain waves are in alpha from age six to twelve, and after age twelve, beta.

> Never underestimate the power of implicit memory over your behaviors.

When we are in delta or theta, we don't know the difference between what is real and what is imaginary. It's why children are highly impressionable between the ages of zero and six. During these years, children can learn one, two, and even three languages simultaneously without trying. After age six, it becomes hard work. Below the age of six is when we develop our identity and most of our beliefs about family and the world. We don't lose these beliefs as adults because they become unconscious, implicit beliefs. We don't develop conscious beliefs until we have alpha brain waves. It's why almost all people come to believe, on an unconscious (implicit) level, that they are not good enough. It can come from a comment or even just a frown from a parent (Lipton 2019). In fact, implicit neuro-networks begin to develop during the third trimester of the unborn child. This explains why a mother who has an unwanted pregnancy can pass on feelings of being unwanted and unlovable to their child. The child eventually begins to put language to these feelings later in life, but can't identify why or where they came from.

Emotions are not logical or rational. Some feelings are so strong we may even believe something is real when it isn't. As adults, we can sometimes translate our "feeling thoughts" into words on a conscious level. It's like having two brains. The logical brain might know that we are not a failure, but the feeling brain makes us feel like a failure anyway. The logical brain may know that we are not overweight, but the feeling brain feels like we are fat. This is how eating disorders such as anorexia or bulimia develop. The feeling thoughts and beliefs are implicit thoughts and beliefs. We also call them automatic thoughts because they originate in the autonomic part of the brain. They come lightning fast, and we usually don't know they are present on a cognitive, conscious level. Being mindful is a way to tune into those thoughts so you can do something about them.

Donny eventually grows into adulthood and becomes Don. He's now married to someone he loves, and knows she loves him. One day, Don is putting a bowl of food into the microwave when his wife raises her voice and yells, "Don't put that in the microwave!" There may also be an angry tone to her voice. Don quickly yells something nasty back, throws down the dish, and storms out of the room. He doesn't speak to her for several hours while he immerses himself in a football game on TV. Later, Don starts to feel bad about his behavior. He then goes to his wife, apologizes, and asks why he wasn't supposed to put that dish in the microwave. His wife tells him that the dish has gold trim around the rim, and she was afraid he was going to wreck the microwave, so she panicked.

What happened in that scenario? The raised, yelling voice with an angry tone triggered Don's implicit brain. His implicit brain went into first a fight mode (yelling something back), then a flight mode (fleeing the scene), and finally a freeze mode (shutting down all conversation). It was an automatic reaction caused by a triggered implicit memory of his dad. Don never once thought about his dad, but at that moment he wasn't thinking logically or rationally. He wasn't thinking, "This is my wife, whom I love and who loves me." Instead, he was feeling stupid and feeling like a bad person. His implicit brain was reacting like a lion was attacking him, and he automatically protected himself like he would've if he'd touched a hot stove. The emotional brain cannot think logically. It only reacts in a reflex type action of survival through fight, flight, and freeze behaviors.

When we experience the world around us, all the information coming from our five senses passes through our brain's filter. From there, it goes to the limbic system, forming an implicit memory. Finally, the hippocampus moves it to the conscious brain to create an explicit memory. This process, however, can get shut down if we consume a large amount of alcohol. This phenomenon is called a blackout. A person may be talking and doing things, but afterward have little to no explicit memory of anything that happened during the blackout. But there can be an implicit memory of this time that could be triggered afterward.

There is some research showing that adrenaline pumped into the body during a significant traumatic event can also shut down the hippocampus. It's why people with post-traumatic stress disorder (PTSD) often have only a fragmented, if any, explicit memory of the traumatic event. But they will have an implicit memory of the event, which causes them to panic in situations reminiscent of the original event. A soldier may panic during a fireworks celebration, for example. My wife, Juanita, gets extreme anxiety driving up narrow, windy forest roads because of an experience she had as a teenager. While at a bush party, a stranger invited her to another bush party down the road. She went along for the ride, but he turned up a windy forestry road where he raped her and threatened to kill her. In her case, she has a clear, explicit memory of the event. She never connected her fear of driving on windy forested mountain roads with this event, however, until I pointed it out to her. I have heard of someone else becoming highly agitated by the smell of a certain cologne because their rapist wore that particular cologne. At that moment, the person may have no idea why they're feeling such heightened anxiety.

Examples of the Power of Implicit Memory

I had a female client who had an excessive fear of the dark. She could give no reason why, except that she recalled a dark room and her mother screaming. During our therapy session, using a technique that I will explain in a later chapter on psychotherapy, she remembered being raped by her father and her mother discovering it happening. The therapy helped her overcome her fear of the dark. Her original fear of the dark was an implicit memory.

Another client's husband was severely injured in a terrible car accident. She couldn't drive by the place where the accident took place without feeling heightened anxiety in her body (implicit memory). After therapy, she no longer experienced this discomfort.

It was the intake day for another six-week round of addictions treatment at my place of work. I opened the front door to greet one of the new group members. I proceeded to step outside to give her a hand with her luggage. In doing so, I tripped on her foot and did a face plant into the paved driveway. My glasses shattered, I began to bleed near the corner of my right eye, and I had severe pain on one knee and shoulder. I was rushed to the hospital, and diagnosed with a concussion. After a week of complete bed rest, I returned to work with a black eye. For several weeks after that incident, every time I reached for that doorknob, I felt an instant of fear in my body (implicit memory). I never felt it with any other doorknobs. The implicit memory disappeared after a while, but my explicit memory of what happened is still intact. Some people can fully recover on their own, whereas others need therapy to return to normal again. My implicit memory linked to that doorknob disappeared because I didn't avoid opening that door or other doors. People often begin to avoid the situations in which their traumatic explicit memory occurred, which ingrains the implicit memory, causing it to become "permanent."

A client came to me with a phobia about Styrofoam. He couldn't attend AA meetings because the coffee was served in Styrofoam cups. He couldn't open gifts because he was afraid there would be Styrofoam in the packing material. He disclosed in therapy that as a child, his babysitter sexually abused him with Styrofoam. After a single session using a specific treatment, he could rub Styrofoam on his face and eat off Styrofoam plates. His fears were implicit. He knew there was no logical reason for his fear of Styrofoam, but he would freeze up in the presence of it.

Siegel (2011) relays a time-honored story from the nineteenth century. A woman had a malfunctioning hippocampus and, therefore, minimal explicit memories. It seems that this woman would visit with a doctor, but then she wouldn't recognize him upon returning to him. The doctor would have to reintroduce himself to her again to continue in conversation. One day, the doctor hid a pin in his hand. When he greeted her and shook her hand, the sharp prick of the pin caused her some pain. At their next meeting, the doctor introduced himself as usual. But when he reached out to shake her hand, she pulled her hand back. When asked why, she replied, "Sometimes doctors do things that hurt you."

She developed a feeling belief (fear) about doctors in this case, but was unable to access its origin because of her malfunctioning hippocampus. She had no explicit memory. She didn't recognize the doctor as the one who hurt her, but the word *doctor* triggered an implicit flight response. Do you have excessive fears of dentists, doctors, police officers, authority figures, men in general, or women in general? These are examples of implicit memories created by previous painful situations or relationships. Occasionally, we can develop an implicit response by vicariously witnessing another's trauma, reading about it, or watching it in a movie.

We are only born with the fear of loud noises (called the startle response,) which can be observed in all babies. Some of us unlearn this fear later in life. All other fears are learned because of implicit memory, given to us by God to keep us safe.

One day, my parents, my three-year-old sister, my wife, Nellie, and I were taking a leisurely drive on an old highway in the mountains. We came upon a parking lot, somewhat hidden in the forest. We drove in, parked, and then got out to stretch our legs. There was a fort-like fence around a large area with no sign indicating what it was. I found a small gap between two of the wood slabs making up the wall, so I peered through it. I was surprised to see a large mountain lion resting near the wall. A gentleman came out of a door in the fortress and asked us what we were doing. We explained that we'd just stopped to stretch our legs and inquired what this place was. He told us that it was where they made Hollywood movies using tame animals.

After we'd promised not to take any pictures, the gentleman brought the mountain lion out on a leash and allowed us to pet it. The four of us adults were highly nervous about the whole thing, but my three-year-old sister didn't hesitate at all. Then the gentleman asked my little sister, "Honey, would you like to ride on a bear?" She quickly responded in the affirmative. At that age, all she knew about bears were teddy bears, so why not! Of course, my mom started to have a fit; the rest of us quickly calmed her down, even though we were also highly anxious about it. The man brought out three bears, each on a rope leash, picked up my sister, and sat her on the back of the middle bear. She thought it was just great!

My sister had not yet developed a negative implicit belief about bears. Thank goodness she eventually did because these implicit memories keep us safe while hiking in areas where bears live. I repeat, our implicit brain does not think logically—only emotionally.

I've had countless clients with a logical understanding of a God of love, but they also have an implicit memory of pain connected to God, which has resulted in a distrust of God. Often it is a negative implicit memory of church, but it gets linked with God. The implicit memory usually wins, and they stop going to church. Implicit memories often trump logical thoughts unless you are very mindful of it in the moment, and consciously choose to push through the powerful, painful emotions. It can take a lot of time in therapy to overcome implicit memories that are self-defeating.

Implicit memory can also be a great benefit. One of my sons had a near-catastrophic motorcycle accident. His motorcycle slipped on wet pavement, and fell on its side with his leg pinned between it and the road. Fortunately, he was wearing leather clothing. An implicit memory of this accident led him to slow down when driving his motorcycle.

Implicit memories are not always emotionally charged. When we first learn to drive, everything is very intentional. After much practice, we operate our vehicles without consciously thinking through every action, making it possible to talk and listen to music at the same time. Most of us have occasionally experienced highway hypnosis. We suddenly have this sense of anxiety because we have no memory of driving the last few blocks. We were so deep in other thoughts, yet our unconscious memory safely negotiated the driving for us.

One of the worst kinds of implicit memory is a negative self-belief. I may fail at something and come to believe, "I am a failure." Then I have a difficult time trying again. I may get teased about my weight, and then develop an eating disorder because I believe, "I am fat." I may get laughed at for a mistake I made in speaking, and now have a fear of public speaking because I believe, "I'm not good enough." Someone may say something mean about my facial features, and I come to believe, "I am ugly." Any of these examples can develop into generalized social anxiety. Some of these implicit negative self-beliefs become so strong we consciously think they are correct. Usually, however, we know they're irrational and not true, but still experience a fight, flight, or freeze reaction in some situations.

Perhaps you've had conversations with people who won't fly because of severe fear. No amount of logic, no amount of statistics on deaths from driving versus deaths from flying, no reason will convince the person to fly. In fact, they may be able to quote you all the statistics themselves.

Self-Sabotage

The word *self-sabotage* is used a lot these days. It's a concept that most of us have experienced. If you haven't, you may simply be unconscious of it. This is where mindfulness of possible self-sabotage can really be valuable because then you can stop it before it happens.

Self-sabotage is ultimately the result of an implicit belief. If I believe that everything I try always fails, it probably will. If I believe that I don't deserve to be with a healthy person, I'll most likely do something to sabotage the relationship. If I believe that I'm permanently damaged, I'll probably never be able to become healthy. A great part of the effectiveness of counseling has to do with a person's belief that the therapy will work. One of my children claimed that they could never succeed at math. I knew enough not to argue with them, saying, "Yes, you can do math!" With that remark, I would have painted them into a corner, and they would probably end up proving me wrong.

> Shame is the feeling you get when you
> believe you are not good enough.

Self-sabotage is a close relative to the placebo effect. The placebo effect has been shown to be a real and powerful phenomenon (Rankin 2013). For example, giving a sugar pill to test subjects and telling them that they will probably have a side effect of nausea and perhaps even vomiting, a majority of the subjects will experience nausea and some will even vomit. Our beliefs can be very powerful.

An Iceberg Model of Human Behavior

Using what I learned about the brain, I developed a model to explain how this works in the mind and body. Many psychologists have used an iceberg model for similar things. Mine is unique, as far as I know. I chose the iceberg model because we can only see about fifteen percent of an iceberg. We call it the tip of the iceberg. About eighty-five percent is invisible (except when you go to a pristine place like Glacier Bay, Alaska; there you can see some of the iceberg below the surface, before it disappears deeper down).

The tip of the iceberg represents the behaviors that we and others see. Sometimes our actions are life-enhancing, and sometimes they are self-limiting. Addictions, fighting, arguing, gossiping, lying, and stealing are examples of self-limiting behaviors. Scripture refers to these behaviors as sins. I prefer self-limiting behaviors because it is more descriptive of why we would want to avoid them. Sin is sin because it has negative consequences and, therefore, is self-limiting. We can't always foresee the negative consequences because we are human and finite. This is where trusting God comes in. If God labels something as a sin, there must be a reason.

Just below the surface of our self-defeating human behavior is anger. This fits the model because anger, an emotion, is not visible. To the person experiencing the anger, however, it might be somewhat visible in that it could be felt in the body—in the stomach, the face, the shoulders, and such. In other words, anger is the one thing below the surface that there might be some awareness of in the moment, even before it is expressed in outward behaviors. Anger may also be visible to others by observing specific behaviors (tip of the iceberg) characteristic of aggressive expressions of anger. Passive expressions of anger may be totally invisible to anyone, including the angry person! There is more about this in a later chapter about anger.

Anger is usually a secondary emotion. Shame, guilt, sadness, and fear are examples of primary emotions that are painful. We don't like to feel these emotions, so our brain automatically goes to anger because anger is an anesthetic to pain. The same location in the brain registers both physical and emotional pain. Pain is pain. Anger is an anesthetic to both physical and emotional pain. I believe that's one reason why fighting in a hockey game is sometimes allowed or even encouraged. The anger can help the athlete push through physical pain and play harder.

ICEBURG MODEL OF EMOTIONAL DYSFUNCTION

Self-defeating Behaviors:

- *substance addictions*
- *process addictions*
- *arguing, fighting, violence*
- *depression, excess anxiety*
- *withdrawing, shutting down*
- *exaggerating, lying*

Just Below the Water's Surface:

Anger, Resentment, Fear

False Guilt & Shame

- *low self-worth*
- *negative identity*

Negative Self Belief (A Lie)

Wounded Heart

- *emotional abuse*
- *physical abuse*
- *intellectual abuse*
- *religious abuse*
- *sexual abuse*
- *injustice*
- *death of a loved one (especially by suicide)*
- *divorce of parents*

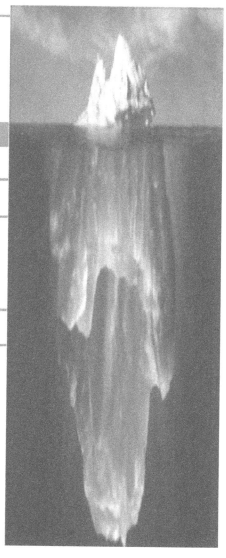

ICEBURG MODEL OF EMOTIONAL HEALTH

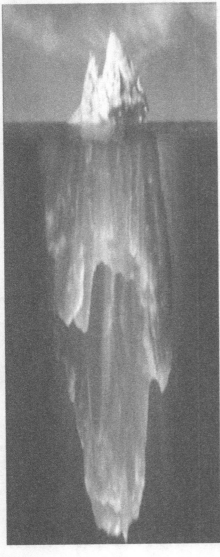

Positive Behaviors:

- *assertiveness*
- *balanced life*
- *healthy lifestyle choices*
- *healthy relationships*

Healthy Feelings of Self-worth

- *positive identity*

Positive Self Belief (The Truth)

Forgiveness of Those Responsible for Core Wounds

Below the anger, in the iceberg model, can be the uncomfortable primary emotion of shame. Shame sometimes arises out of the other emotions. If I am sad or afraid, for example, I feel like I am weak. This results in feelings of shame because, as a man, I have come to believe, on an implicit level, that real men aren't weak. Men can develop an implicit belief that men must always be strong because our culture continuously reinforces this idea. The implicit belief that I must be strong creates shame for being weak, and that results in anger, making me feel strong. Shame is a painful emotion, and anger is the anesthetic.

Juanita pointed this out about me one day. We were traveling down highway I-5 on our way to southern California. As we got near Redding, we decided to drop in and see my aunt. While we were visiting her, she disclosed that she was very close to dying of cancer. Deep down, I knew that it would be my last time seeing her, but I was suppressing that thought because I didn't want to feel the pain. Once we were back on the road, Juanita said, "Aren't you sad that you won't see your aunt again?" I snapped at her in anger. I have no memory of what I said, but I'm sure it wasn't pleasant. I was instantly flooded by an implicit reaction, and went into a fight mode. Without skipping a beat, Juanita said something like, "It's okay to be sad. Your aunt is dying, and you won't see her again." My counselor's brain kicked in with that comment, and I thought of the iceberg model. I was feeling shame for feeling sad, and I went to anger to beat down the pain of shame.

Shame is often below the anger, even if you don't feel it. Shame is sometimes called the invisible emotion because anger can anesthetize it so quickly. Below the shame is a negative core self-belief: "I am not good enough," "I'm a failure," "I am unworthy," "I am weak." If there is no shame below the anger, the anger will be expressed appropriately. Anger itself is only an emotion. It's not right or wrong. It is how it's expressed that counts.

These negative self-beliefs arise from a core wound. Remember Donny's experience, "I am stupid," "I am a bad person." Emotional wounds are the worst kind of wounds because they don't show a visible scar. One of the biggest lies ever told was, "Sticks and stones may break my bones, but words will never hurt me." Words can wound deeply. Imagine a physical wound like gashing your arm open on a nail. Let's say you do not cover it with a bandage. You can imagine that it may not heal because you would be continually rubbing it open against things. Every time you rub it against something else, it begins to sting and bleed again. An emotional wound is like that, except we can't see it. We can't put a bandage on it. When you're in a situation that is similar to the original wound—being criticized, mocked, or teased—you feel the pain of it all over again as if it just happened. You don't consciously remember the memory. You are feeling the feelings of the first memory and other memories that are similar to it. This is called a trigger. Your immediate reaction of fight, flight, or freeze is merely self-protection or self-preservation. It is like touching a hot stove. You react, and it is not your conscious choice. In a future chapter on psychotherapy, I will discuss how we can heal these wounds and desensitize the triggers.

Back to Paul's Experience

"But I can't help myself, because it is sin inside me that makes me do these evil things. I know I am rotten through and through so far as my old sinful nature is concerned. No matter which way

I turn, I can't make myself do right. I want to, but I can't. When I want to do good, I don't, and when I try not to do wrong, I do it anyway. But if I am doing what I don't want to do, I am not really the one doing it; the sin within me is doing it." (Romans 7:17-20). Sounds like an implicit memory response.

"O wretched man that I am! Who shall deliver me from the body of this death?" (Romans 7:14 King James Version). Have you ever felt like Paul? I have. Paul uses an illustration of "the body of death" that we are not familiar with. In Paul's day, sometimes the punishment for murder was to tie the dead body of the victim to the body of the murderer, mouth to mouth, eyeballs to eyeballs. Then they let the two of them rot together in a dungeon. And Paul said, "This is the kind of experience I am having."

In answer to his question, "Who will deliver me from the body of this death?" he says, "Thank God! The answer is in Jesus Christ, our Lord" (Romans 7:25). If it were not for the grace of God, we would have no hope.

How Can Science Help?

It is an implicit memory that I inevitably help people heal through therapy. Therapy helps reduce automatic reactionary behaviors. I use a two-fold approach of science and Scripture whenever a client is open to it. When a client is not open to spiritual things, I can use only science, but it can still bring a lot of relief and healing to the implicit brain. It always starts with awareness. An awareness of my wounded heart can begin the process of healing. If I take my car to the repair shop or my body to the hospital, they need to diagnose what is broken first, to fix or heal it. I will go into more depth on this in the chapter, "Psychotherapy, a Bridge to Freedom."

Think back now to the words of Paul when he said that he doesn't understand himself. When I say that some of this type of behavior is because of the way God created the brain, I am not saying that our sinning is God's fault. If our brain did not work this way in a sin-filled world, we would probably not survive more than a few years of life.

Scientific information like this can be very beneficial to understanding human behavior. By now, I hope you can see how science can make a significant contribution alongside Scripture as a source of help with making changes in our lives. The science of psychology (the study of the mind and human behavior), however, has been a controversial topic among Christians since the days of Sigmund Freud because the earliest psychologists were very openly anti-religion. They taught that religion caused mental illness. It was not until the 1970s that many Christians began to see psychology as a division of science like biology, chemistry, or physics. This was when scientists began to do double-blind studies to test hypotheses in the field of psychology.

Psychologists would now agree studies have shown that a healthy spirituality enhances mental health. Most psychologists now refer to their work as a bio-psycho-social-spiritual approach to healing. Humans are complex organisms.

Scripture is not a science textbook.

We need to keep in mind that Scripture is not a science textbook. The Bible is not intended to be a psychology textbook. But it supplies crucial background assumptions by which we can shape and judge psychological theories and conclusions (Van Leeuwen 1996). For example, Scripture refers to the four corners of the earth. We do not have to believe that Scripture is wrong because we are now aware of the spherical shape of the planet. It was how people understood the earth at that time in history. It's also a poetical way to describe the earth in specific contexts.

My philosophy has been to embrace and use well-founded scientific evidence in the realm of psychology if it does not violate my personal conscience as a Christian. Other Christian counselors may be different than me. A second criterion that I use is asking "How beneficial is it to help my clients heal and make positive changes in their lives?"

Scriptural teaching on the topic of grace is great, but we all still struggle, like Paul, with certain behaviors. No one is sinless. Paul began with the words, "I don't understand myself at all" (Romans 7:15). He even goes so far as to say in verse twenty-three, "There is another law at work within me that is at war with my mind. This law wins the fight and makes me a slave to the sin that is still within me." Paul had no understanding of how the brain operates as we do today. An understanding of this science can help in the process of changing behaviors.

Scripture makes over six hundred references to the heart. It talks about hearts of flesh and hearts of stone. For example, God spoke about writing his law on our hearts (see Hebrews 10:16). At the time, there was no understanding of the brain and its connection to emotional sensations in the body, such as the bowels or the heart. The brain sends signals to the parts of the body, by which we become aware of the emotion. An awareness of how my heart (brain) was wounded is the beginning of healing.

Helping All People

With a scientific knowledge of the body, medical doctors can treat the body for diseases such as diabetes, arthritis, gall stones, and sometimes cancer. Counselors, equipped with the scientific knowledge of how the brain works, can treat depression, anxiety, and PTSD. There is a treatment for triggers and flooding, but it is not perfect. We will always have to contend with the flesh.

When I taught high school biology, I would take a slice of a human brain out of a jar of formaldehyde. I would dry it off and then pass it around the class, letting each student feel it on their skin. I did this to emphasize that our brain is a piece of meat, just like every other organ in the body. It is essential to feed the brain proper nutrients and oxygen to keep it functioning well. An additional aspect of the brain is that the thoughts we think and words we speak out loud change the brain's chemical structure. And it reaches even further. A healthy brain equals a more robust immune system and a healthier physical body. The brain is where the Holy Spirit communicates with us. Let's keep it healthy through a good diet, aerobic exercise, and sufficient sleep. Investing time in a marriage relationship (changing our thoughts and emotions) helps the physical heart in similar ways as time spent in working out in the gym and eating a healthy diet (Chen 2018).

Whenever I share this information about the brain, people perk right up and experience a sense of relief. The relief comes from knowing that they are not a moral failure or that they are not alone. It all becomes clear and makes perfect sense. This knowledge does not excuse sin. It helps us understand that we are not going crazy. Too many people get so discouraged with themselves in the behavior department that they give up and throw in the towel. They believe that there must be something wrong with them, and God will eventually give up on them, if he hasn't already. I can give them this knowledge and give them hope at the same time.

Understanding is a bridge to freedom. Be free!

4

Where is God When it Hurts?
Suffering—A Bridge to Freedom

"Nellie didn't make it, Don. She's gone." These words were repeating in my mind over and over. It was the longest night I have ever endured. I was in bed, my two and four-year-old daughters on one side of me and my five and seven-year old sons on the other side. We were all clinging to one another out of pain and despair. I have never felt so alone in all my life. "Nellie didn't make it, Don."

Shortly after my encounter with Sibonde and the steel drum, Tenga, my best friend, who was an African teacher on staff, came to me with a heavy heart. It was his birthday, and he was feeling discouraged about his life. He thought that he had been a failure as a Christian, and had no idea what to do about it. As I listened to him talk, I began to relate to what he was saying.

Since my conversion in college, I'd continued my relationship with God. I did this by taking time early every morning to study Scripture and pray. Now, with no electricity in the early morning or evening hours, and a full workday during daylight, I had let that practice slide completely. I'd justified it because I was a busy missionary teacher. The difference between my friend and me was that I knew what to do about it, and he didn't. I shared with him my story, and that I also wanted to get back what I'd lost. Eventually, I shared these thoughts about the importance of having a relationship with God with some of the other faculty as well. They asked me to prepare some sermons on this topic, and to hold a short nightly series for the students to hear.

Just after we'd started the nightly meetings, our oldest son, Kerry, got extremely sick. Nellie, a trained nurse, diagnosed it as hepatitis A. There were many reports of deaths in the surrounding area, and we had been wondering what was going on. It was serious, and the local clinic did not have the resources for treating any kind of challenging medical issues.

We had the only vehicle in a hundred kilometers in any direction. At that time, however, it could not be trusted to make the eleven-hour journey to the hospital.

Nellie had just made the treacherous journey to the local clinic at the bottom of the mountain. On the return trip, too many people had squished their way into our vehicle. It's how they do things in that part of the world. For example, they push as many people into the back of a van-type bus. The driver accelerates, and then slams on the breaks, so everyone gets thrown forward. Then they quickly push a few more people in through the back door, and shut it quickly before anyone falls out.

Nellie couldn't convince some of them to get out of the car. As a result, a rear spring broke on the way back home, making it dangerous to drive very far on such rugged roads with four small children. What would we do if the car completely broke down somewhere in the wilderness while trying to reach the hospital eleven hours away?

Nellie came down with the same symptoms shortly after Kerry recovered, but her case was worse. I continued calling for help on the radio with even more earnestness, but I was getting no reply. I remembered hearing that everyone at our mission headquarters was away for some meetings, but I kept trying.

Then a friend drove up to our house with a woman whom I'd never met before. He'd brought her to look after our four children and myself while Nellie went to the hospital. The woman was the wife of another missionary. They had no children, and her husband could more easily survive without help than we could.

We needed to wash our laundry by hand, hang it on a rope to dry, and iron it to kill any Mango fly eggs. The iron was heated by a chamber containing hot coals from the fire over which we cooked our food. There was no such thing as fast or instant food, except for bananas. Everything was screened for bugs and small stones and then washed before cooking. Anything that we could not peel was soaked in bleach water. I was teaching full time, and continuing with the nightly revival meetings. I needed help with my children while Nellie was away at the hospital.

The students were keen to come and listen night after night. In this part of the world, they had reduced Christianity to keeping the Ten Commandments in order pass the final judgment and enter heaven. It was a very behavior-focused approach. What I was sharing was revolutionary and life changing to these people. The sermons were on the topic of having a personal relationship with a God who could be trusted. The students and the staff had never heard anything like it before. They were eager to listen night after night.

My Eldest Son's Words

I remember the night like it was yesterday. I had no idea how Nellie was doing, but I wasn't overly worried because she was in the best hospital in the country—or so I thought at the time. That night, I was speaking to the students and staff on the topic of faith (trust). One of the key parts was my emphasis on what it means to have faith in God. Having faith or trusting God means that we can pray, "God, I believe (have faith, trust) that you can heal, but if you choose not to, I will continue to love and trust you anyway." I had no idea how much I was preaching to myself that night.

I left that meeting, exiting the church into the inky darkness. The friend who had taken Nellie to the hospital met me there. He hugged me and whispered in my ear, "Don, I am so sorry. Nellie didn't make it. She's gone." He almost had to carry me up the hill to my house. I gathered my four children together in my bedroom and told them that their mommy had died, and we would not be seeing her until we got to heaven. The four of them went stone silent. We hugged and hugged and finally crawled into bed. I have no memory of how we made it through that first night. Trauma can do that to your mind.

We went to the hospital, where we all saw her body. I told the kids to say goodbye to their mommy, but Kerry just matter-of-factly said, "Why would we do that? She can't hear us." It was so hard to absorb what was happening.

My Second Trip to Africa

I ordered a post mortem exam because I wanted to know the cause of Nellie's death. I went home to Canada, but never did receive the report in the mail as promised. A year later, I returned to the hospital only to find out that the post mortem report was missing.

"Things like this happen when there is malpractice involved," I was told by a German doctor. All the European doctors had been on safari during the time Nellie came to the hospital. From what he'd heard, they didn't give her anything but plain saline with no vitamins or dextrose. He also informed me that women in their mid-thirties die of hepatitis A more than any other population group. I had to forgive quickly. There was nothing I could do about it.

During that first year back in Canada, I raised over $10,000 as a memorial fund in honor of Nellie. I brought it back in person to be sure that the money went towards finishing the girls' new dormitory on the school campus. I also returned with a bronze marker for Nellie's grave. I made this trip with a good friend, who came to support me and to see the Africa that I'd come to love. We'd truly lived in storybook Africa—lions, giraffes, elephants, zebra, monkeys—the whole works.

Before Nellie's death, Tenga secretly told me something no one else on campus could know. His father had arranged a marriage between him and one of the eleventh-grade students on campus. Tenga was one of the faculty and my best friend. He couldn't talk to his fiancée except in a teacher-student relationship, and she had almost two years to graduate before they could marry.

Nellie and I used to arrange secret meetings for them at our house. Tenga would come in the back door, and, later, his fiancée through the front door. We would close all the curtains, eat dinner, and play table games together so the couple could get to know each other. Another reason for returning to Africa with my friend was to attend their wedding. My friend and I got to sit at the head table at their reception. The "wedding cake" was a whole roasted goat. The bride and groom made the first cut in the goat and fed each other a piece.

My Third Trip to Africa

Sixteen years later, I had the privilege to travel back to Africa again with my youngest daughter, Jody, who was then nineteen. We went together as a part of her school mission trip to Kenya to build a medical clinic for the Maasai. The Maasai are an interesting tribe that has never embraced Western culture or dress. They braid their hair with a mixture of mud and cow dung, and spend their days herding cattle. Someone told me that you could count on one hand the number of Maasai who had converted to Christianity to that point in time.

At the end of the project, Jody and I went down to Tanzania for a few days. We visited Nellie's grave with the bronze marker now in place. We hugged each other and cried. We saw the girls' new dorm in use and the words over the main entrance, "Nellie Wren Straub Hall." As I was touring Jody through the science building that I had taught in, something caught my eye. On one of the shelves, I spotted something that was a part of an extensive collection of biological specimens that I'd left behind. I handed Jody a large jar and exclaimed, "Jody, this is the placenta that you were born with!" It blew her mind. We took a picture of her holding it.

Nellie's Funeral

They held a funeral for Nellie on the campus we had lived on, and buried her by the river, beside the path that I'd walked every day for over two years. My children were staying with a missionary family in Arusha, so I was with some friends who had come to be with me at the funeral. I did not sleep the night before the funeral. I could hear the loud wailing down on campus. It was their tradition that people would take shifts to mourn loudly throughout the night.

Almost immediately after the funeral ended, I came down with hepatitis A and malaria at the same time. They wasted no time driving me right past the hospital Nellie died in and across the border to Nairobi, Kenya. I have no memory of the journey because I was unconscious. I woke up, isolated from all visitors in a strange room, in a strange country, knowing no one. My children and friends were all back in Tanzania. I spent one month recovering, never leaving that hospital room once. I put together a lot of jigsaw puzzles in thirty days! I weighed only ninety pounds when I was released.

By the time I returned home to Tanzania, my friend had sold all of my possessions, except for a few clothes and necessary items, so that the five of us could travel back to Canada. He purchased my car for his own family, and sold the one I had ordered from Japan. This was the family that took care of my children while I was in Kenya. I have so much gratitude for what they did for me.

How ironic that when I returned to Africa a year later for a short visit (my second trip), I did the same for this friend's wife. A truck had hit his car the day before I arrived in Tanzania. The day I came, he was in Nairobi with a broken neck. I helped his family deal with things so they could follow him back to America for surgery. The car that he'd bought from me was available for my friend and me to travel around Tanzania.

At Nellie's funeral, I recall praying that God would raise her from the dead, just like Jesus raised Lazarus. Deep grief can do that to you. I believed God could do it, and every cell in my body ached for it to happen.

Then a thought passed through my mind, "Why would God do that for me when, right at that very moment, someone else somewhere in the world was praying the same prayer?" It's not a stretch to believe that every second of every day, a heart is crying out to God in pain over the loss of a loved one.

During the funeral reception, a missionary I didn't know came to me. Placing a hand on my shoulder, he said, "Don, I don't know why God did this to Nellie, but he is trying to teach you a lesson about something." I wanted to punch this man in the nose. He might as well have cut me open and poured salt into the wound with what he'd said. It reminded me of how Job's three friends spoke to Job when he was at his lowest point. His words stuck in my mind like Velcro.

After recovering from hepatitis A and returning from Nairobi, I tossed and turned one night, thinking of what that missionary had said. I began to feel that I must have been a lousy missionary, and God was punishing me. That same morning, I "happened" to read the story of John the Baptist, who was beheaded by Herod. When they told Jesus about John's death, Jesus pointed out that John was one of the greatest of the prophets. It changed my perspective on being a lousy missionary. I was still struggling, however, with why God would do such cruel things. If God didn't kill Nellie himself, then why did he allow it to happen? Where was God when my children and I needed him the most?

Later that day, I received a telegram from a missionary who'd moved back to America. His telegram was medicine for my soul. He'd written, "Don, Nellie's death was not the will of God. An enemy did it."

The words, "Nellie's death was not the will of God" sent me on a path of searching for the truth regarding suffering. Isn't God in control? If so, doesn't that make everything that happens God's will? It never occurred to me that death was not God's will, but it made sense. It was never God's will that humankind would sin and die. God's nature is to bring life, not death. Why would a loving God want anyone to die? Death can't be God's will. Why would any suffering be God's will?

Suffering is Not God's Will

I have often been puzzled by some of the things Christians say. "God is in control." "Everything happens for a reason." "God disciplines his children through suffering." "It was not God's will to heal so and so." "God took my child for a reason." "God saved him from dying to give him a second chance." Job's three friends said many similar things about God, but Job refused to buy into it. In the end, God affirmed the admonishments Job gave to his friends. If it were not for the first two chapters of the book of Job, we might come to the same conclusions as the three friends of Job—Job must have done something terrible, and God was punishing him for it.

Another interesting book is *Man's Search for Meaning* by Victor Frankl (2016). Frankl was a Jewish psychiatrist who spent several years in some Nazi prison camps. The first two-thirds of his book, describing life in a prison camp, is extremely difficult to read. The amount and severity of pain that the prisoners endured is unimaginable. I visited Auschwitz, one of those camps that Frankl lived in, and I cried my way through the piles of spectacles, combs, and brushes. I cried in the gas chambers and at the ovens.

Frankl was one of the few survivors of the Holocaust. To survive, he had to find meaning in his life and meaning in his suffering. He speaks about this in his writings on logotherapy, his method of helping patients.

There are three ways that people find meaning in life. The first is by a career or work, including volunteer work. The second is by experiencing relationships and love. Frankl goes on to say that the third avenue to meaning is found in suffering, by rising above it and growing from it (Frankl 2006).

"Well, Don, God did this to Nellie to teach you a lesson." How could anyone say that to someone who is suffering, let alone believe such a thing? I had to find answers to my questions about suffering and God's role in it. I began to listen to how Christians talk about God and suffering. "God is so good. My aunt was healed of cancer!" "I found the job of my dreams. God is so good!"

God does not cause suffering and death.

It was not what people said, but what they did not say that struck me. "My aunt died of cancer" (silence). "I can't find any job to pay my bills" (silence). Do you hear in the silence, "God is not good?" Is that the implication? Sometimes we say more by what we don't say. It seems that many times, Christians contradict themselves without realizing it.

Remember those school days when we would take a daisy and begin plucking the petals off? "She loves me," pluck, "She loves me not," pluck, "She loves me," pluck, and so on until there were no more petals and we supposedly had our answer. Is that what we do with God? "My aunt was cured of cancer. He loves me." "I just lost my job. He loves me not." Is God some arbitrary ruler, choosing to make some suffer and reward others, preferring to heal some, and let others die?

I know of an extended family who had a family ritual. Whenever they got together, they would spend some time taking turns sharing any news. When someone shared some good news, that person would end with the words, "God is good." Then the entire family would chorus, "All the time." If someone shared some bad news, that person would end with, "God is good." Then the entire family would chorus, "All the time." If God is not good all the time, then God is not good. If God does not love all the time, then God is not love.

I believe I've read every book written by Phillip Yancey. My favorites are *Reaching for the Invisible God* (Yancey 2000), and *Disappointment with God* (Yancey 1992). It was years, however, before I read anything by Yancey that I came to my present understanding of suffering and God's role. Yancey added so much more understanding that supported my conclusions.

The Law of Love and Freedom

Why is there suffering if God is love?

If God isn't love, he wouldn't be God.

But then why does he allow suffering?

Let's start with the word *love*.

Love is the greatest force for good in the universe.

Love makes life worth living.

There would be no meaning or purpose in life without love.

Almost everyone will agree with these statements. This truth about love is why it is so painful when we are not loved. Love is a basic need equal to oxygen, water, and food. During World War II, babies were dying in orphanages that didn't have enough helpers to hold the babies. Even though they were given enough milk via a bottle propped up for them to feed, they died from the lack of a loving touch. We were created for love and connection.

But here is the thing. You cannot have love without having freedom. Freedom must go with love. Nazi prison guards could force a prisoner to do anything: kill someone, eat human excrement; anything but one thing—love them. You cannot force someone to love you. Love is a choice, a free choice. Instead of having children, I could have bought a Chatty Cathy Doll with

75

the pull string on the butt that robotically says, "I love you." That doesn't cut it, though. That's not love. There is a significant risk in having children because they have the freedom to choose not to love back. It's why it is so sweet when one of my sons or daughters says, "I love you, Dad," at the end of a phone call! There is nothing better in the world than to hear those words. Why? Because they don't have to say them. It's a choice to say the words, "I love you."

Humans have always intuitively known the value of freedom. It's why many have gone to war to reclaim freedom. Many great movies are about fighting for freedom: *The Hunger Games, Star Wars, Braveheart.* The list is endless.

> Love cannot exist apart from freedom.

In the movie, *Braveheart*, William Wallace is in a jail cell praying, much like Jesus in Gethsemane. He prays for the strength to endure what he is about to experience. In the next scene, Wallace is walking through the crowd with a beam tied to him like a cross. People are shouting curses while throwing rotten vegetables and garbage at him. In the next scene, Wallace is stretched out on a cross, and as the ax comes down to behead him, he cries out one powerful word: "freedom!" As a result, he inspires Scotland to unite as one and fight for freedom from England's tyranny.

Scripture says, "It is for freedom that Christ has set us free" (Galatians 5:1 NIV). Jesus came "to redeem those under the law" (Galatians 4:5 NIV)— "redeem" means to set free from slavery. "For you were called to live in freedom" (Galatians 5:13). We can use our freedom to cause pain and suffering or for love and healing. God's will is that we choose to use our freedom to love; it is never his will for us to choose to use our freedom to hurt and cause pain.

Scripture declares, "Dear friends, let us continue to love one another, for love comes from God. Anyone who loves is born of God and knows God. But anyone who does not love does not know God—God is love" (1 John 4:7-8). God does not just practice the action of love, he is love. Love describes the nature of God.

I used to wrestle with the question, "Why didn't God destroy Satan and spare us all this pain?" I began to create in my mind a way to answer my question. I pretend that I'm having a dispute with someone. We are arguing over something. Each of us is claiming to be right and giving our evidence, trying to convince the other person. You walk into the room, and stand there watching and listening to our debate. Finally, I pull out a gun and say to the person I'm arguing with, "I'm right, end of story." Then I shoot the person dead. Now, I turn to you and say, "I am right, aren't I?" How would you respond to that? "Yes, sir. Whatever you say." What we are left with is only fear, not love. There can be no loving, trusting relationship. God wants lovers, not puppets on a string. This requires love and trust, freely given.

Let me go back to my belief that the law of God is not an arbitrary set of rules. Life is not like a game of Monopoly—if you land on this square, go directly to jail, do not pass go, do not collect two hundred dollars. Instead, I see God's law as a scientific law. The law is a description of how the universe works. If you steal from someone, the consequence is pain and suffering. My sin doesn't just result in another person's pain but in my pain as well. Much of our suffering is a consequence of our own poor choices, but much of it is also the result of other people's choices.

Free Will

If God is love, he would have to be a God of freedom too. You cannot have love without freedom. God knows that he can't say, "Love me, or I'll break your arm." This kind of language kills love and creates fear. But this is how we interpret much of the Bible.

When I came across two verses in 1 Chronicles 10 that contradicted each other, I had to find a way to harmonize them. Verse four says, "So Saul took his sword and fell on it." Verse fourteen says, "So the Lord killed him, and gave the nation to David, the son of Jesse." Who killed King Saul? Saul (by suicide) or God?

Another example of this seeming contradiction is in the story of David. "This is what the Lord says: 'Out of your own household I am going to bring calamity on you. Before your very eyes, I will take your wives and give them to one who is close to you, and he will sleep with your wives in broad daylight'" (2 Samuel 12:11 NIV). As we read later in 2 Samuel 16, one of David's sons, Absalom, does this. We know that God cannot sin. God did not force Absalom to do this. This was the choice of Absalom, perhaps the result of David's poor example as a father.

> Suffering is God's will only in that freedom is God's will.

My conclusion is that because God is love, God runs his universe on the principle of freedom. God also, therefore, takes responsibility for everything that happens as a result of this freedom. God doesn't make a multitude of decisions about what to allow and what not to allow in the universe. The will of God is that we have freedom because, without it, we cannot have love. Whenever you have freedom, there is the possibility that someone will use it to do something that causes suffering.

Therefore, suffering is God's will only in that freedom is God's will because freedom is necessary to have love. To say it even more emphatically, God is often described in Scripture as doing what he does not prevent. God does not contravene a human's free will.

Living with Pain and Suffering

Flying home from Los Angeles one day, I sat next to two children about ages four and six. They were traveling alone. The stewardess wanted to make sure they understood the safety rules, so she asked them if they had flown before. "Yes," the youngest said, "a hundred times." Later, he said to his sister, "Isn't it weird? We don't want to leave Mommy, and then we don't want to leave Daddy, and then we don't want to leave Mommy, and then we don't want to leave Daddy."

My eyes filled with tears listening to them talk, and, a bit later, he fell asleep leaning against my arm. The fear that these little ones must experience is beyond my comprehension. What kind of fears did my children experience after their mother died? Does Jesus notice the fear of children?

After returning from a month in the Nairobi hospital, I was still recovering from hepatitis and malaria. I was resting on a couch one morning while my four kids were in church next door. I was still weak, depressed, and feeling sorry for myself. In walked a young man, who I didn't know. He pulled up a chair by the couch.

He introduced himself as the husband whose wife had come to take care of us while Nellie was in the hospital. He started by saying how sorry he was for my situation. I appreciated people expressing themselves this way, even though their words seemed hollow. No one could know the pain and fear for the future that

I had after Nellie died. Then he said something that made me so angry I wanted to punch him in the nose.

"I know how you feel," he said.

How could he know how I felt? He was a young missionary with no children and a young, beautiful, healthy, and very much alive wife. How dare he say something so rude. No one could know how I felt.

But he kept right on talking. He explained that, after college, he had married, and together they had taken over his parents' farm. Having his own farm had been his dream since childhood. Life on the farm was great, until one day he came home from the fields to find a note on his kitchen table. His wife had written that she didn't love him anymore, and she'd left him to live with the real estate agent in town.

I suddenly felt ashamed of myself. It was a good thing that I hadn't punched his lights out because now I understood that he did know my pain. All I could do was lay there and cry. I wasn't crying because of my sadness for his experience or my own loss of Nellie. I was crying because I was glad, even happy, to know that the last words Nellie had spoken to me were, "I love you, Don."

I was crying because I realized that there are worse things to fear than death. Recently I gave the eulogy at my father's funeral. I shared a story of my dad telling my brother-in-law, Dave, that he didn't want to die. He hoped to live until Jesus returned. Dave had replied to my dad, "Dan, there are a lot of worse things than death." Sure enough, my dad got Alzheimer's disease. He didn't know who I was for almost two years before he passed away. Yes, there are worse things to fear than death!

> God chose to run the universe on the principle of freedom, which resulted in both suffering and love.

Jesus said there are worse things to fear than death. "And do not fear those who kill the body but cannot kill the soul. Rather fear him who can destroy both soul and body in hell" (Matthew 10:28 ESV). In other words, Jesus said, "Not being a part of the kingdom of God is the only thing to be afraid of."

Jesus is not saying that you'll never have fear in life, even as Christians. Fear is as natural as pain. It can be shown scientifically that everyone experiences fear to some degree or another. Any person incapable of this emotion would not survive long in a hostile and dangerous world. There are, however, marked differences in the way people respond to fear.

There are 350 places in Scripture where God says, "Fear not." Most of them may sound rather cold or commanding. "Don't be afraid. That's an order!" But read these statements in the context of a loving Father. Any loving father (or mother) would recognize the natural fear in their child and would hold them close and say, "Don't be afraid. I'm right here."

God chose to run his universe on the principle of freedom, which has resulted in both suffering and love. Love is a verb, an action, an action that creates emotions of joy, happiness, contentment, and more. Whenever I hear another story of heartache and pain, I immediately thank God for freedom because, even though there is pain, freedom makes love possible. That is my way of coping with personal pain and the pain that I experience when I listen to my clients.

Joni Eareckson Tada, in her autobiography, *Joni: An Unforgettable Story* (Eareckson 2001), uses a helpful illustration. Suffering is subjective and on a continuum. On one end, someone may be irritated by a fly buzzing around their head. On the opposite end of the continuum, someone may have caught on fire. When you are suffering, consider the fact that there is likely someone suffering more than you. You will then see your suffering from a new perspective. Joni became a quadriplegic in her teens by diving into shallow water. It took time, but she rose above the pain and became an author, painter, and singer. Her story is remarkable. There are many stories of other people as well, such as Nick Vujicic, who was born without arms or legs. Nick speaks to millions of people around the world, encouraging them to find purpose no matter what life throws at them.

As a counselor, clients continuously share stories of pain and suffering every day. I take a metaphorical shower to cleanse my mind at the end of each day. The worst stories involve children. It is beyond me how parents can do such cruel things to their children.

One of my clients was ranting about how he gets triggered by the word *God*. I explored that with him for quite some time. He was exposed to a lot of religious abuse growing up. Then I asked him if he would mind if I shared my personal belief about God and suffering. He gave me the green light, so I basically shared the law of love and freedom I just described above. He was very receptive to a God like that.

A client told me of being forced to stand beside the garbage cans along the road until the garbage collector came. Her mom told her that, hopefully, the garbage collector would take her too. Another told me of a parent forcing him to stand in the snow with bare feet and no coat for long periods. Another client shared about a parent tying her to a bed for several days at a time, with no toilet breaks or food. Another client told an account of her parent pimping her out for money. Another client told a story about his parent locking him into a clothes dryer while she went out to drink at the bar. I could fill a book with accounts of childhood abuse shared by my adult clients.

Now, they come to me for help with their messed-up lives and addiction to alcohol and drugs. These are the natural consequences of their parents' treatment of them as children. I genuinely believe, however, that almost all parents do not intend to inflict pain on their children. Parents do the best they can with the tools they have. Some parents have very few tools. It doesn't matter whether I purposefully pick up a vase and heave it at the wall, or I accidentally knock it on the floor with my elbow. The vessel is still broken. All we need to know is what is broken, so we can fix it.

"I do not leave unpunished the sins of those who hate me, but I punish the children for the sins of their parents to the third and fourth generations" (Exodus 20:5). This verse is a part of the second commandment of God's law. Choosing to see this law as a description of how the universe operates, I understand this verse as saying that the actions of parents will affect the lives of their children and their children's children. The punishment is the pain and suffering that are the natural consequences of our sins. A great book that helped me unpack this concept is, *Hurt People Hurt People: Hope and Healing for Yourself and Your Relationships* (Wilson 2001). When a parent hurts a child, the consequence is that the child passes the hurt on to their children by hurting them in similar ways. The hurt continues to be passed on for generations until someone breaks the cycle. Instead of hurting children, the role of a parent is to teach them to love. Once again, in this verse, God seems to be taking ownership of the consequences (punishment) that people experience because of the freedom we have been given by him.

An Unbelievable Second Loss

"Don, there is absolutely nothing we can do now except to make Penny as comfortable as possible until she takes her last breath. You need to make a decision about the removal of all life support."

Sometimes it's not due to the actions of someone that causes pain and suffering, but just because our world is so broken by sin. Penny, my second wife, is an example of that. She inherited a gene for celiac disease. Even though Penny could not eat bread herself, she used a large bread mixer to make six loaves of bread for us weekly. We had no idea that she was so sensitive to gluten. When she inhaled flour dust, it caused significant diarrhea and inflammation of her bowels. It created a complete blockage. After one surgery that removed five feet of small intestine, she developed another obstruction. She had a drain placed into her stomach to let out any liquid. Nothing could pass through her intestines. She ate no solid food for over twelve years. To stay alive, she was given nutrients intravenously (parenteral nutrition or TPN). A doctor implanted a permanent line into a primary blood vessel near her heart. Both of us were trained to manage the equipment needed to do this daily "feeding." They don't train most nurses in the special procedures that we had to learn to do at home. The materials and supplies that were delivered weekly to our house cost our Canadian medical health care system about one million dollars per year. Without it, she would die. The first year I called her my one-million-dollar wife, then my two-million-dollar wife, until she passed away in the twelfth year as my twelve-million-dollar wife. Our doctor claimed that she held a world record for remaining alive on TPN.

After eleven years, the original vein wore out, and infection took over. The doctor had to move the line to another place in her body, and soon that wore out. After the third vein, the infection finally ended her life. She passed away lying beside me in a hospital bed. Once again, I experienced profound pain, and the loss of my partner of twenty-three years. Nellie's death was swift and unexpected. Penny's death was slow and expected—daily for twelve years. I calculated that Penny spent at least one-third of our married days in a hospital room. I underwent a grieving process for twelve years leading up to her last breath.

By this time in my life, I had a firm understanding that it wasn't God's plan or will that Penny suffered like this through all those years. We decided early on in our marriage to live life as fully as we could instead of living every day as if we were at the edge of death. We would pack up her supplies and travel by car or even by plane to visit our family. One time, we were late for a connecting flight in Vancouver only to discover that all her life supports went to California along with the plane we'd just missed. It meant we had to go to a hospital overnight for TPN and other medicines while waiting for a flight the next day.

God is Always Present No Matter What

One of my go-to verses of Scripture has always been Romans 8:28. "And we know that in all things God works for the good of those who love him, who have been called according to his purpose." I interpret this to mean that God does not cause bad things to happen, and bad things that happen are not God's will. God can, however, turn a bad situation into something beneficial if we choose to trust him through it.

Penny's positive attitude inspired many people. Our church bought her a Lazy Boy recliner rocker, so she could sit comfortably in church each week. Even though she had constant pain, she also had a fun sense of humor. We would joke about going to an all-you-can-eat buffet so she could drink all the pop she wanted while I ate the food. She could drink, go into the restroom, empty the pop through her drain hose, and then repeat.

My wife now, Juanita, was one of Penny's close friends. Juanita and her sister would often come to our home and clean for Penny, and give her medications when I was away on a business trip. After Penny's death, once Juanita and I had been dating a while, she told me a story about Penny. Once again, it illustrates her sense of humor and attitude in the face of pain, and her daily realization that life for her would end soon. Penny gave Juanita and her sister a list of women and made them promise not to let any of the women on the list marry me after she passed. "Was your name on the list?" was my first question in reply to Juanita. We had a good laugh about it together. Penny was a special person to a lot of people.

Pain – The Gift Nobody Wants

Dr. Paul Brand and Philip Yancey wrote a book together: *The Gift of Pain*. Dr. Brand spent his life working in a colony of leper patients. Throughout my life, I wrongly understood that leprosy was a disease that caused parts of your body to "rot" away. Disfigurement was why they always covered their faces in the movies I'd watched. The truth is that leprosy is caused by bacteria that attack the nerve cells that detect pain. Without these cells, a person might pick up a hot object and never know it until the tissue is damaged so badly that it later falls away. Rats may eat the ends of fingers or toes during sleep.

Dr. Brand created a device whereby a leper could know when something was too hot or when too much pressure was applied to their fingers. An alarm would go off, signaling the leper to drop it or back off. It was interesting that, if the person really wanted to do something, they would often ignore the signal and keep on doing what they wanted to do. This would, of course, result in damage (Brand and Yancey 1993). I find that so many of my clients do not listen to their bodies. The body is telling us things, and if we ignore what the body is saying, it could be fatal. Humans can be very odd this way.

A counselor friend of mine used to tell the following story.

A man had a neighbor who had a dog. The neighbor's dog would lie on the front porch and howl all day. One day, the man went to his neighbor and asked, "Why does your dog lie on the porch and howl all day?"

"That's easy," said his neighbor. "The dog is lying on a nail that's sticking up through the porch."

"Why doesn't he move then?"

"I guess the pain is not great enough."

Unless the pain of not changing is great enough, we do not change. I call it the law of pain.

Everyone knows the experience of touching something hot that they didn't realize was hot and having a reflex reaction. This automatic pulling away reaction saves the flesh from burning more than it would without it. Pain is a significant gift, in that sense.

"Dear brothers and sisters, whenever trouble comes your way, let it be an opportunity for joy. For when your faith is tested, your endurance has a chance to grow. So let it grow, for when your endurance is fully developed, you will be strong in character and ready for anything" (James 1:2-4).

> Unless the pain of not changing is great enough, we do not change.

Most of us are familiar with the phrase, "No pain, no gain." It's a part of the law of pain as well. Pain accompanies any positive change. To achieve less pain, one must experience, for at least a short time, greater pain. Working out at the gym, attending counseling sessions, studying for an exam, and getting a root canal at the dentist are a few examples. Perhaps some of the pain of the dentist is in the wallet, but the pain is worth it in the long run.

Many people have come to God after they've tried everything else. In AA, it's called hitting bottom. Some people think they have hit bottom, only to discover that there is a deeper bottom. One of my clients said it this way, "We only hit bottom when we stop digging." Suffering has a way of bringing us closer to God if we allow it. In the world of addiction, people often say, "If it doesn't kill you, it will make you stronger." I usually correct them with, "If it doesn't kill you, it will make you stronger if you learn from it."

God Knows Your Pain

"As evening came, Jesus said to his disciples, 'Let's cross to the other side of the lake.' He was already in the boat, so they started out, leaving the crowds behind (although other boats followed). But soon, a fierce storm arose. High waves began to break into the boat until it was nearly full of water. Jesus was sleeping at the back of the boat with his head on a cushion. Frantically they woke him up, shouting, 'Teacher, don't you even care that we are going to drown?' When he woke up, he rebuked the wind and said to the water, 'Quiet down!' Suddenly the wind stopped, and there was a great calm. And he asked them, 'Why are you so afraid? Do you still not have faith in me?'" (Mark 4:35-40).

What kind of storm is blowing in your life? Right now, I suspect that some readers are weathering out tornadoes or hurricanes. Fears entirely drench you. Your heart may be aching from the strains caused by severe winds of trouble. Right now, your minds may be having a difficult time concentrating because of worry that thunders louder than my words. You may be afraid of the future. And yet, you appear calm and dry on the outside. People ask you how you are doing, and you reply out of habit or custom, "Fine." No one knows the severity of the storm you are in, and you are unsure if you want others to know, and yet part of you longs for someone to listen to you unload your burden. You tried praying, but it seems that God is sleeping on the bottom of the boat.

Maybe today you are experiencing fair weather, but you have had some of those stormy days. One thing I can guarantee is that there will be more stormy days ahead. It is part of being alive in a fallen world.

Economic Storms

Some of these storms are financial storms. Perhaps the recession knocked out your retirement savings. Maybe your area was hit by a hurricane or an earthquake. Maybe your company downsized, and you are now unemployed. Have you ever considered that most of us are only a few months away from becoming homeless if our financial conditions changed in any of these ways?

The fear of not being able to support your family is a genuine fear for some of you today. But many of you cannot relate to these fears. Instead, a lot of you are probably like me. Far too often, I find myself worried over trivial things.

I heard a song recently. The message basically said that this world has everything you want but nothing that you need. Isn't that the truth?

Here is what Jesus says to those who have financial fears, "So I tell you, don't worry about everyday life—whether you have enough food, drink, and clothes. Doesn't life consist of more than food and clothing? . . . Why be like the pagans [those who don't know the truth about a loving God]who are so deeply concerned about these things? Your heavenly Father already knows all your needs, and he will give you all you need from day to day if you live for him and make the kingdom of God your primary concern" (Matthew 6:25,32-33). Make the kingdom of God your primary concern! There are greater things to fear than lack of finances. Be concerned about the kingdom of God!

Let's try to get a picture of how much wealth a few of the wealthiest people in the world have, compared with the average person in America. Using some simple math ratios, let's say I was sitting on my couch at home, and a quarter fell out of my pocket into the cushions and out of sight. That isn't much compared to my total assets. But if one of these wealthy people sat on their couch and that same fraction of their total assets fell out of a pocket, it would be over a million dollars! Any one of them is welcome to come over and sit on my couch! The truth is that we, you and I, (not just the very, very rich) are among the five percent of the wealthiest people of the world.

Whenever I face a financial storm, I begin to worry. Yet, I try to look on the brighter side of it. I consciously force myself to do this because my mind naturally wants to run downhill and feel sorry for myself. I try to find something positive and focus on that, so I don't play a pity party with myself.

I returned home from a business trip to discover that Penny had driven into a light post, destroying both the car and the post. Insurance would not cover it because she was driving under the influence of prescription pain killers (I was angry with the doctors, who'd refused to listen to me and have her driver's license taken away, but that was water under the bridge. She lost it after that accident).

I had to look at this financial storm in the most positive way I could. It could have been worse—much, much worse. Penny might have been killed herself or injured or even killed someone else. We could have faced a multi-million-dollar lawsuit without insurance coverage. The police officer said that he could have jailed her for it. There was much for which to be grateful. Remember, someone is likely suffering more than you.

Relationship Storms

Maybe some of you have weathered or are presently experiencing relationship storms. Perhaps you are a parent whose heart is fearful right now about a prodigal son or daughter who is still out there, lost in the world. Maybe they are in the cruel world of drugs or prostitution. I can relate to this storm. When I look back on this storm, it seems like only a dream. I can still picture myself spending nights lying face down like a bear rug in front of my fireplace, crying out to God to look after my son, and to bring him back home safe. I was so afraid.

During the day, I would have the sensation that I'd swallowed a cannonball and was carrying it in my gut. It was difficult to concentrate on work. You may know what I'm talking about.

Those were days when I couldn't seem to find any bright side to look on. The only thing that I could do was to think about how Jesus wept when his friends hurt. I would focus on the fact that Jesus loved my son even more than I did, and Jesus was even more concerned than I was. Believing this was the only thing that brought relief. Parents! Do you know that God loves your children more than you do? When you fear for your own children's salvation and wonder why God doesn't do anything to help, remember that God loves them even more than you do.

Paul says, "When we were utterly helpless, Christ came at just the right time and died for us sinners. Now, no one is likely to die for a good person, though someone might be willing to die for a person who is especially good. But God showed his great love for us by sending Christ to die for us while we were still sinners" (Romans 5:6-8). Many parents would at least like to believe that they would die for their son or daughter if they knew that it would save them by doing so. Think about it. Jesus died for your son or daughter even when he knew that for some of them it would be totally in vain because they would still spurn his love. He died for them anyway.

"God is in control," is a widespread phrase used by some Christians. There is even a song by that title. The phrase, "God is in control" is found nowhere in Scripture, but it does seem to be an intuitive way to think. Several verses appear to support this belief, but all of them are saying that God is present and with you. He is helping you get through these trials. They do not mean that God controls what happens. God doesn't override our free choice to do what we choose to do. Love requires free choice.

Very occasionally, God creates a miracle. A miracle may be defined as something that goes against the natural laws of the universe. I share more about miracles in a future chapter. A miracle may override gravity or disease, but a miracle is never used to override someone's freedom to choose.

Maybe your fear of the future is the result of the relational storm of divorce, or perhaps you fear the possibility of divorce as you currently struggle in your marriage. Divorce was something that I never worried about. I think I felt secure in my marriage because I knew my wife loved God more than me. If your spouse knows that you love God more than you love yourself, more than you love your toys, and yes, even more than them, it will give them a sense of security in the marriage. It isn't that I never had any relational storms in my marriage. You'd have to be brain dead not to have any conflict in a marriage. Relationships, especially marriage relationships, take work, but the effort it takes to work through the conflict is worth it.

Parents, you'd be surprised at how your children fear divorce. Every time you fight, they fear the worst. I have heard it openly expressed when counseling children. My university instructor taught that the best thing parents can do to build security in their children is to make out on the couch in front of them. They will do summersaults over it.

I believe that God knows the pain of divorce through experience. After Adam and Eve sinned, God could no longer walk and talk with them face to face. Genesis 3:23 says, "So the Lord God banished Adam and his wife from the Garden of Eden." The meaning of banished is essentially the word *divorced*. This is why God says, "I hate divorce" (Malachi 2:16). God hates divorce because he knows how painful it is.

Global Storms

Occasionally, throughout history, our world faces a global storm. World Wars I and II touched most countries of the world. These were periods of global pain and suffering. The Spanish flu of 1918 killed between fifty and one hundred million people world-wide, six hundred thousand in the US. As I write this, our world is in another pandemic—Covid-19. The stock markets have crashed. People are quarantining themselves, and governments are calling for a lock down in some places. Shelves in grocery stores have been cleaned out. Most businesses are closed, and people are unemployed and worried about how they're going to pay their bills and feed their families. Some fear for their physical lives, and others are treating it like it's a joke. I can no longer shake hands, and I am always mindful of social distance. All in-person worship and other in-person meetings have been cancelled. At this point, we do not know if and when our global crisis will end.

There are, however, so many great stories of people caring for their neighbors. People are bringing groceries to elderly people who can't get out. They are looking for ways to encourage each other. Crisis can bring out the worst and the best in human beings. It's all a choice as to how we look at it—crisis or opportunity?

Is Jesus Sleeping in Your Boat?

Does it seem like Jesus is asleep in the bottom of your boat? Was Jesus sleeping in the boat during the raging storms of the death of my wives? No! The church is called the body of Christ for a reason. The church became the hands and feet of Jesus for me. People surrounded me with their presence. Some brought food; others phoned and emailed me. Shortly after arriving home to my parents after Nellie's death, I was sitting in a doctor's waiting room with my son. While waiting, we saw a delivery made to the secretary. It was a huge basket of goodies for Christmas. It was apparent that it was a big surprise, and she was very excited about it. When our turn came, they put us in a private waiting room for the doctor. The secretary came into the room with the basket and said, "I heard about your family at church last week. I decided that you need this basket of goodies much more than I." Words were not enough to show how that made us feel at that time in my life.

I'm sure you've all heard of the great redwood trees of California, several hundred feet high, and so broad that they have cut a hole in one for cars to drive through. Did you know that the redwoods have very shallow root systems? They always grow in groves, large groups of them together. If they grew alone, they could never withstand the storms that blow, but by standing together, they're not blown down. Don't ever underestimate the value of belonging to a community of people who care for each other. Don't isolate yourself from community. You need to connect with a group of people and develop those relationships. When the storms of life strike, you'll be glad you did.

Friends and family are not even enough to carry you through the biggest storms of life. I have come to believe that our fear of the future is inversely proportional to our trust in the God that holds the future. The less you know and trust God, the greater will be your fear. This is not to say that we should never experience the emotion of fear. Courage is only courage when there is fear. Faith is not required when there is complete certainty.

Why could Jesus remain asleep in the boat while his best friends feared for their very lives? Why does Jesus allow us to experience the storms of life that cause us to fear? God sometimes calms the storms in people's lives because they do not have enough faith to pass through the storm.

> God can calm a storm, but he would
> rather calm us in the storm.

Sometimes God calms the storm, but sometimes instead of calming the storm, he calms us. Scott Krippayne sings a song, "Sometimes He Calms the Storm," written by Benton Kevin Stokes and Tony W. Wood (Stokes and Wood 1995).

Sometimes He calms the storm
With a whispered peace be still
He can settle any sea
But it doesn't mean He will

Sometimes He holds us close
And lets the wind and waves go wild
Sometimes He calms the storm
And other times He calms His child

Do you get it? Jesus could sleep on the bottom of the boat in that storm. Surely, he was aware of the storm around him, but he didn't fear because of his trust in his Father. He would rather have had his disciples ride the storm out in faith than work the miracle of calming the storm for them. I know this is true because Jesus had only one comment to make to them concerning this storm, "Why are you afraid? You have so little faith" (Luke 8:26). The greater miracle is not the miracle of calming the wind, the rain, and the waves. The greater miracle would have been the calming of the disciples, growing a trust in them that would keep them calm through the duration of the storm.

But then, when and where does that kind of trust come? It comes from the experiences of going through life's storms with Jesus. This storm on the lake was nothing like the storms that the disciples faced after Jesus ascended to heaven. This storm helped to prepare them for even greater storms. We know how the disciples faced their future storms. They could look their persecutors in the eye and say, "I don't care what you do to me, beat me, stone me, throw me in prison, I will not stop preaching about Jesus." We know how they could face martyrs' deaths. It was because they could look back on the times that they spent with Jesus, and they knew by their personal experience that he could be trusted.

They finally learned what Jesus had longed for them to learn. There are worse things to fear in this life than death: the fear of missing out on the kingdom of God. Take that one thing in life seriously. Paul said it this way, "For to me, living is Christ and dying is even better" (Philippians 1:21).

One evening in college, I was invited to a Bible study. As we sat cross-legged on the floor, I flipped through my Bible and came across those words, "dying is even better." I read the verse aloud, and it led to a conversation about death. This is how I explained it that night. Let's say that I am driving a car, and, suddenly, out of nowhere, I am hit head-on by another vehicle. In slow motion, it goes like this: I see the car, I hear the crunching of metal and feel the forward thrust on my body, I feel the impact of my head, I hear a trumpet blasting, I feel myself rising through the air, and I see Jesus with his arms spread open to hug me. I was tearing up writing those words.

The very next day, after that Bible study, I was driving with four others to a wedding in a city several miles from the college. We came across a terrible accident. It was so bad that it was impossible to tell what kind of vehicles they were. I saw a severed foot on the road, and then I saw my friend, now dead, with a frozen scream on his face. Eleven people died that day, five of them friends. Immediately, Philippians 1:21 came to my mind. "To die is gain," rang in my head. I am undone thinking about that day.

Jesus doesn't cause the storms of life that make us so afraid and suffer so much. They are the result of sin, and God allows them because sin must play out its natural course to bring about an eternal solution to sin in the universe. Love will win in the end. The kingdom of God will prevail, but, in the meantime, there will be storms. Where did we ever get the idea that, if you are a Christian, you will have a more comfortable life with less pain? You can't find that in the Bible. God is more interested in your character than your comfort. Just because Jesus can sleep on the bottom of the boat doesn't mean that the boat will never sink, and none of us will drown. But Jesus promises us that he will be with us in the storms. In the end, everything will be okay. If it's not okay—it's not the end!

There is a saying that I used to often quote, "God only allows you to go through what you are capable of handling." I moved away from that quote to, "God only allows you to go through what he can carry you through." Later, I completely threw out both of those quotes because they imply that God is up there, deciding what experience of suffering that you will or will not go through. God values freedom, and sin brings suffering. Now my quote (paraphrasing Romans 8:28) is, "No matter what life throws in your path, God can carry you through it, and make something good out of it."

> No matter what life throws in your path, God can carry you through it, and make something good out of it.

When we are afraid of these storms, like the disciples, usually our first cry to God is, "Please calm the storm! Take it away!" Sometimes Jesus does calm life's storms that cause us to be so afraid. But I believe his preference, and the greater miracle, would be for us to allow him to calm us in the storm.

Suffering is a bridge to freedom. Be free!

5

Adopted
Acceptance—A Bridge to Freedom

"Hello, Don, a baby boy was born yesterday. The mother is only seventeen and wants a good family to adopt him. Would you and Nellie be open to adopting him?" It was my doctor who had called late on a Saturday evening.

We'd just arrived home from camping in the mountains. It was only the end of April. It had snowed, so we'd packed up and went home early. We didn't hesitate to do adventurous things like this, even though Kerry, our only child at the time, was not even two years old. Nellie was a seasoned Alaskan who had grown up in a village that had very few amenities, such as electricity and running water. I was the one who struggled with the primitive living conditions in Africa.

We were young and adventurous in those days. Our doctor suggested that we have a home birth when Nellie was pregnant with Kerry. Home births had a bit of a comeback in the 1970s, and it sounded cool to us. I got to deliver my first child while the doctor coached me from the sidelines. My mother was also there for support. I discovered why, in the movies, someone always yells, "Boil some water!" whenever a baby is being born. The hot water is for the hot chocolate to celebrate the birth! The next morning, I called the school principal to bring my science class on a school bus to my house for a field trip. I laid out the placenta and umbilical cord on the kitchen table for them to see. Each student took a turn holding a baby less than twenty-four hours old. The teenagers were spellbound.

Several months later, I invited my class to our house for a party on a Saturday night. Together we watched a program on primetime television. The show featured Nellie, Kerry, and me regarding our home birth.

When Kerry was four days old, we flew to Alaska to show him off to Nellie's family. It was not our first choice to take him there so young, but we'd already booked our flights, and he had been born two weeks later than expected.

More than a year later, Nellie, Kerry, and I went to California to visit relatives for Christmas. We went to Disneyland, and then we were planning to go to Universal Studios with some aunts and uncles. Nellie, who was pregnant, felt a bit off. She confided in her uncle, who was a physician. His advice was to live life as usual as possible, but to avoid anything crazy like wild roller coaster rides. His philosophy was that a miscarriage was nature's way of preventing the birth of a child who would probably not survive.

Halfway through our tour of Universal Studios, we stopped for a break. Nellie headed off to the restroom. When it was time to resume the tour, she hadn't returned yet. I sent one of her aunts to see what was going on. They called a staff doctor, and the tour left without us. Nellie aborted twins in the restroom. They were still very tiny in size, and there were no complications. An ambulance escorted us out. There was no charge for their medical services, and they gave us each a rain check to return any time for a free tour.

The Adoption of Kris

Our doctor, who'd called that Saturday night to ask us about adoption, knew about our unfortunate experience during the Christmas season. After hanging up the phone with our doctor, I told Nellie about the newborn boy needing a family. The miscarriage was still heavy on our hearts, and we were silent for the rest of the evening, each of us thinking and praying about this opportunity.

The next morning, I broke the silence with the question, "Do you want to go to the hospital and get the baby?"

"Yes, let's do it!"

That afternoon, we met the baby and his mother, who was from the US. Nellie and I drove the mother to where she was staying at the time and brought Jeremy David home with us. Jeremy David was the name of a first cousin about the same age as Kerry, so we renamed our new son, Kris James. It was love at first sight.

The next day, Kris's skin had a yellow color. Nellie knew that jaundice meant Kris had a high level of bilirubin, which could be dangerous. They admitted Kris into another hospital, and we had to leave him there under a special lamp for a few long days over the weekend. That weekend, Nellie and her teen girls' choral group were singing in a church. I will never forget one song they sang, the well-known Gaither song, "Because He Lives." Nellie was not only the director of the group, but she also sang with them. Tears were running down her cheeks as she sang the verse about holding our newborn baby as a solo. When they'd chosen the song and practiced it this way, we had no idea that Kris would be part of our family.

Kris was legally adopted several months later. We did our best to conceal the fact that Nellie was pregnant at the time of the interview with the social worker. We feared that it might prevent the adoption. Our third child, Leanne Cheri, was born eight months after Kris!

Right from the start, Kris was as much a part of us as any of the other kids. But because he came so unexpectedly, there was one time when we left for town without him! We lived in the country, outside of the city. Halfway to town, we had to do a U-turn to retrieve him. It's hard to understand how it made no difference to us that he was adopted. As he was growing up, we continually told Kris about his adoption, that we'd chosen him, and loved him as much as our other three children.

Throughout his life, Kris struggled with depression. I came to understand that even within the womb a mother can imprint on the unborn feelings she's having regarding the baby. An adopted child generally has a feeling belief of not being wanted, and, therefore, of not being worthy and valuable. It's an implicit belief, which makes it even more powerful. The development of the fetus is affected by the pregnant mother's emotional state with long term consequences—especially her stress, anxiety, and depression (Divecha 2018).

I heard Dr. Gabor Maté, M.D. (2009) share what his mother had told him about his experience of being born into a Jewish family in Europe at the time of the Holocaust. She'd had to call in a nurse because Gabor was crying nonstop. The nurse informed his mother that all the Jewish babies were crying. There is an unexplainable bond between the mother and the child that is profound and life-affecting. A child can begin to have chronic feelings of rejection just from a frown on their mother's face. A baby is sensitive to the size of the pupils of their mother's eyes, which change according to the mother's emotions.

There were a couple of times when I really noticed Kris's depression, and it led me to ask him if he wanted to find his biological parents. He consistently refused the offer. Then, one Friday afternoon when he was 19, I asked him again. This time, he agreed. He explained that he had wanted to in the past, but he hadn't wanted to make us feel bad.

I wasn't sure where to begin the search. I only knew Kris's mother's name and the state she came from. I called the largest library in the province to inquire if they had phone books in their database. They did. All they required was a last name and the state. They could then fax me a list of all the phone numbers in the state with that last name. We went for it. I gave the librarian my school's fax number, but because my wife, Penny, was out with the car, I had no way to get the list. I asked her to fax the list to the school, but also to pick one random name from the list and give me their phone number. There were several names on the list to choose from.

Kris and I prayed first, and then I dialed the number. A gentleman answered the phone. Within a couple of minutes, I had the phone number of someone who was most likely Kris's grandfather. Kris could hardly contain himself as I dialed the next phone number.

After a short and probably awkward introduction, it became apparent that I had the right person. The gentleman asked, "Would you mind repeating that to my wife? Let me pass the phone to her."

"Hello, my name is Don. I prayed, and then miraculously found your phone number. I have reason to believe that my adopted son is your grandson."

"If he is, he was born on April 9, 1977," she responded matter-of-factly.

That was Kris's birthday. This led to a conversation; after that Kris's biological mother called us. She lived within a day's drive from us. One weekend, I gave Kris the keys to our car, and he journeyed with a friend to meet his biological mother and two half-sisters.

When he returned, he was walking on air. He couldn't stop talking about how he and his sisters were so much alike. They even cracked their knuckles in the same order as he did. The connection with his biological family really helped Kris.

To this day, Kris keeps in touch with his biological mom. His grandfather wrote Kris a very kind letter, appreciating Kris's exceptional character, validating us for how we had raised him. His grandparents came to our house for a visit. They also came to Kris's wedding. Recently, Kris called me to say that he'd taken his four-year-old son to visit his great grandparents. These kinds of reunions by adopted children with biological families are rare. We feel very blessed by how it turned out, and privileged to know this wonderful family.

A few years after Kris's wedding, Kris's biological grandfather called me with a surprising request. Two of his grandsons were living with their dad near where I lived at the time. One of them had just died under strange circumstances while acting a part in a movie being filmed. He was Kris's first cousin. I was a pastor at the time, and I accepted his invitation to conduct the funeral.

Kris was commercial fishing in Alaska, so he couldn't attend the funeral. There was a picture of Kris's deceased cousin at the funeral. My mouth fell open, and I teared up immediately. He was the exact image of Kris. It was the most difficult funeral I have ever conducted.

Adopted by God

"How we praise God, the Father of our Lord Jesus Christ, who has blessed us with every spiritual blessing in the heavenly realms because we belong to Christ" (Ephesians 1:3). "Spiritual blessing?" What is that? It's a rather vague term. The words, "has blessed us," are in the past tense. Spiritual blessings are found in "heavenly realms." What does that mean?

Paul uses the term "heavenly realms" again in Ephesians 1:20b, "seated him [Christ] in the place of honor at God's right hand in the heavenly realms," and Ephesians 2:6, "For he raised us from the dead along with Christ, and we are seated with him in the heavenly realms—all because we are one with Christ." When God brought Christ to sit on his right hand in the heavenly realms, he brought us too! This sentence is in the past tense.

On the Damascus road, where Saul was traveling to persecute Christ-followers, he was blinded by the light and heard Christ speak.

"'Saul! Saul! Why are you persecuting me?'

'Who are you, sir?' Saul asked.

And the voice replied, 'I am Jesus, the one you are persecuting!'" (Acts 9:3-5).

Jesus identifies with us so closely that he told Saul that Saul was persecuting Jesus himself by persecuting his followers. One of Paul's common expressions became, "those who are in Christ" (Romans 8:1 NIV), and "seated us with him in the heavenly realms in Christ Jesus" (Ephesians 2:6 NIV). There are so many more verses that use the phrase *in Christ*.

God desires to bring us close for warm intimacy.

"Long ago, even before he made the world, God loved us and chose us **in Christ** to be holy and without fault in his eyes [some translations say, "in his sight"]. His unchanging plan has always been to adopt us into his own family by bringing us to himself through Jesus Christ. And this gave him great pleasure" (Ephesians 1:4-5, emphasis mine).

God is not satisfied with a distant view of us from the heavenly realms. He prefers to bring us up close for warm intimacy. This is the language of a father with his children or a bridegroom with his bride.

"Long before he laid down earth's foundations, he had us in mind, had settled on us as the focus of his love to be made whole and holy by his love" (Ephesians 1:5 The Message). The word *adopted* is used in most translations. God's plan has always been to include us in his family life.

Some think of adoption as being below blood birth in order of importance. Paul, however, is addressing Roman culture. A natural child could be cut out of an inheritance, but an adopted child could never be excluded. Inconceivable! Jesus is a natural son or heir, and we have been made joint-heirs with Jesus through adoption.

"So you should not be like cowering, fearful slaves. You should behave instead like God's very own children, adopted into his family—calling him 'Father, dear Father'. For his Holy Spirit speaks to us deep in our hearts and tells us that we are God's children. And since we are his children, we will share his treasures—for everything God gives to his Son, Christ, is ours too" (Romans 8:15-17).

Jesus prayed, "Abba, Father" (Mark 14:36a). *Abba* is an Aramaic word meaning "Daddy." It is the most intimate way of saying "Father."

Abba is an Aramaic word meaning "Daddy."

Paul encourages us to pray the same way: "Because you are his sons, God sent the Spirit of his Son into our hearts, the Spirit who calls out, 'Abba, Father'" (Galatians 4:6 NIV).

It's not about the wealth that we inherit because this family never dies. We inherit the Father himself—we experience being in the family itself! We are wanted, chosen, welcomed, known, accepted, and embraced. We get to taste, feel, and experience the family life ourselves.

The Father's dream for us is to be brought into his house, and not just brought into his house but honored as family members at his table. We are seated not only at his table but at his right hand in close conversation with him. It is not just a conversation, but a friendship that is so close and personal, so real and intimate that everything the Father is and has is shared with us. That is adoption!

Acceptance is a bridge to freedom. Be free!

6

My Acceptable Addiction
Self-awareness—A Bridge to Freedom

My doctor reached for his prescription pad and began to write.

"Oh, no!" I thought, "He's writing me a prescription for medication." He tore off the page from the pad and handed it to me.

It read, "Clean out your desk and do not return to work until further notice.,"

To this, I replied, "I have two desks" (two leadership positions).

The doctor took back the slip of paper, crossed something out, and rewrote it: "Clean out both desks and do not return to work until further notice." I thought it would be a few weeks, but it turned into almost a year. That was over ten years ago.

I am currently employed almost full time as an addiction counselor at a forty-two-day live-in addictions treatment program funded by the government. I was privileged to be hired, not only as one of the two clinical therapists, but to also help create the curriculum and program. We take a best practices approach that is based on the latest research. It is a bio-psycho-social-spiritual approach to addiction because humans are complex beings. What we eat and how we exercise affects our emotions and spirituality. Our emotional health affects our immune system, digestion, and circulatory system. Our emotions affect our relationships and vice versa.

Myths About Addiction

There are several myths about addiction. One of the most common myths is that addiction is a genetic disease. The reason people made this conclusion was that it was observed to run in families. But there's been no "addiction gene" discovered. The environment, however, is a much more valid reason for addiction. Families tend to repeat dysfunction through the generations.

Another popular myth is that addiction is a moral failure. All a person needs to do is say "no." This philosophy makes the addiction worse because of the shaming that usually accompanies it. It is too simplistic.

The truth is that addiction is the result of changes in brain neural pathways. It is a slow process that changes the way the brain functions. It is a slow process, and a lot of work to change it back again to a non-addicted brain.

Imagine that there is a paved path going through the wilderness, but you wish to create a different path that leads to a different place. It would require trampling down weeds and moving obstacles in the way. It would take hard work, traveling the same path repeatedly before the path would become as easy to travel as the paved path. Keep in mind that the old pathway is still there. This illustrates how our brains create new neuropathways that have different outcomes when moving from addiction to sobriety.

> The ideas that addiction is genetic or
> a moral failure are myths.

Addiction does have some of the features of an illness. Still, a disease model by itself does not even come close to understanding what addiction is all about. It's far more than a medical issue. Gabor Maté studied the worldwide scientific literature on the research of addiction. He discovered that the research is nearly unanimous regarding the nature of substance addiction. Addiction can be thought of as a chronic brain condition. Like other mental or physical conditions, there is no reason to blame or shame a person for relapse any more than you would when someone's rheumatoid arthritis flared up again (Maté 2008).

The Development of Addiction

The research that has been done on the brain since the invention of instruments like the CAT (computerized axial tomography) and MRI (magnetic resonance imaging) scans is phenomenal. We now know that, unlike animals, most of the development of the neural connections in the human brain takes place after birth. How well a child is nurtured by their parents determines the number of neuro-connections in the brain. The brain of a child that is neglected or abused has far fewer neural connections than the brain of a child who is nurtured well. The fewer the neural connections, the more susceptible a person is to addiction (Maté 2009). A brain with fewer neural connections does not experience the same feeling of being loved as a brain with many neural connections. This is because there is a lower output of natural opiate-like chemicals produced in the brain. Among other functions, these chemicals moderate both physical and emotional pain and create the feeling of being loved. People who have a cocaine addiction, whom I have counseled, will often say things like, "Cocaine feels like a warm hug," or "I have finally found love and a home in cocaine." Studies of the brains of adults who were raised in abusive, chaotic environments, reveal brains that are far younger than typical adult brains. As counselors, we notice the behaviors of people in addiction to be more adolescent in nature than mature adults. This is arrested development due to their inadequate childhood environments.

> How well a child is nurtured by parents is
> the greatest determiner of addiction.

I never refer to my clients with an addiction as "addicts." The words *addict* or *junky* are labels that we put on people or ourselves. Labels like these can shame. When we label them as addicts in society, it separates them from the rest who "are not addicts." The truth, however, is that we're all addicted to something. We are addicted to sin. "If we say we have no sin, we are only fooling ourselves and refusing to accept the truth" (1 John 1:8). This is why it is unfair to label some people according to their specific addiction or sin. People with addictions already carry enough shame, and shame is pain. The unconscious brain does not distinguish between physical and emotional pain. Pain is pain.

I prefer to use the words *people with an addiction*. As I have said, the primary cause of addiction is pain. The question is not, "Why the addiction?" The question is, "Why the pain?" In fact, we could replace the word *addict* in any sentence with the words, "someone with so much pain, they don't know how to cope with it." This is why I spend most of the counseling time looking at and healing the pain that is the root of the addiction.

The good news is our brains never stop developing. Science has now embraced the concept of neuroplasticity. This is the opposite of what I was taught in university when I took my degree in biology over forty-five years ago. We now know that our brains continually change throughout life. The brain can repair itself through psychotherapy.

Probably the most critical factor in recovery from addiction is that a person must live in an environment of unconditional acceptance. The person needs lots of love and compassion to change their addicted brain to a sober brain. This is why every child needs to develop a healthy brain in the first place, something most people with addictions never had the chance to do. This is the environment that Jesus wants his church to be. We are called the body of Christ in Scripture. We are his hands and feet in this world. My definition of recovery is "learning to love again, beginning with yourself."

> The most critical factor for recovery is an environment of unconditional acceptance.

When we think of addiction, we usually think about alcohol and drugs. There are also process addictions: sex, pornography, gambling, food, shopping, social media, religious activities, work, and more.

Some of these things are good things, and even a necessary part of living. But when any of them get out of balance with other important things in life, they become problematic. I always thought that it was just a joke to use the word *workaholic*. Now I understand that these process addictions result from a chemical change in the brain as well. There is little difference between how different types of addiction work. This is because all thinking and behaving results in chemical changes in the brain. In this sense, every addiction is a chemical addiction.

Substances, in themselves, are not necessarily addictive. Many people undergo surgery using opioids as an anesthetic, or take prescription opioids for pain. Still, only a few of them become addicted as a result. Some become addicted because the physical pain becomes chronic, and others because they have unresolved emotional pain.

> Addiction is primarily about coping with pain.

The idea that certain substances are addictive in and of themselves came from many studies of rats. When rats were given a choice between water and morphine, for example, the rats eventually began to choose the morphine over the water and became addicted. But when one scientist, Bruce Alexander, looked at the experiments, he noticed that the addicted rats had been put in an empty cage, alone. Bruce decided to run the experiment differently. He built two types of homes. Some of the rats were put into cages and left alone, like the previous experiments. Some of the rats were put into cages that were filled with a community of rats. The community of rats were also given all kinds of toys, everything a rat could want. He called it Rat Park. He discovered that the rats in Rat Park used only a small fraction of the morphine compared with the amount used by the rats kept alone in cages. It wasn't the drug that caused the addiction but the environment (Hari 2015).

This is most likely why addiction is more prevalent in certain subcultures of our society. These subcultures are usually characterized by poverty and feelings of separation and rejection by the majority culture. Historical abuse happens when the younger generation learns their history of mistreatment, such as with slavery or the creation of Indigenous residential schools. They feel the pain of shame for being who they are (Maté 2009).

My Socially Acceptable Addiction

Let's look at my socially acceptable addiction, workaholism. Workaholism is the addiction we often brag about, and sometimes give awards to people who have it. I have heard people say, "I haven't taken a vacation in years." It can be especially true within the church. I recall, as a pastor, saying, "If you want to get something done in the church, give it to the busiest person."

Interestingly enough, I received the "Above and Beyond Award" from our district leadership just before my near burnout, recovery from which took close to a year. I call it a near burnout because I've completely recovered from it through therapy. I've met many others that have never been able to fully recover.

My life has been a pattern of taking on more than a full load of work. Aside from my fulltime work as a teacher, I would take on extra projects, such as leading mission projects to third world countries, church youth leader, chairperson of a building committee, a member of the school board, and more. When I was young, I never gave it much thought. Now when I look back, I can see how the workaholism affected me, regardless of what my young body felt at the time. It started to really catch up with me during the last few years of my ten years as a pastor. At that time, I was a pastor of a church with a couple of hundred people. I was, however, a teacher in (and later the principal of) a kindergarten to grade twelve school at the same time. The church offered me this "opportunity," but, in embracing it, I must take ownership of my mistake.

I started to get an underlying feeling that something serious was wrong in my life. I couldn't put my finger on it, but then others began to see symptoms as well.

I was not sleeping much. I ignored it because I was enjoying the ride, and I didn't think I needed to sleep that much anyway. Quite often, I would wake up at two or three in the morning. Because I couldn't sleep anymore, I would get up and begin working on something. I thought that this would tire me out so I could go back to bed and fall asleep. The trouble was, most of the time, I would work until it was time to get up. Committee meetings would last late into the night. Because I had two leadership positions, I had committee meetings most nights of the week.

Something inside of me kept saying that I couldn't continue this pattern forever. On the other hand, I was enjoying it! It felt good to get things accomplished. It felt good to receive the thanks and praise for jobs well done. A burn out is now called "compassion fatigue." People who are caregivers are very susceptible to it. Now I understand that I was getting high on my own adrenaline. When your system keeps pumping out adrenaline like this, eventually you get adrenal burn out. I developed an allergy to my own adrenaline. This gave me a chronic cough for about twenty years that was triggered by stress.

I started to get worried when I would have panic attacks in the middle of the day. I'd sit at my desk and shake when I couldn't concentrate enough to read a paragraph. I would walk to the far end of the school to do something, and then couldn't remember what I'd come for when I got there. I had so many urgent things to do I couldn't decide what was most important. When my wife, Juanita, and I would go for a walk, she'd complain that I wasn't present with her. She said that my mind was somewhere else— lost in space. I was building a school schedule in my mind, one that usually took more than fifty hours to satisfy all the required criteria.

Finally, some close friends who themselves had experienced a burn out, saw the signs and did an intervention. They made me promise to go see a doctor. I promised them that I would be as honest as I could with the doctor. This was when the doctor told me to clean out both desks and leave work until further notice.

During my stress leave, I went for a two-week session at Silver Hills Guest House and Spa. The leader of the wellness program, Phil Brewer, spent a lot of time helping me. I discovered that I was in worse shape than I'd thought. Another staff member at Silver Hills gave me a couple of excellent books to read. The first was, *Never Good Enough: Growing Up Imperfect in a "Perfect" Family; How to Break the Cycle of Codependence and Addiction for the Next Generation,* written by Carol Cannon (1993). The other book was *Broken Toys Broken Dreams: Understanding and Healing Codependency, Compulsive Behaviors, and Family* by Terry Kellogg (1990). I began to see that I had all the textbook symptoms of addiction. I became aware that I was a workaholic and of how it had developed.

Like all addictions, workaholism is not just about the behavior. There are attitudes and beliefs that one holds that drive the behavior. To cure the workaholism, I had to identify and change the beliefs that supported it. Today, as a person in long term recovery, I don't just have to hold myself to an average of forty hours of work per week, I have to work on thinking differently to stay within that limit.

Abuse

Our attitudes and beliefs originate in childhood. Addiction usually originates from growing up in an environment that doesn't provide proper nurturing. Homes that are abusive and neglectful, physically and emotionally, lay the foundation for addiction. There is, however, a type of abuse and neglect that's often overlooked. Research shows that children who grow up in extremely conservative religious homes are also susceptible (Cannon 1993). Children raised under "zillions" of rules and who are continually chastised by their parents, never feel that they're good enough. I call it religious abuse.

Stephen Covey created the metaphor of an emotional bank account. We are continually making deposits and withdrawals in all our relationships. Deposits consist of giving compliments, speaking words of gratitude and appreciation, and performing acts of kindness. Withdrawals include criticizing, pointing out faults, and unfair treatment. The magic number to keep a relationship in the black is a five to one, positive to negative ratio (Dollard 2017). A parent probably believes that they are helping their child every time they correct them. But if it's not balanced by at least five positive messages to each negative message, the child's account goes into the red. Children develop a negative perspective of themselves, resulting in feeling beliefs of never being good enough and feelings of shame.

My intention is not to blame parents or to shame them. It's not about blame; it's about awareness. I cannot change what I'm not aware of. I believe that parents do the best they can with the tools they have. The amount of information available to my parents in the 1950s was minimal and far below the quality of information that we have available today. I have watched, with pride, my adult children as parents. In many ways, they are doing a better job than I did. If I knew what I know now, I would have been a different parent.

Let's not forget that parents have been wounded themselves. It has been said that hurt people hurt people. Abuse can come from anyone and in many forms. Following is a list of types of abuse. I've built this list from multiple sources, including my experience of listening to clients. The book, *The Emotionally Abusive Relationship* by Beverly Engel (2002), can provide greater depth to this topic. Most of these types of abuse can be grouped under "Emotional Abuse." Many people that I share this with discover that they'd been abused in ways that they never considered as abuse. If one grows up with abuse, it may seem normal rather than abusive.

<u>Physical abuse</u> involves whippings, beatings, spankings that are over the top, being slapped on the head, dragged by the ears, burned, doused with ice water, etc.

<u>Intellectual abuse</u> is when your opinions are ridiculed or attacked, or you're not allowed to differ from another person's point of view.

<u>Physical neglect</u> is when you are not fed enough food or provided basic necessities, such as clothing, shelter, or medical attention.

<u>Emotional neglect or deprivation</u> is when parents don't show enough interest in a child. They don't talk to or hold and hug their child sufficiently. They are distracted and, therefore, emotionally unavailable to their children. Parents with an addiction are often neglectful of their children's needs. Parents or even spouses who are workaholics are often not available as much as they should be.

<u>Physical abandonment</u> is when a child is left alone in the home or the car for long periods. It's also when they're not picked up at a designated time and place as promised. It also includes when parents divorce, and one parent's involvement with the child significantly decreases. The death of a parent is a type of abandonment. My month in the hospital on the heels of their mother dying was an example of abandonment. It's not how an adult perceives it. It's about how the child perceives it.

<u>Verbal abuse</u> is when you are continually being put down, called names, being criticized, or shamed. There is a difference between criticism and constructive feedback. Criticism involves assigning labels, such as useless, ugly, irresponsible, or lazy. It can also be through using words like *always, never,* or *only*. These words make things all-encompassing in nature. Criticism attacks a person's character, personality, and identity. A negative identity produces shame (false guilt). For example, "I am useless." Unlike criticism, constructive feedback involves pointing out unhelpful behaviors. I may have failed to be responsible for something, but that does not make me an irresponsible person. No one is perfect. It's important to point out mistakes in a person's behavior that need to change. It can become abusive, however, when we don't meet the five to one ratio of positive to negative remarks.

<u>Boundary violation</u> is when your need for privacy is not respected. It's when someone walks in on you in the bathroom or your bedroom without knocking (especially from the adolescent years and on). It's when someone goes through your personal possessions, computer, or cell phone. Of course, parents must monitor young children's behaviors.

<u>Sexual abuse</u> is when a child is exposed to nudity or sexual content at inappropriate ages. Blatant sexual abuse is inappropriate touch and rape.

<u>Role reversal</u> is when a parent expects a child to meet his or her needs. The child ends up parenting them. This is common when a parent has a heavy substance addiction.

<u>Emotional "sexual" abuse</u> is when a parent uses the child to meet their own emotional needs. This creates an unhealthy bond between them. It often happens when one parent is out of the picture (emotionally or physically), and the other parent substitutes the spousal relationship with a relationship with a

child. It could also be when a child feels responsible for keeping the parent in a good mood.

Social abuse is when a parent interferes with their child's access to friends their age or fails to teach their child essential social skills. A spouse controlling a partner's social life and limiting their friendships is also social abuse. Homeschooling children without providing them with opportunities to associate with their peers is abusive.

Religious abuse is when religion is used to manipulate you to comply with rules. It's also when hellfire is used to coerce you to obey or believe. It happens when God is portrayed as someone who is watching every move that you make in order to find some fault with you. You are being abused if you're told that when bad things happen to you, God must be punishing you for something you did wrong.

Chaotic abuse happens when an environment has very little stability. There is constant discord and chaos. This could be due to someone being extremely and chronically sick, or someone having to move a lot. I went to twelve schools in the first twelve years of my education. My children often had to do their school homework on the floor of their mother's hospital room. Any of these examples of chaotic abuse may be situations that are unavoidable, but there are still usually negative consequences that arise from a lack of stability.

I recall an illustration of how parents sometimes use God to manipulate children to do what they want them to do. Children then grow up thinking that Christianity is a list of do's and don'ts, rather than a relationship with Jesus.

Mom and dad say to Billy, "Billy, do you love Jesus?"

"Yes," says Billy.

"Well, then take out the garbage."

And all the way to the garbage, Billy is wondering if he really does love Jesus.

When parents make God the scapegoat in an attempt to get their children to do what they want them to do, this neuro-associates emotional pain with God.

The idea occurred to me that adults sometimes talk to children about concepts that a child's mind is incapable of understanding. A wrong or inadequate understanding can be worse than no understanding. For example, I wonder, how can a child fully comprehend the concept of Jesus dying in our place for our sins? I can only see harm done when you give a child the impression that God would kill you for stealing a cookie or pinching your little sister. "Jesus died, so you don't have to die for stealing a cookie." To a child's mind, how could these infractions warrant the death penalty? This is religious abuse. Heavy concepts such as these must be introduced to young minds very thoughtfully and at appropriate stages of development. I've often wondered why Jewish children didn't go to the temple until the age of twelve. I believe that children are not accountable for their sins until they reach a particular developmental stage. But we still need to teach them right from wrong.

I once overheard a parent say, "Now children, don't giggle when you thank Jesus for the food. Jesus doesn't like it when you disrespect him like that. He might give you a tummy ache if you are disrespectful." This is religious abuse.

This was the religious environment that I was raised in. In my experience, it's quite typical of Christian schools, churches, and homes. We might talk about a relationship with God, but we often model and emphasize behaviorism.

A Journey Toward Healing

Healing my workaholism meant taking a hard look at my own false beliefs and unhealthy ways of thinking. I call it stinking thinking. After I unpack this, you might say, "Don, how could you think that way? Surely you knew the truth, didn't you? You were even a religion teacher and a pastor."

Let me first explain something that psychologists call dissonance. Dissonance is a lack of harmony. It's when we believe two opposite things at the same time but cannot harmonize them. For example, I believe that I am created in the image of God, but I also hold beliefs like, "I'm useless," "I'm a failure," "I'm not good enough," "I'm ugly," or "I'm weird."

I may believe that God is love, and he forgives me of my sins by grace and not by my works. But I can also have thoughts like, "The reason I got sick is because I was disobedient to God." I might think that, "The reason I'm having financial problems is because I'm not paying my tithe or giving large enough donations."

Most of the time, the truthful beliefs are held in our conscious minds. We can say them and preach them, but the lies are held in our unconscious minds. The lies are often only feeling beliefs. I feel guilty, even when I'm not guilty of anything I can put my finger on. I feel I'm not good enough, even when I know I've done my best.

Following are some of the patterns of self-defeating behaviors and false ways of thinking that are often linked to addiction.

I go to my addiction when I'm in emotional pain to relieve that pain. This is more obvious when you consider substance addictions like alcohol. Work was my way of numbing the pain of a wife who was chronically ill, could end up in the hospital, and die at any time. The reason I say that I was a workaholic is because the amount of time spent working was detrimental to my own wellbeing and emotional health. This went on for over twenty years, and it only got worse with time.

This is especially typical behavior for men because men do not generally like to talk about their feelings as much as most women. Men often hold their emotions in by distracting themselves with work, sex, eating, or adrenaline-producing sports and such. As men, we need to learn to talk about our pain in open and honest ways instead of pretending that everything is great. Men need to stop thinking that they must be strong all the time. Workaholism is not necessarily about work. It's more about having to be busy all the time.

I felt guilty or lazy if I took the time to relax. I would take my briefcase to the beach because I felt that I always had to be productive and efficient with my time. This was a product of my German heritage. Regardless, it's not wise to live out of balance between work, play, and rest. We use the expression, "burning the candle at both ends," for this. We are borrowing from our future life force to accomplish more than we need to accomplish today. We lose more than we gain, but we don't find that out until it is too late. I am referring, for example, to my habit of attending committee meetings on so many evenings, and then getting up at three o'clock in the morning to begin a workday.

I had difficulty saying, "no." It felt selfish to say "no" to anyone who needed my help. I lacked boundaries in my life. Having balance is called temperance in Scripture. "And every man that strives for the mastery is temperate in all things" (1 Corinthians 9:25). I will address the topic of self-care more fully in another chapter.

Underlying Unhealthy Beliefs

There are particular unhealthy beliefs that underlie the inability to say "no" when someone asks for help. One driving force is fear of rejection or judgment. What will people say if I say, "no?" Will they still like me? Will my job always be secure?

We call this being a people pleaser. Here's the dilemma of a people pleaser who is a leader of an organization: it's impossible to please everyone. I was trying to please the conservatives on the one hand and the liberals on the other hand. I wasn't happy unless everyone was happy. It can get exhausting, trying to make everyone happy.

I had negative core beliefs about myself, "I'm not good enough," and "I have to get it perfect before people will like me." We call these automatic thoughts because we think them so fast, and so often, we're not always aware of them. They are powerful, and they get us into trouble.

To feel good enough, I would go ahead and volunteer myself once again, even when I knew I didn't really have the time or the energy. I read a great book by Joyce Meyer that pointed this out so clearly to me, *Approval Addiction: Overcoming Your Need to Please Everyone* (Meyer 2008). Another reason I was addicted to work was because I was addicted to approval, even if it was my own approval at times. No matter how much I accomplished, it was never enough to satisfy me. It feels good when people say things like, "That was really great, Don." "Wonderful job." "We need you, Don." But in the end, I was my own worst critic, always beating myself up with thoughts of not being good enough.

One of the most challenging tasks in my recovery from my work addiction was to realize that I was not indispensable. I had to believe that others could take over for me and do just fine without me. As a counselor, I must remind myself that I'm not anyone's savior. After doing all that I can, I remember that they are adults who have choices. They are responsible for their own recovery. I am just a facilitator in that process.

Another result of my negative core belief, "I am not good enough," was handling constructive feedback. I was very defensive. Receiving this kind of feedback triggered my core negative belief, and I would automatically go to a survival mode of fight, flight, or freeze. This, of course, continually got me into trouble with people because I'd become defensive. No one appreciates someone who is always "right."

I understand now that there are always two or more valid perspectives to every issue (depending on the number of people involved). It works better to listen actively. Active listening involves non-verbal communication like eye contact, audible sounds, and words of acknowledgment. It also means being able to rephrase what someone has said until they know you understand them. This validates their perspective.

The antidote to defensiveness also includes taking immediate ownership of mistakes. I now continually tell myself, "I don't have to be perfect. I don't have to be right. I could be wrong. I am enough, even if I am wrong."

I had to change my way of speaking. Instead of blurting out, "That's not right, it's this way . . ." I began to say instead, "I might be wrong, but I think . . ." or, "It's only my opinion, but I suggest . . ." Another thing I had to learn was to say something like, "Thank you for the feedback and ideas. I will take them into consideration." Implementing these changes made a world of difference in my relationships.

Who Am I?

I have heard people say things like, "I'm going to India to find myself." The problem is, wherever you go, there you are. These people lack an identity—the answer to, "Who am I?" I also had to discover the answer to the question, "Who am I?" That might seem like a very odd question, but it is a fundamental question to being emotionally healthy. I would gamble that most of us couldn't give a satisfactory answer to that question.

Codependent people tie their identity and self-worth to external things. These things could be a career, money, possessions, designer clothing, or body image. My identity was tied up with my job (I am a teacher, a pastor, a counselor). If you link your identity to external things like these, and then you lose those things, you're left without an identity. This happened to me when I "retired."

Here is what I need to tell myself continually: "I am not what I do." "I am not what I own." If I don't continually remind myself of these things, I would never feel good enough; I would never feel I had enough. How much money does it take to satisfy a person? A little more. In Africa, I had a poster on my living room wall that read, "Happiness is not having what you want, it is wanting what you have."

The truth is, "I am enough." I am enough just the way God created me. I am a child of God. I have worth, and I have value. I am worthy, not because of what I've done, not because of what I do, or not because of what I own. I'm not worthy because Jesus died for me. His death for me shows my worth to him. I am worthy simply because I exist. Here lies the most significant breakthrough I made in my recovery. I don't have to prove my worth to anyone, including myself or God.

"I will be a Father to you, and you will be my son. . ." (Corinthians 6:18).

"So you should not be like cowering, fearful slaves. You should behave instead like God's very own children, adopted into his family—calling him Father, dear Father. For his Holy Spirit speaks to us deep in our hearts and tells us that we are God's children. And since we are his children, we will share His treasures—for everything God gives to his Son, Christ, is ours, too" (Romans 8:15-17).

I am an educated person. I know these things with my head, but not necessarily with my heart. This creates dissonance. With my head (my logical mind), I believed God loved me. Still, my feeling beliefs prevented me from believing how kind God was and that his thoughts towards me were always loving. My biological parents were not perfect. They did the best they could with the understanding they had. The truth, however, is that my dad was a workaholic too. He was not often present in my life as much as I wanted him to be. When I did something wrong, he would yell at me. My parents would continually correct me and find fault with me. At least that's how I perceived it at the time. I'm sure my parents meant well and believed they were helping me become a better person. The criticism was seldom about immoral issues. It was about more general things, like not cleaning my room well enough or not getting my work done fast enough. Things had to be done correctly. I'm sure now that my parents had no idea how I was interpreting all of this. I truly believe my parents did the best they could with the tools they had, but they fell far short of my Father God. I, too, fell short as a father to my own children when I followed the same pattern.

I Am Enough

Today, I can see God smiling affectionately, maybe even giggling when a few little children are giggling so hard at the table that they can't pray. I cannot see God giving them a tummy ache for being children.

I don't feel guilty and beat myself up for falling asleep in prayer or while reading my Bible. I now see myself as a child, curled up on the lap of my heavenly Father, falling asleep in his arms. I picture him looking down on me with a tenderness that I had for my children when they fell asleep while I was reading them a bedtime story. Jesus kept coming back to this issue over and over. Look at so many of his illustrations and references to the Father in heaven.

"You parents—if your children ask for a loaf of bread, do you give them a stone instead? Or if they ask for a fish, do you give them a snake? Of course not! If you sinful people know how to give good gifts to your children, how much more will your heavenly Father give good gifts to those who ask him" (Matthew 7:9-11).

"Not even a sparrow, worth only half a penny, can fall to the ground without your Father knowing it. And the very hairs on your head are all numbered. So don't be afraid; you are more valuable to him than a whole flock of sparrows" (Matthew 10:29-31).

"If a shepherd has one hundred sheep, and one wanders away and is lost, what will he do? Won't he leave the ninety-nine others and go out into the hills to search for the lost one? And if he finds it, he will surely rejoice over it more than over the ninety-nine that didn't wander away! In the same way, it is not my heavenly Father's will that even one of these little ones should perish" (Matthew 18:12-14).

Of course, all children who have missing fathers, physically or emotionally, suffer the same symptoms. Every boy and girl needs to hear their father say, "You have what it takes. I believe in you. You are worthy and valuable." If we didn't get these messages from our earthly parents, now as adults we could realize that we have a good Father in God who says these things to us. You have a good Father. For many who have experienced severe abuse at the hands of a father, that is very difficult to believe.

Children develop implicit beliefs about God through what they experience from their parents. An absent parent means an absent God. A harsh parent means a cruel God, and a strict parent means a rigid and judgmental God. Even if we learn an explicit view of God that is loving and accepting on a cognitive level, our implicit feeling beliefs cause dissonance.

If you want a great book about this topic, I recommend Brennan Manning's book *Abba's Child: The Cry of the Heart for Intimate Belonging* (2002). The author is a Catholic priest who fell into alcoholism as a result of his hard work in ministry. His book is the story of his struggle to move into an intimate relationship with Jesus.

"The Spirit you received does not make you slaves so that you live in fear again; rather, the Spirit you received brought about your adoption to sonship. And by him, we cry, 'Abba, Father'" (Romans 8:15).

The truth is, "God sees me as worthy and valuable."

You can count on that promise. It's a certified check that you can take to the bank and cash. This check will not bounce. It is God's guarantee.

I hope you have accepted God's guarantee of salvation. I hope you have received his free gift of forgiveness and eternal life through Jesus, but forgiveness and being saved is not the end goal.

The good news is that you can come home to a good Father. He treasures you and values you more than his own life. He sees me like I saw my children when they were born, and holds me like I held them in my arms for the first time. Instantly, I knew that each child was the most precious thing on the face of the earth. I would give my life for them. I knew their great value even though they hadn't even graduated from kindergarten. Each of my children is valuable beyond measure.

The good news is that you are enough to God, and there is no need to prove that to him, to yourself, or anyone else. You are enough just because you exist. You are God's child. You are worthy and valuable. An awareness of this is the beginning of healing and sets you free.

Self-awareness is a bridge to freedom. Be free!

7

Is Self-Love an Oxymoron?
Boundaries—A Bridge to Freedom

"I have no medicine for you. I need this medicine for myself."

It felt incredibly selfish to say these words, and I was uncontrollably sobbing as I made my way around the circle during an experiential exercise in group therapy. Being a pastor and counselor makes it especially difficult to tell someone that I cannot help them. But it was this exercise that saved my life. If it weren't for this exercise, I would not have gone to the doctor about my symptoms of burnout as soon as I did. I believe that.

My group counselor made me say these words twenty-five times to twenty-five people in my group. I have participated in this kind of exercise in a couple of programs over the years: "Breakthrough," in Kansas City, Missouri and "Connections" in Kelowna, British Columbia. There's also a similar program called "Choices," in Fort Worth, Texas, and Calgary, Alberta. I recommend these experiential-type weekend programs. I found "Breakthrough" by HeartConnexion (see heartconnexion.org) to be the most spiritually-focused program of the two that I've attended. The emphasis in these programs is not on workbook-type information but on games and exercises that you actively participate in with others.

The experiential method of learning is more effective in creating change because it activates the right side of the brain. The left side is linear in nature and processes information. The right side is the more relational and creative side of the brain. When we balance the use of our left and right brain, we call it horizontal integration. In experiential learning, we don't just sit and take in information. We play games where we walk around and interact in a variety of ways. We make use of multimedia and especially music. I find it interesting that in the Old Testament there is a lot of sensual activities in worship. There were sacrifices, fire, incense, smoke, and dramatic ceremonies to illustrate the truth of the gospel. The sacrificed lamb would eventually represent Jesus, who would come to save the world.

Programs like the ones in which I participated inspired me to create my own program, "Bridges to Freedom," which is also the name of my private counseling practice. I have been doing "Bridges to Freedom" several times a year for over seven years now. People find freedom, and make considerable changes in their thinking and living as a result of one weekend.

I want to go into more depth on what is necessary to both prevent and recover from addiction. A key ingredient is self-care. As I mentioned in the previous chapter, my definition of recovery is "learning to love again, beginning with yourself." Unfortunately, most people in addiction have never loved themselves well. On the other hand, I've found most people in addiction to be very caring people. Invariably, caring comes up on almost everyone's list of strengths. I warn them, however, that a great strength can also be a great weakness. It is possible to care too much.

> My definition of recovery is "learning to
> love again, beginning with yourself."

As a youth, I was taught, "Love God first, then your neighbor, then yourself last." It sounds very spiritual and holy. One day, I began to ponder Jesus' words, "Love your neighbor as yourself" (part of Mark 12:31). Jesus was quoting Leviticus 19:18. What struck me was that if I didn't love myself well, then I am commanded not to love my neighbor well either! It doesn't say, "Love your neighbor more than yourself," or "better than yourself." It says, "as yourself."

The word "as" could act as an equal sign (=) in a math equation: $3 + 7 = 10$ could be written as $10 = 3 + 7$. Love yourself as you love your neighbor would be just as valid an equation.

I know many people who are uncomfortable with the concept of self-love. But we must keep in mind the meaning of love. Love is a pure and holy thing. God is love. Love is a verb. Love may be thought of as an emotion, but primarily it is an action that creates pleasant emotions. To love ourselves means to take loving actions towards ourselves. Love cannot be a sin. Love is the opposite of sin. Some refer to unconditional love as if there were some other kind of love. If love isn't unconditional, then it isn't love. Just like you can't force someone to love you, you can't buy love either.

Love is a Verb

Love is a verb! Love is caring, nurturing behavior. Self-love or self-care means taking time to rest, sleep, exercise, relax, work, play, pray, and eat healthy. God asks us to extend grace to others, why not to ourselves as well? God asks us to forgive others, why not ourselves as well? Why would I treat myself any differently than God does? If I should speak politely to my neighbor, why not be polite in my self-talk. Do you find yourself beating yourself up with abusive thoughts about yourself? Stop that stinking thinking! Use healthy self-talk.

Is it righteous to be a doormat? Is it healthy to be a people pleaser? Are you allowed to hold your own opinion about something?

Inevitably, I ask every client working on addiction the question, "Why are you here?"

Some provide answers such as, "I'm here for my spouse, for my children, or for the judge."

I say, "Wrong answer. Recovery doesn't work unless you are here for yourself. The best gift you can give your spouse or your children is a healthy, sober you!" Is that being selfish?

Boundaries

Cloud and Townsend (1992) are known for their books and workshops on boundaries. Their book, *Boundaries: When to Say Yes, How to Say No, To Take Control of Your Life,* has been a lifesaver for many. The book provides practical guidance on the topic of boundaries. We can't put boundaries on other people because we have no control over others. We must not attempt to put boundaries on others because it kills love. I am not referring to parents placing boundaries on children. There are appropriate boundaries for different ages of development. Neither am I referring to other types of unequal relationships such as teacher-student, employer-employee, and police-citizen. I am referring to coworkers, spouses, classmates, and fellow church members. But, at times, we must put boundaries on ourselves to protect ourselves from harm. The problem lies in knowing what boundaries are necessary and appropriate. Healthy self-care must be distinguished from being selfish towards others.

Love is not love without freedom, but it could also be said that love is not love without boundaries.

After the awareness of my addiction to work, I had to begin to place boundaries on myself. Simply put, I had to learn to say "no" to some things. Before one can say, "no," one needs to know when to say, "yes." In other words, you need to know what your values are. Sometimes you need to know the difference between what is good and what is better or best. There are a lot of good things to do, but our limited time may only allow us to choose what is best and say "no" to some good things.

One of the most challenging things for me to do as a counselor is to tell someone that I have a full load, and I cannot help them; that they will have to look for another counselor. I need to remind myself that I don't want to end up on stress leave again. I need to remind myself that I am not the only counselor in the city.

My daughter, Leanne, gave us our first grandchild. Tyler is now thirteen years old, but he cannot speak one word. He cannot feed himself. Tyler wears diapers. But he can walk, and he can be quite destructive. Tyler must be watched with one hundred percent of someone's attention if he's not restrained. We love Tyler to pieces, but Leanne learned that she must place boundaries on herself, even though doing so felt like she wasn't being a good mother. Juanita, my wife, could give Leanne emotional support for this situation. Juanita adopted two baby boys, both of whom she raised primarily as a single parent. One of them has special needs. Even though she felt guilty doing it, she made use of respite care to stay sane and healthy.

Leanne has two other younger children to give time and attention to. She arranges respite care for Tyler to have time for herself and the others in the family. I have seen families disintegrate when there are no boundaries. Leanne is a marvelous mother, and it makes her feel guilty to put Tyler in another person's care for a few days. This is necessary, however, if she is going to be the best mother to all three of her children and a good wife to her husband. It's important for husbands to understand this as well. I've often had to tell mothers to take some time for themselves. If they don't, they begin to get moody and irritated with their children. Fathers must step up to the plate and encourage their wives to take time away while they take responsibility for the children.

Consider the announcement airlines give on every plane before takeoff. "Before helping someone else with their oxygen mask, please put your own mask on first." You can't help someone else if you faint from lack of oxygen. Leanne often says that having Penny as a mother for twenty-three years taught her how to love and care for someone with special needs. All my children learned good work ethics. They had to help with more household chores than the average child during those years that Penny was so ill. God can bring good out of anything when we allow him to work. I had to put boundaries on myself through those years to protect myself and the children. I had to put Penny in respite care so we could take a break and do things that she wasn't able to do with us. It was not fair that my children had to spend so many days after school in a hospital room doing their homework on the floor. But Penny and I both agreed, so I implemented boundaries around that problem even though some people thought I was selfish.

> We need to be able to say "no" to some things.

Jesus set an example in this. "Yet despite Jesus' instructions, the report of his power spread even faster, and vast crowds came to hear him preach and to be healed of their diseases. But Jesus often withdrew to the wilderness for prayer" (Luke 5:15-16). Jesus did not heal every person who needed healing. He was human in the sense that he had limitations like us. "As evening came, Jesus said to his disciples, 'Let's cross to the other side of the lake.' He was already in the boat, so they started out, leaving the crowds behind" (Mark 4:35-36). He then let the disciples take care of the boat while he went to sleep on a pillow.

Parents have the challenging task of knowing when to apply pressure to children to perform and when to back off. No parent is perfect, and we often do this poorly. What you do to a child may hurt, but that's okay if it doesn't harm. A doctor might thrust a needle into a baby's butt, causing the baby to cry, but it does not harm the baby. Telling someone that they have ketchup on their face may cause a bit of embarrassment, but it does no harm. It helps someone in the long run.

One time I was teaching a class of junior high students. There was snickering going on among some girls in the back of the classroom. I ignored it. Then I noticed a foreign exchange student from Thailand in the front row holding up a piece of paper, trying to get my attention. I stopped and leaned forward to read his broken English, "Fly down!" He, at least, was not worried about embarrassing me because he saw the greater good of telling me the hard truth!

Sometimes we must have those hard conversations with people for their own good. If we are people pleasers, we will let those conversations fall by the wayside, but later, things will probably get worse. Many couples stuff things away until they burst out with angry words and emotions. Not every action that we think is loving is indeed loving. If our goal is simply not to hurt anyone, we may be harming them in the long run. Some parents are overprotective and enabling.

Codependency

In the book, *Love is a Choice: The Definitive Book on Letting Go of Unhealthy Relationships,* the authors employ the commonly used metaphor of love cups (Hemfelt et al. 1989). Some call them love buckets. According to the metaphor, if you have a full love cup, you have a healthy sense of self-worth, self-esteem, and self-love. You know how to fill your own love cup. You have boundaries and take care of yourself. If you have a partially full love cup, you wrestle with low self-worth and self-esteem, have poor boundaries, and insufficient self-care.

A partially full love cup represents a codependent person. A codependent person is rarely partnered with an independent person. Independent partners take good care of themselves. They realize that they are not responsible for their partners. They're also good at setting boundaries on themselves to protect themselves.

What I find fascinating is that codependent people generally attract codependent people. Codependent people find people who "complete" them—opposites attract. But a person must be complete and okay in themselves to create a healthy relationship. Two independent people can have an interdependent relationship, as opposed to a codependent relationship.

Independent people generally attract independent people. Codependents in a marriage relationship continuously complain and make demands on each other. "You never say anything nice to me." "Why don't you spend more time with me?" They are attempting to get their partner to fill up their own love cup. In the end, they keep sucking each other dry. Independent people know how to fill their own love cup continuously without the need to have another person fill it. They don't need their partner to make them feel good about themselves because they are already satisfied with themselves. They can freely give love to their partner, knowing how to refill their own cup by loving themselves. Within a healthy interdependent relationship, there is no jealousy or clinginess.

Interdependent couples can enjoy time together or apart. One partner can say, "I'm going out tonight with my friends." The other partner will respond by wishing them a nice evening out. I think it's great that my wife, Juanita, takes a weekly night out and occasionally a weekend with her sisters and best friends. Juanita doesn't like to fly. She has no interest in visiting foreign countries, but she's okay with my annual trips to various places with a buddy or one of my sons.

Scripture says, "a man leaves his father and mother and is joined to his wife, and the two are united into one" (Mark 10:7-8). It takes two whole (independent) people to become one. It's multiplication rather than addition: 1 x 1 = 1. Two half (dependent) people cannot become one because ½ x ½ = ¼. Also, if one of the two in a relationship is codependent with a parent (hasn't emotionally left their mother or father), the relationship will become even more unhealthy. My university professor used to say, "The person left home physically, but not up here," pointing to his head.

Children raised by parents who have full love cups are well-nourished and mentored. They learn how to love themselves and how to fill their own love cups. Children raised by parents with partially full love cups have low self-esteem and don't know how to love themselves. Quite often, a codependent parent will form an inappropriate bond with a child. This sets up a codependent relationship between the parent and the child that extends into the child's adult life. The adult child both resents the parent's help, but at the same time cannot live without the parent's support.

I prefer the word *external dependency* instead of the more commonly used word *codependency*. External dependency takes place when a person needs external things to feel a sense of self-worth or value, such as money, career, possessions, or a perfect body shape. In the broadest sense, external dependency is defined as an addiction to people, behaviors, or things (Hemfelt et al. 1989). I believe that we all have a "God-shaped" space within us that only God can fill. Humans try to fill this space with things like toys, money, sex, and relationships. But nothing can fill that void except God. Only when we come to understand that God loves us, and we are therefore worthy and lovable, can this void be filled. Each person needs to have their own personal relationship with God.

I believe that unless you really know how to love yourself, you cannot properly love someone else. Love is caring, protecting, nurturing, building up, maintaining, improving, honoring, respecting, and valuing.

Codependency is attempting to feel worthy
and valuable through external things.

If someone says, "I love ice cream."
I would say, "No, you don't. You really, really like ice cream."
You can't love ice cream, because love is a verb, an action.
Someone else says, "I love myself."
Yes, you can love yourself because love is a verb. But love isn't love if it doesn't have boundaries.

Boundaries are a bridge to freedom. Be free!

Emotional Dishonesty
Honesty—A Bridge to Freedom

Juanita and I were driving our motorhome to go camping at our favorite place. It's a long, narrow, windy road for much of the way. Driving a huge vehicle makes me tense, and I was really focused. She took a profile picture of me driving and posted it on Facebook. Later, I read the first comment, "Throw on a smile, my friend!" The comment was something I wouldn't have given a thought about years ago, before my training in counseling. With new understanding, I now cringe at the words. We live in an emotionally dishonest society.

"Hey, how are you doing?"

"Fine."

We're always "fine," "good," "great," even when we are anything but those things.

When I arrived in Tanzania, one of the first things they taught me was how to greet people: "Habari gani?" This literally means "News?" They emphasized that we must always reply with "Nzuri," which literally means, "There is no bad news!" It's the equivalent of "Fine" or "Good" in our culture. Emotional dishonesty appears to be a multi-cultural tradition.

In some circles, it's a sin not to smile. After all, doesn't Scripture say? "Always be full of joy in the Lord. I say it again—rejoice!" (Philippians 4:4).

One of my good friends has a practice of greeting me with, "Don, how are you doing?"

"Fine."

"No, Don, how are you really doing?"

Suddenly, my jaw drops. Busted!

I don't believe that I've ever heard one sermon in church on the topic of emotions. I have, however, listened to sermons on honesty. It's time to put the two together. Scripture has much to say about honesty. "But you [God] desire honesty from the womb, teaching me wisdom even there" (Psalm 51:6).

Our marriage, family, and church relationships have suffered from emotional dishonesty. Emotional dishonesty creates an inauthentic connection. There is no real intimacy: in-to-me-see.

One day, I overheard a mother say to her young son, "Stop your whining. Big boys don't cry!" At first, I cringed at those words. Then I felt guilty because I'm sure I've said those same words to my sons at one time. Truthfully now, do big boys cry? Absolutely, they can cry. But in our culture, men need to be strong—whatever that means? I believe that real men cry.

Why Emotion?

The devil did not create "negative emotions." God did. Right there, our language betrays us. The phrase "negative emotions" implies that some emotions are bad. There are no bad, wrong, or negative emotions, just emotions. Perhaps we could classify them as comfortable or uncomfortable emotions. But every emotion serves a purpose. Emotions are a part of God's design. There are over six hundred references in Scripture to the heart. The heart often symbolizes the emotional side of being humans. "My heart is troubled and restless. Days of suffering torment me" (Job 30:27). We often feel emotions in our bodies as a physical sensation. We may actually feel the emotion in our heart (the chest). But we may also feel them in our stomach area and other places. "Look, O Lord, for I am in distress; my stomach churns, my heart is wrung within me" (Lamentations 1:20 ESV). Emotions help us deal with the bad stuff in a fallen world. They give us useful information. Emotions are vital to mental and physical wellbeing.

If you feel no emotion, it means you are dead. If you feel almost no emotion, it means you are either intoxicated or dissociative. Dissociation happens when the brain shuts down and goes into a freeze response. As long as you are alive, you will feel emotion. There is, however, a window of tolerance for each of us. If our emotion exceeds a certain level of tolerance, we fall apart or shut down.

If you throw a handful of spaghetti into a pot of cold water and wait, it softens, but then it tastes like glue. You need to add heat to cook the spaghetti. But if you don't turn the heat down at the critical point, the pot boils over onto the stove, and you have a big mess. Like cooking spaghetti, we must learn to manage our emotions, not try to get rid of them. Using alcohol and drugs to numb feelings is not a healthy way to exist. Mindfulness exercises are wholesome methods to manage emotions, and there are no ill side-effects. Some mindfulness exercises are included near the end of this book.

More than a hundred years ago, the earliest psychologists viewed emotions as a sign of poor mental health. Among other symptoms, fainting, outbursts, nervousness, and irritability were hallmarks of hysteria, a psychological condition only attributed to women (Pearson 2017). This was used to justify laws forbidding women from voting or owning property. Men were thought of as being mentally healthy because they displayed low levels of emotion. Unfortunately, many of these myths still linger in our culture today. Many psychologists believe that the reason males do not often display emotions is more culturally-induced than genetic. Men are equally as emotional as women. They have learned to shut them down—big boys don't cry (Hick 2018). Music is one area in which men can express emotions. I've observed that most recording artists on popular radio are male. Listen to their singing. Men have and can express emotion.

Emotions can play an essential part in problem-solving (Schwarz and Skurnik 2003). In his book, *When Your Body Says No*, Gabor Maté (2012) summarizes the research on how suppressing emotions like anger or experiencing severe stress is linked to several diseases. Heart disease, irritable bowel syndrome (IBS), multiple sclerosis, Alzheimer's, arthritis, cancer, and Lou Gehrig's disease (ALS) are among them.

> Every emotion has an important purpose.

Tony Robbins (1991) refers to emotions as action signals. Every emotion is a signal to take some sort of action. Ignoring the emotion without taking appropriate action is unhealthy. It's healthy to allow yourself to have a full experience of catharsis. Catharsis is the purging of the emotions or relieving of emotional tensions by allowing yourself to express the emotions. Once you have taken the appropriate action that an emotion signals, you can then manage the emotions through mindfulness techniques. Don't ignore the information in an emotion and fail to act.

Sadness

Sadness is an action signal to rest and self-soothe. This emotion is telling you to slow down and relax. Crying activates the parasympathetic nervous system (Marcin 2017). This system is the off switch for fight, flight, and freeze reactions. Crying for an extended time releases chemicals that counter pain and help you feel better (Marcin 2017). Tears of emotion differ from tears of lubrication. Tears of emotion contain stress hormones and other toxins secreted in the brain (Marcin 2017).

To grieve well, we must allow ourselves to cry. We often hold back crying because we are afraid we won't be able to stop. In fact, we may have to develop the skill of crying. Some know how to cry, and others don't. You can help yourself cry by going into a dark room and making yourself comfortable. Listen to your body and make vocal sounds that match the feelings. It may be a whimper, howl, roar, or a deep sobbing sound, but let it be expressed vocally (Defoore 2004).

Scripture has some beautiful passages that reveal deep sadness.

"Long enough, God, you've ignored me long enough. I've looked at the back of your head long enough. Long enough, I have carried this trouble, lived with a stomach full of pain" (Psalm 1:12 The Message).

"Doubled up with pain, I call to God all day long. No answer. Nothing. I keep at it all night, tossing, turning . . . And here I am, nothing, an earthworm, something to step on, to squash" (Psalm 22:2, 6 The Message).

"I'm on a diet of tears, tears for breakfast, tears for supper, all day long" (Psalm 42:3 The Message).

"I'm tired of this, so tired. My bed has been floating forty days and nights. On the flood of my tears, my mattress is soaked, soggy with tears" (Psalm 6: 6-7 The Message).

Fear and Anxiety

Fear and anxiety are action signals to do something to keep ourselves safe. In psychology, we are careful to distinguish between these two words by defining them differently. Fear is about the present. I experience fear when there is a rattlesnake on the floor in the room with me. Anxiety is always about the future (Forsyth and Eifert 2007). I experience anxiety when I think rattlesnakes are lurking in the grass behind my garage. Fear and anxiety feel the same, only the intensity may differ. People differ in the levels of intensity when feeling these emotions. For this reason, you can never know how another person feels.

The central aspect of fear and anxiety is that we must become mindful of real danger versus perceived danger. Living daily in a state of anxiety due to perceived danger is unhealthy. Many people suffer from too much stress (feelings of anxiety). Some stress is necessary because real danger or real challenges are present. But some stress is unnecessary because there is no real danger present. We just perceive that there is danger. If I see a rattlesnake in the grass, then the threat is certainly real. If I am triggered by seeing only tall, dry grass, my anxiety is due to an implicit memory of an experience in the past creating a perceived danger in the present. If rattlesnakes live in the area, the anxiety is there to keep me safe from a real danger. I could, therefore, walk heavy-footed to scare any snakes away. It is only a perceived danger if rattlesnakes do not live in that area of the country. If you see a poisonous snake, there is a real danger, and your impulse of fight, flight, or freeze could save your life.

Recall the illustration of touching a hot stove. The first impulse may be automatic, without your conscious choice. But when we react in the absence of real danger, it can sometimes get us into trouble. Anxiety is the emotion that causes the most trouble. The implicit brain takes control at that moment, and you react in fight, flight, or freeze when there may be no reason to do so. Implicit memory is only an emotional reaction. The implicit brain uses no logic. In these moments, if it is possible, we need to use our logical brain to make a conscious decision about how to respond appropriately. But we often react before the rational brain can do this.

If the danger I am experiencing is in the present, we call that emotion fear. In that case, I need to keep myself safe in the moment through fight, flight, or freeze. If I am thinking about the future and feeling anxious or worried, we call that anxiety. Anxiety tells me that I need to act now to prevent a potential danger in the future. Check the smoke alarm batteries. Make sure the stove burners are turned off. Drive slower and more cautiously. Put some money into savings. The list of examples could be endless. If I have already done everything I can to protect myself, and there is no danger in the present, I move on to managing my anxiety through mindfulness exercises.

We must consider anxiety as our friend and embrace the emotion rather than running away from it. We need to talk to ourselves like this, "Anxiety is my friend. Anxiety keeps me safe." When we attempt to eliminate anxiety in the moment through avoidance, we increase our anxiety in the long run (Forsyth and Eifert 2007).

Let's say that I'm driving down the road on a hot summer afternoon. I get thirsty for a crushed ice beverage, and I see a corner store that sells them. I pull into the parking lot, go to the back of the store, and fill my cup. As I am standing in line waiting to pay for my beverage, someone bursts through the door and shoots a gun in the air. The person proceeds to order us to get down on the floor and hand over our wallets, threatening to harm us if we don't cooperate.

Flash forward. I am driving down the same road, and I get thirsty for a crushed ice beverage. I see the same corner store, but I get a knot in my stomach from a wave of anxiety (perceived danger), so I drive right on by. If I drive right on by, I have just reinforced my anxiety towards that corner store. If I keep trying to avoid my anxiety, I begin to avoid other corner stores. After some time, I could become anxious about going into larger stores or malls and perhaps develop full-blown agoraphobia—I stay home and order everything to my door.

Anxiety is your friend because it keeps you safe.

The way to prevent this scenario from happening is to embrace my anxiety as my friend. I need to carry the anxiety with me instead of running from it. I stop at the corner store, go to the back of the store, fill my cup, pay for it, and enjoy drinking it. I must have some positive experiences to reverse the implicit memory of anxiety linked to the corner store.

There is wisdom in the Serenity Prayer: "God grant me the serenity to ACCEPT the things I cannot change, the COURAGE to change the things I can, and the WISDOM to know the difference." We cannot change an emotion, such as anxiety. Emotions do not come with an off switch like a light. We must accept our anxiety at the moment. It's our friend, keeping us safe at that moment. Then we must have the courage or commitment to do something with our body to complete the task at hand rather than withdraw from it.

Some fascinating research done over a span of eight years showed that our beliefs and attitudes about stress or anxiety are more important than the amount of stress. Those who believed that stress makes you physically ill, were the only ones who actually suffered physically from stress (McGonigal 2013). Anxiety is my friend is literally a healthy attitude to hold.

I Have No Expectations

When I was in counseling myself, my counselor taught me two mantras to remember. A mantra is a phrase that we say repeatedly. These two mantras have given me a sense of peace in my life like nothing else has.

The first mantra is, "I have no expectations." Why is it a good mantra? There is no such thing as common sense. The idea of common sense implies that we are born with it. That's impossible. We learn everything, and we must be taught something to learn it. Neither do we learn everything we are taught. Common sense does not exist. Therefore, when I see someone doing something or not doing something that I consider to be "common sense," I have an expectation. When I have an expectation, I set myself up for disappointment. When I am disappointed, I become a victim. A victim has no power. When I have an expectation and a person does not meet my expectation, I give that person my power. That's when I lose control and react in a fight, flight, or freeze response. It doesn't turn out well, and can ruin the rest of my day. "A person without self-control is like a city with broken-down walls" (Proverbs 25:38).

When I take my grandchildren to Knott's Berry Farm or Disneyland, I repeat to myself, "I have no expectations." That way, I can enjoy the journey, because it's not about the destination or outcome. There will be long line ups. One of my grandchildren may not want to go on a ride that everyone else does. Having no expectations keeps me patient, so I can enjoy the time with them. As much as I do enjoy roller coasters, it's not about how many of them I can ride. It's about making sure my grandchildren enjoy their day. With this approach, I end up enjoying the day too.

One time, I was explaining this mantra in a workshop. My faithful volunteer who does audiovisual for all my "Bridges to Freedom" weekends, challenged me. She pointed out that when she drives, she expects people to stop at stop signs and red lights. It must have been a bit late in the evening because her comment seemed reasonable. The next day, however, it struck me that when I took my bus driver's training, they taught me defensive driving. When you drive defensively, you never assume that a vehicle is going to do anything. For example, you check for a dipping of the front of the vehicle to indicate braking. When a pedestrian is standing by the side of the road, you try to get eye contact to know that they see you. When you are driving a busload of sixty-four children, you must drive without expectations.

There is one exception to the mantra, "I have no expectations." It is putting expectations on ourselves. We need to put expectations on ourselves, though we must not set our expectations too high. This is partially why I came close to a burnout. I have been a perfectionist throughout my life. There is no such thing as perfection, so I was hooped from the beginning. I wasted time and energy in ways that were useless by trying too hard. Sometimes we need to lower the bar of expectations on ourselves. "I have no expectations."

I Let Go of the Outcome

The second mantra is, "I let go of the outcome." This is similar but not the same as the first mantra. In life, there are many things that we have no control over: the weather, the government, and, most importantly, other people. We only have control over ourselves. This brings us back to the Serenity Prayer. We need wisdom about what we have control over and what we don't. For anything that we have no control over, we need to let go of the outcome. I do everything that I can possibly do to solve a problem, but after that, I must let go of the outcome. To not let go of the outcome creates a lot of unnecessary anxiety. "I let go of the outcome."

If anxiety is a necessary emotion to keep us safe, then what do we do with Jesus' remarks about worry?

> I have no expectations and I let go of the outcome.

"So I tell you, don't worry about everyday life—whether you have enough food, drink, and clothes. Doesn't life consist of more than food and clothing? Look at the birds. They don't need to plant or harvest or put food in barns because your heavenly Father feeds them. And you are far more valuable to him than they are. Can all your worries add a single moment to your life? Of course not. And why worry about your clothes? Look at the lilies and how they grow. They don't work or make their clothing, yet Solomon, in all his glory, was not dressed as beautifully as they are. And if God cares so wonderfully for flowers that are here today and gone tomorrow, won't he more surely care for you? You have so little faith! So don't worry about having enough food or drink or clothing. Why be like the pagans who are so deeply concerned about these things? Your heavenly Father already knows all your needs, and he will give you all you need from day to day if you live for him and make the Kingdom of God your primary concern. So don't worry about tomorrow, for tomorrow will bring its own worries. Today's trouble is enough for today!" (Matthew 6:26-34).

I interpret this to mean, "get your priorities straight." It does not say or imply that we have nothing to do in finding food and clothing for ourselves and our families. But when you worry, you don't embrace your anxiety as a friend. The result is that you freeze up from anxiety and become helplessly paralyzed. You lack the courage to move forward in positive ways. Instead, as I've already stated, recognize your anxiety as an action signal to keep yourself safe. Do all you can do, and then, after that, you have no choice but to let go of the outcome and trust that God is right there with you just like he promises.

Scripture has many references to people having fear and anxiety. The first incidence was Adam and Eve. "When they heard the sound of God strolling in the garden in the evening breeze, the Man and his Wife hid in the trees of the garden, hid from God. God called to the Man, 'Where are you?' He said, 'I heard you in the garden, and I was afraid because I was naked. And I hid'" (Genesis 3:8-10 The Message).

I believe that, beginning with Adam and Eve, the most significant damage that sin has done to humankind is to create within us shame and an unhealthy fear of God. There is a healthy fear, which might better be described as respect. But I am talking about being afraid of God, and not being able to trust that God deserves respect. Only through an intimate relationship with God can we get to know him well enough to learn to trust and respect him.

God's people are not perfect. Here is another reference to God's people having fear. Fear is a natural emotion to keep us safe. "God! God! I am running to you for dear life! The chase is wild. If they catch me, I'm finished: ripped to shreds by foes fierce as lions, dragged into the forest and left unlooked for, unremembered . . . Stand up, God. Pit Your fury against my furious enemies. Wake up, God. My accusers have packed the courtroom" (Psalm 7:1, 6 The Message).

"God is love, and all who live in love live in God, and God lives in them. And as we live in God, our love grows more perfect.

So we will not be afraid on the day of judgment, but we can face him with confidence because we are like Christ here in the world. Such love has no fear because perfect love expels all fear. If we are afraid, it is for fear of judgment, and this shows that his love has not been perfected in us. We love each other as a result of his loving us first" (1 John 4:16-19).

I believe a mindfulness approach to managing anxiety does not conflict with Scripture. Mindfulness means being able to focus your attention on your own thoughts. The acronym for the mindfulness approach that I prefer to use is ACT: Acceptance Commitment Therapy (Forsyth and Eifert 2007). Accept your anxiety because you cannot change it. Commit to doing what you can do and do it. In the end, you must let go of anything you have no control over. "I let go of the outcome."

Guilt

I discussed this emotion in an earlier chapter about the two brains. The emotion of guilt is an action signal to apologize, ask forgiveness, and make amends. Forgiveness is like a reset button on a relationship. I go into more depth on this in the chapter on forgiveness.

Shame is the only emotion that God did not create, and that Christians do not need to feel. I believe that we'll feel shame anyway because we live in a fallen world, but God understands. Guilt and shame feel identical. In review, shame is false guilt. Shame is the result of a lie we believe about ourselves at the moment. We can defeat shame by recognizing the lie and replacing it with the truth of God. The lies come from implicit memories of abuse. Satan, the father of lies, capitalizes on those lies.

> Shame serves no purpose because it is false guilt.

Addressing those who were out to kill him, Jesus said, "For you are the children of your father the devil, and you love to do the evil things he does. He was a murderer from the beginning and has always hated the truth. There is no truth in him. When he lies, it is consistent with his character; for he is a liar and the father of lies" (John 8:44).

Anger

Anger is an action signal to protect yourself and your loved ones from injustice. Anger is an appropriate emotion when there is an injustice. If people didn't get angry at injustice, then nothing would be done to correct the injustice. Some have gotten angry at racism and have written a book about it to help others. Others have worked on passing laws to protect people from racism. If a person never gets angry in the face of injustice, there is a good chance that person is sociopathic. If you ever wonder whether or not you are a sociopath, you most likely are not. Sociopaths don't have a conscience and cannot think in that way.

Anger is generally a secondary emotion. Because anger is such a central emotion that causes many problems, I have devoted a whole chapter to the emotion of anger. For now, let's just look at some Scriptural references describing some of God's people expressing their anger.

"May the LORD cut off all flattering lips and silence their boastful tongues" (Psalms 12:3).

"Harass these hecklers, God. Punch these bullies in the nose. Grab a weapon, anything at hand; stand up for me! Grab the spear, aim the javelin, at the people who are out to get me!" (Psalm 35:1-3 The Message).

This chapter is about being honest about your emotions. If you are feeling angry towards someone, you might as well talk to God about it because he already knows what you are thinking.

Myths about Emotions

Myth #1 – Some emotions are to be avoided. "Smile, my friend." "Stop you're whining. Big boys don't cry!"

Truth – Emotions are neither right nor wrong. They are just emotions. Sometimes the problem is how we express them, or that we don't express them at all.

"There is a time to cry and a time to laugh. A time to grieve and a time to dance" (Ecclesiastes 3:4).

"Then Jesus wept" (John 11:35).

Myth #2 – I am responsible for another person's emotions.

Truth – I am not responsible for another person's emotions.

I am responsible for my own actions towards others. If I behave rudely or disrespectfully towards another person, I must own it, apologize, and make it right. But if someone is emotionally upset about something I say and do, I'm not responsible for their emotions. They are most likely being triggered by their own painful implicit memories at that moment. It's their baggage from their past.

There are many ways that children can pick up the impression that they have power over and, therefore, responsibility for another person's emotions. Following a hug, a parent may make a simple comment to a child such as, "Oh honey, you make mommy feel so much better." This comment may seem rather endearing, but it is a type of emotional abuse.

I believe that it's important that parents emphasize to their children that it is not the child's fault that they (the parents) are sad, worried, or angry. Children are egocentric, which means that they make everything that happens about themselves. Emotionally honest parents would explain to their child that they are sad, and it is okay for people to be sad sometimes (Burney 2011). It's okay to hug, but it is still okay to be sad, anxious, afraid, or angry. Parents need to model how to express emotions in healthy ways. It would also be valuable for parents to model how to self-soothe.

> Learn to be comfortable with another person's emotions.

A television host, producer, and writer, known as Mister Rogers from "Mister Roger's Neighborhood," acted as an excellent adult role model for teaching children how to manage, talk about, and express emotions. As an ordained pastor, Fred McFeely Rogers considered children his ministry. There are two movies about him that are well worth watching.

As described above, a male who was taught to feel responsible for his mother's emotions could grow up feeling responsible for his wife's emotions. When she cries, he may immediately try to fix her as an attempt to help her feel better. I used to say things to my wife like, "You shouldn't feel that way about that situation." Even though I was only trying to make her feel better, I finally learned that it was a hurtful thing to say. A woman might resist these kinds of approaches, and feel angry that her husband does not have any empathy for her. She doesn't want to be fixed. She just wants to be understood, hugged, and to know that her husband is okay with her tears. This illustration could easily have the male and female roles reversed in some relationships.

If you are uncomfortable with someone else's emotions, then you are the one who has a problem. Learn to be comfortable with your emotions, and learn to be comfortable with others' emotions. It usually doesn't help to say, "I know how you feel." No one can truly know how another person feels. Just validate their feelings, and allow them the space to feel. Emotions are neither right nor wrong, they are only emotions.

Emotional Honesty

As I said earlier, we are taught by our society to be emotionally dishonest. We are always "fine" or "good." It's an emotionally unhealthy society where attitudes support the belief that it is shameful to be human (make mistakes, not be perfect, etc.). Likewise, when people are held to be less worthy because of their gender, race, or physical appearance, that society is emotionally degenerate (Burney 1995).

God understands your emotional humanness. I remember when some magazines had scratch and sniff ads for perfume. I wish I could put scratch and hear songs in a book. If I could, I would fill this book with songs. Music is the language of the heart, the language of emotion. One such song that is appropriate for this chapter is Amy Grant's song, "Better Than A Hallelujah," lyrics written by Sarah Hart (2009). One key line says, "We pour out our miseries, God just hears a melody." The gist of the song is that God prefers honesty about our emotions over pretending that all is well by singing "Hallelujah." Listen to the song on YouTube!

Honesty is a bridge to freedom. Be free!

9

Thank God for Flat Tires
Gratitude—A Bridge to Freedom

Most Christians have heard of a book called *God's Smuggler* by Brother Andrew. It's about a Christian who smuggled Bibles into countries where they were illegal. I've wondered if smuggling wheel rims and tires count if you need them to do missionary work?

Aside from fuel, I also needed better tires for my car. The ones that came with the car from Canada had a four-ply rating. I discovered that, in Africa, they use a twelve-ply rating. These more robust tires are needed because the thorns that grow on African bushes can easily puncture a four-ply tire. I discovered that the hard way. So, I went tire shopping, but all the tires in Tanzania were for sixteen-inch rims. My car had fifteen-inch rims.

I came up with what I thought was a clever plan. We needed textbooks at our school, and there were none for sale in the country. Since the school did not have money for textbooks, I decided to hold an auction on my front porch to raise some money for textbooks. I could legally bring textbooks from Kenya into Tanzania but not car parts. I rationalized that no one would know if I was bringing in wheel rims and tires if I was driving with them on the car when I crossed the border. But I really hadn't thought things through.

Back to the Beginning

Before I moved to Africa, I connected with the American teacher that I was going to replace. I wanted to know what I should bring with us. The answer was everything! We could not count on being able to purchase the basic necessities in Tanzania.

We filled a shipping container with a Toyota Land Cruiser, some furniture, a propane stove and fridge (neither of which we could use since there was no propane), an upright piano, and a gasoline-powered clothes washer with rollers. We even found an old sewing machine that operated without electricity. As well as the shipping container, there were over 250 apple boxes. We shipped a six-year supply of everything necessary to survive and a few extra treats. We bought used clothing for four children, ages eight months to five years, which they'd grow into over the six years we were planning to live in Tanzania. I built the kids' beds, an indoor fort, and a desk out of the wood crates our shipment came in.

The day we arrived at the school campus where I'd be teaching, we discovered that we'd be living in a newly built house. It was unlike any other building in the area. It had indoor plumbing with a tub, toilette and sink, and a kitchen sink. All the other homes for faculty were dark and dingy, and residents had a separate kitchen outside of the house due to the smoke from a cooking fire. We could never get propane for our stove, so we used charcoal to cook on the ground outside our back door.

Others used a five-gallon plastic bucket to take a bath, but we had a bathtub like back home. Because the water was so cold, we could only make the children bath once a week. Bath night was the worst day of the week for our kids. They would scream in pain when getting bathed. After our things arrived, I built a solar hot water heater on the roof of our house. It supplied water that was too hot to touch, but became the perfect temperature for a bath when mixed with the icy water. After that, we'd occasionally invite one of the other staff members to come our house for a bath, which was a real treat for them.

They told us that the new house was built for the girls' dean when the girls' new dormitory was completed. The funds came from a worldwide offering collected for this specific reason. But the headmaster said that the staff decided to let us stay in the house because it solved the current dispute among them as to who would get the new house. The American carpenter who was building the dormitory was living in the missionary's house, which was no better (only larger) than the other homes on campus.

Our Christmas tree was a bamboo branch, and all we had to decorate it was white paper snowflakes. On Christmas Eve, we prepared little goodie bags of cashews that were available in the city, and brought them to each of the other faculty homes. We sang them a Christmas carol or two. Most of them were grading papers and such because Christmas was not a big thing for them. But the next day, they held a big pot luck just to cheer us up.

Little did we know that all our personal belongings would arrive in Africa almost a year after we did. We purchased foam mattresses to put on the cement floor. Other than that, we had no furniture until our shipment arrived. We did everything sitting on the floor, including eating. By the time our shipment came, almost every article of the kids' clothing was too small for them. Nellie's and my clothing was well worn. My shoes had holes in the soles, and most of my shirts had holes in the elbows. We'd brought some cheap dishes and plastic cutlery in our suitcases, but, towards the end, all our forks had missing prongs.

Nellie and I did our laundry by hand, kneeling beside the bathtub using freezing cold water. Scrubbing the clothing together to clean them was why the clothing wore out more quickly. Before our things came from America, we had to triple the diapers used by our two youngest children. We hung our clothing on one small rope and the bushes behind our house. We had to use an iron that was heated by coals from our cooking fire.

One time we missed ironing one baby blanket for Jody, who was only one year old. She broke out with what looked like large pimples all over her body. They turned out to be larvae from mango flies that laid their eggs on the blanket while it was drying. That was the reason for ironing everything. It wasn't to make them look good; it was to kill the larvae. It was quite the procedure to remove larvae from the body. We first applied some petroleum jelly to the spot. This cut off the air supply and made them wiggle to the surface. Then we had to squeeze each larva out like you'd do when popping a pimple. The pain was so great, Jody screamed while we did this to over fifty larvae. I know by experience how great the pain was because I got a couple of larvae in my body. Have I mentioned yet how much we, in America, have to be grateful for?

When I returned to Canada after Nellie died, it was almost Christmas Day. While visiting my parents, I went to a shopping mall. After living in Africa for so long, the mall looked like everything was lined in silver and gold. The contrast with what we were used to in Africa is impossible to describe. I wanted to stand on one of the benches in the middle of the mall and yell at the top of my lungs, "Hey all you Canadians, stop your complaining. You have no idea how fortunate you are! You should be more grateful."

Trips to the City

We had no drapes on our windows, so it was like living in a glass house. It was common to see the faces of children, noses pressed against our windows, watching us live. After several months, I finally went to town and had some drapes made. Getting to town without a car meant walking about fifteen kilometres down the mountain and hoping to catch a bus that had no routine schedule. Being a mzungu (Swahili for white man, but which literally means "someone who roams around aimlessly") had its advantages. A bus conductor would reach out to grab my hand and pull me through the crowd of people who were all trying to board the bus simultaneously. I always felt safe in Tanzania because they treated us like royalty. I never worried about my kids getting lost because someone would bring them back to us. Once, we thought that Jody, age two, had wandered off. All kinds of people were scouring the paths looking for her. We ended up finding her sleeping in our bedroom closet with the cat as her pillow, the cat's tail in her hand.

After the long walk down the mountain came the ten-hour ordeal of riding on a very crowded bus with no air conditioning. Most people had to stand, but they made sure that the mzungu had a seat, even if it meant holding someone's chicken or a baby without a diaper. You couldn't tell if I was sweating or had wet my pants at the end of the tortuous trip. Have I mentioned the word gratitude yet? It seems appropriate to remind ourselves how much we can be grateful for.

The return trip was the same, except now I had to carry all my purchased items. I did not trust giving them to someone to put on the roof of the bus. They could easily go right over the top and down to someone on the other side of the bus. I recall one especially difficult return trip. I had run out of water, but had yet to make the long hike back up the mountain in the hot equatorial sun. I gambled and drank from a muddy puddle. It was a choice between getting sick from contaminated water and dying from inevitable dehydration. I used my shirt to screen out most of the mud.

In the area where we were residing, there didn't seem to be malaria. The species of mosquito that carry the protozoa didn't live so high in the mountains. I did, however, get malaria twice from a couple of trips to the city. On one trip, I got so sick that I had to immediately return to the city for help. After the long walk back down the mountain and a ten-hour overnight bus ride, I stood for what seemed like hours in a line at the clinic. This was followed by another line to pick up my medicine. From there, I went to the church headquarters to do some business. I remember standing at the door of one of the offices. A person asked me if I was okay. That's the last thing I remembered until I woke up on a bed in another clinic. I didn't know about the clinic designated for foreigners only. Apparently, I was given the wrong medication at the other clinic. My blood pressure had plummeted, and I just about died. Have I mentioned how much we can be grateful for?

Our Container Finally Arrives

Finally, the day came when I was informed that our container had arrived. Apparently, it got lost in a transfer between ships in Israel. I went alone by bus to the port city of Dar es Salaam. As it turned out, it wasn't easy to get my container through customs. There was an illegal but widespread custom of government employees asking for "Chai (tea) money." In other words, "Pay me some money, and I will do what I'm supposed to do for you without charge." I refused to pay chai money. That meant several extra days of waiting. They were attempting to squeeze the chai money out of me. I would spend day after day walking the streets, returning once each day to see if I could get my goods.

On the fifth day, a gentleman handed me some papers and told me to go to a desk that he pointed out to me. He told me not to go to another desk, which he also pointed to. After he left, I felt suspicious of this man because he was the one who wanted chai money, so I went to the desk that he told me not to go to. Sure enough, that was where I was supposed to go. The other desk would have put me through many more unnecessary hoops. Next, I arranged for a truck to load up my stuff and follow me home. But first, I had to get my car running. That was when I discovered that getting a set of license plates could take months. When I saw my car, however, I realized that the people on the other end hadn't followed my instructions to remove my Canadian license plates. They were supposed to be returned before shipping the car. This was a small miracle. License plates in Tanzania never expire, so I just drove with my plates that said "Beautiful British Columbia," and no one raised any questions.

At first, my car wouldn't start because the battery was dead. It had been in storage for a year. I paid for the battery to be recharged, but, after getting home, I realized that the repair shop had stolen my battery and replaced it with an older one. That's when I learned never to lose sight of my car while anyone was working on it. Driving home was my first experience driving on the left side of the road with a steering wheel on the left side of the car (the vehicle had made for North America). Did I say anything about how much we can be grateful for?

Moving Our Things In

At last, I pulled into the school campus with our car, followed by a moving truck. But now I would have to face the music.

For a year, I had been considered the wealthiest person in those mountains. That was with only the suitcases of stuff we'd travelled with. I was so embarrassed about all the things I'd had shipped. It was already dark, but the truck dumped out the enormous wooden containers storing the boxes and furniture. I worked along with the night watchman most of the night. We used a crowbar to dismantle the containers so the contents could be carried to my house in the morning. The path to our house first crossed a river via a couple of fallen tree trunks. Then the trail was a steep upward climb the rest of the way.

In the morning, about 150 students formed a parade. Each of them took a box on top of their heads. Most of them made a second trip with more boxes and larger items. Finally, two of the strongest carried the piano over the logs across the river and up the narrow path. It was unbelievable to see their strength. On our end, we drew the curtains shut and put everything inside the living room. We had no idea where we would put it all. Most of it we stored in the attic.

Later that day, I met with the entire student body and faculty for joint worship. I explained to their curious minds what we had in those 250 boxes. At least I did my best. I explained to them in words that I thought they could understand. I said, "Pretend you were moving to a place across the ocean where you knew that there were no beans, rice, cornmeal, mangos or bananas. Wouldn't you bring a six-year supply of those things? Well, that's what's in those boxes, except that they're Canadian things." They all nodded their heads in the affirmative, but I still knew that they wished they could see just what we had in those boxes. Did I say anything yet about how we have so much to be grateful for?

The Auction

I found it almost impossible to teach Chemistry and Physics without textbooks. After all, the students had to pass the "Cambridge Entrance Exam" to graduate from high school. It was interesting trying to teach students how to calculate the cost of using an electric clothes washer when they had no idea what a clothes washer was. We didn't even have electricity anywhere in the area. I really needed some textbooks with pictures.

About six months after we unpacked, it occurred to me that we could raise enough money to buy the school textbooks if we sold most of the things we didn't immediately need. We learned that we could have more items shipped back at the end of our three-month furlough, which would come after the end of our third year there. The word was spread about the auction sale. I used what Swahili I knew and conducted the day-long auction from my front porch. They had never seen an auction before.

At one point, the entire audience began laughing hysterically. I couldn't figure out what was so funny. I was trying to sell an empty jar. Even a used jar or tin can had great value there. I was saying "Chupi! chupi!" over and over. One of the students who was helping me whispered in my ear, "Say, chupa! Chupi means underpants!"—that was a word not spoken publicly in that culture.

Learning a new language can be embarrassing at times. In that culture, whenever you greet someone older than yourself, you say, "Shikamoo," which literally means, "I hold your feet." The reply is always, "Marahaba," which means, "I am honored." One day I was replying, "Maharagwe," to a bunch of children, and they all started to giggle and ran away. I found out later that I had said, "beans" instead of, "I am honored!"

We made more than enough from the auction to buy the textbooks needed for the school. To purchase them, my family made a trip to Nairobi, Kenya. What a difference there was as soon as we crossed the border. The city of Nairobi had everything like back home. We even ate pizza in a restaurant, although the pizza had carrots, broccoli, and peas on it!

My Attempt to Smuggle

One morning while in Nairobi, I left my family at the guest house and struck out on my own to buy rims and tires for our car. I located a wrecking yard, but it was not yet open for the day. A man came to my car and claimed that he worked there. He was waiting for work to begin for the day. After I told him what I was looking for, he looked at my unique mag wheels, which were very rare in Africa in those days. He assured me that he could get me a very high price for those. I could trade my fifteen-inch mags and tires for sixteen-inch steel rims and tires and make a large profit. All he wanted was half of the profit for his help. I got greedy and went for it.

He jumped into my car and directed me to another part of town. We were first going to buy some cheap sixteen-inch rims with tires. I was already getting suspicious that he was not on the up and up. We pulled over, and he instructed me to stay in the car until he returned. I waited quite a while, but then suddenly a taxi pulled up beside me. The guy jumped out, and then proceeded to toss four rims with tires into the back of my car. He grabbed my money and handed it to the taxi driver. Then, acting like he was in a real hurry, he hopped in and yelled for me to drive fast. Suddenly, I started to sweat. I began to think that he might have just stolen the wheels from someone.

Everything became a blur after that. When we got back to the place where we'd started from, the stranger told me to go inside, get them to switch the wheels, and then they would surely buy my mag wheels for a very good price. After that, I was to bring back the money and give him half the profit. That seemed weird to me because I thought he was employed there.

He got out of the car, and I drove into the facility. I talked to the owner about buying my mag wheels. The owner took one look at the wheels that I'd just bought and exclaimed, "You just bought four sixteen-inch rims and tires, but your car can't take sixteen-inch wheels!" Then, I told him what had happened. He explained to me that the guys who hang out there don't work for him. They just try to scam anyone who comes there early in the morning. The owner paid me what I spent on the wheels and tires and said, "Good luck finding fifteen-inch tires for your fifteen-inch rims because they don't make them here."

By now, I was really ashamed of myself for trying this scheme. I returned to Tanzania with the same rims and tires I'd left with. I knew it was dishonest to smuggle them into Tanzania. I just thought that they would never know, and I justified my plan because I needed them to do my mission work. I'm glad it didn't work out because, at the border, they specifically asked me if my tires were the same tires I'd left with. That was not what I thought would happen. I'm the kind of guy who would not be able to tell a lie out loud to someone's face. I would have been busted at the border.

There, I got that confession off my chest! It was not one of my finest moments. I carried a lot of shame and guilt about that experience for a long time.

Our Vacation Trip

Shortly after our trip to get the textbooks, we had a two-week Christmas break. Previously, while in Arusha, we'd met some missionary friends who lived on the border of Tanzania and Burundi. They had children the same age as ours, and they'd encouraged us to come visit them. We also had friends from Canada who were working in Rwanda, and they had invited us to their place for Christmas.

One thing that we'd brought from home was an old canvas tent that slept eight to ten people. I set up the tent in our backyard to air it out and repair some holes. Local people would come by and say, "Very rich man, two houses!" I'd had a huge roof rack made for our car that held a bunch of borrowed jerry cans for fuel. We loaded the rack with the tent and supplies and headed off on a 2,000 kilometre round trip. We visited the famous Manyara National Park and Ngorongoro Crater. It was a childhood dream come true. I had never seen so many kinds of African animals in a zoo, let alone in such large numbers. I have an amazing collection of animal pictures that I treasure to this day.

After staying in little huts up to that point on our trip, we arrived on the open plains of the Serengeti. We got to a campsite at dusk. There were a few camper vans there, but we had the only tent. This was not a fenced campsite, and there were all kinds of animals nearby. The kids were already sleeping when we became aware that we'd been surrounded by lions. They weren't making their usual roaring sounds, but were instead producing deep bass-like guttural huffing sounds. The males were probably trying to impress some females. I tried to get Nellie to agree that we should sleep in the jeep, but she just said, "Remember, the guide book said that there's never been a case when a lion attacked a tent in the Serengeti." Then she turned over, and went peacefully to sleep.

I could not sleep. I'm sure that I was awake all night. I was grateful we were alive the next morning!

Eleven Flat Tires

Up to the edge of the Serengeti, the roads had been free of thorn bushes. The road through the plains was more of a two-track cow trail. This was when we started getting flat tires. Obviously, there were no tow truck services or service stations. I had to jack up the car by hand, remove the wheel, and then use another jack to break the seal on the tire. I did this by putting the jack between the tire and the car bumper. This method used the weight of the car to break the seal between the tire and the rim. I learned that trick from watching my dad, who used to fix his own tires. Then I had to get the tube out, patch it, put it back in and pump up the tire with a hand pump. That took considerable time and energy in the hot sun.

I was now black with dirt, and we had no extra water for washing. This happened repeatedly throughout the day. We fell far behind schedule, so we had to sleep in a place where we couldn't pitch the tent. We took everything off the roof and stuffed it in the car for the four kids to sleep on, and the two of us slept uncomfortably on the steel bars of the roof rack. This was the second night that I barely slept, if at all. This time, I was afraid of snakes or bandits in the area.

The next day, we had even more flat tires. After we came to a gravel highway, I made the decision to hitchhike to the next town to bring back help. We pitched the tent by the side of the road for the kids to rest. I was squeezed into a small bus carrying several business people dressed in very fine clothing. There I sat, black as coal from head to foot. They dropped me off at the Catholic mission in the next town.

The nuns quickly put together a basket of goodies for us to eat and sent one of their maintenance workers with a jeep to help me fix the tire and bring my family back to stay for the night. It was dark by the time we arrived back at the car. My family had packed up the tent, and were already in the car with the doors locked. Some nice men in a truck had come by, fixed the tire, and then ordered them to stay in the car because they were worried about bandits.

That was our tenth flat tire on this trip. We were driving to town, with the worker from the Catholic mission following us. Then we got our eleventh flat tire. As we were fixing this tire, he noticed some lights in the distance, and realized that it was the Baptist mission. He left us to go for help. The Baptist missionaries came and brought our family to stay with them for the night. The lights were the only reason we knew that they were there. We found out the next morning that they usually didn't have their lights on at that time of night. They'd been celebrating a family who was leaving the following day, and had stayed up later than usual.

Rescued at Last

During breakfast, we chatted with the Baptists about where we were headed. They knew the missionaries that we were going to visit. All their children had been born at that mission hospital. We had to pause for a few minutes later that morning to ride out an earthquake. It was the first earthquake I'd ever experienced.

After breakfast, the missionary broke some fantastic news to us. He told us a story about how just that past week, when he was in town, a storekeeper wanted to sell him a set of four tires. The missionary hadn't wanted them because they were fifteen-inch tires, and they had no vehicles with fifteen-inch rims. But the man kept pressing him to buy them, and offered him an unbelievably low price. Then the missionary felt compelled to buy them, even though he had no idea why. They became ours at an incredibly low price that morning, and, with better equipment available, they were changed in no time. The new tires were twelve-ply; we had no more flat tires for the rest of the journey, or any time after that.

We had a wonderful time with our friends at the mission hospital. We hadn't known how difficult it would be to cross borders. But we made it through the first border by telling the border patrol that we were friends of the missionaries at the hospital. We stayed in a five-star resort hotel in the capital city of Burundi. The kids had a blast swimming in the pool. It was Christmas Eve day when we checked out and headed for Rwanda. They wanted chai money at the next border, but we refused and waited it out until they finally gave in and stamped our passports.

Christmas was special with our friends. They had no kids themselves but had prepared stockings for each of our kids. On Christmas Day, they took us sailing on a nearby lake, and it drew a massive crowd of spectators. By now, we were used to people watching us and sometimes coming over to feel my kids' hair.

Our return trip had only one glitch. One day, we came to a closed gate spanning the road. The men guarding the gate with machine guns informed us that there was a cholera outbreak. The road was closed, so it would be more than five hundred extra kilometres to go around this blocked road. I insisted that we be allowed to go, and promised we wouldn't stop anywhere and get out of the car. Our cholera immunizations were expired. They refused, but I just stayed there, parked in front of the gate. I knew that it was a scam, and they just wanted chai money. I got out a book and began reading like I had all the time in the world.

After a while, I looked up from my book and saw an open gate; the soldiers were standing with their guns on their shoulders, looking in the opposite direction. I knew what that meant, so I started the car and drove on through. There were no more problems for the rest of the way, and we were so grateful for such good memories and small miracles.

Being Thankful

Guess what the first word was that each one of my four children said when they learned to talk? "Dadda," right? How did you guess? Of course, that's my side of the story. I really don't remember much about those days. I do remember speaking baby talk to my kids, and I had a word that I made them say whenever they got something they wanted: "Tatta!" I believed it was necessary to teach my children as early as possible to say, "Thank you."

"As they entered a village there, ten lepers stood at a distance, crying out, 'Jesus, Master, have mercy on us!' He looked at them and said, 'Go show yourselves to the priests.' And as they went, their leprosy disappeared. One of them, when he saw that he was healed, came back to Jesus, shouting, 'Praise God, I'm healed!' He fell face down on the ground at Jesus' feet, thanking him for what he had done. This man was a Samaritan. Jesus asked, 'Didn't I heal ten men? Where are the nine? Does only this foreigner return to give glory to God?'" (Luke 17:12-18).

Nine Jewish men were healed, and one foreigner. Jesus was not so surprised or astounded that one foreigner came to thank him. Jesus was astounded that nine of his own people did not return to say thank you. Nine Jewish men showed no gratitude, but Jesus healed them anyway. God blesses us daily. Some of us don't recognize the blessings, nor do we give thanks for them, but they come anyway.

"Surely the righteous shall give thanks to Your name; The upright will dwell in Your presence" (Psalm 140:13 New King James Version). You might think that righteous people would be grateful, but nine Jewish men did not return to give thanks. But there are situations in which we don't feel thankful. To give thanks when a person doesn't feel grateful would be hypocrisy. Wouldn't it?

There's a seemingly insignificant verse that you could easily pass by in John, chapter six. "Then Jesus took the loaves, gave thanks to God, and passed them out to the people" (John 6:11). You probably remember the story. More than 5,000 people were fed with only a few loaves and fishes. But notice, the text simply reads, "Jesus gave thanks." In today's lingo, some people would say that Jesus said grace. Jesus thanked God for the food. Recently I've bumped into Christians who feel that there is no need to pray before you eat. It's just a ritual that has no meaning. I taught my small children to recite, "God is great. God is good. Thank you for the food. Amen." If it becomes only a routine, then we have lost the spirit of gratitude and thanksgiving.

For many, it takes a Thanksgiving holiday once a year to force us to say grateful sounding things. I have eaten approximately 75,000 times since I came into this world. I suppose thanking God for the food could become just a routine. But consider these words, "And all the angels were standing around the throne and around the elders and the four living beings. And they fell face down before the throne and worshipped God. They said, 'Amen! Blessing and glory and wisdom and thanksgiving and honor and power and strength belong to our God forever and forever. Amen!'" (Revelation 7:11-12).

How long is forever? I dare say it's a lot more than 75,000 times. The angels never weary of thanking God. They have been at it for trillions of years, and they are still at it. Have you ever struggled with whether to give thanks for the food in a public restaurant?

The book of Psalms is noted for its praise and thanksgiving. Chapters 145 to 150 lists who and what gives thanks to God: angels, kings, the righteous, cattle, beasts, reptiles, birds, sea monsters, and everything that has breath give thanks. The sun, the moon, the stars, the atmosphere, and the hail give thanks too. Even snow, frost, wind, and oceans all give thanks. All of God's own works give thanks to God! After a list like that, surely no one could have an excuse not to give thanks to God.

"Then you will sing psalms and hymns and spiritual songs among yourselves, making music to the Lord in your hearts. And you will always give thanks for everything to God the Father in the name of our Lord Jesus Christ" (Ephesians 5:19-20). These verses are not just good suggestions. It is God's will that we give thanks. And notice the method: "making music to the Lord in your hearts." In other words, with all your heart, give thanks. Don't just give thanks outwardly like some routine habit. Let it come from your heart. Notice that the text says, "give thanks for everything." I went through the same six short psalms again, and listed all the things mentioned just in those verses where thanks is given. Here's a list of some of them (many of them were repeated): God's graciousness, mercy, justice, kindness, faithfulness, and salvation. Give thanks to God because he hears our cries and because he satisfies our desires. But that's not all. The psalmist also lists many simple things that we should thank God for: food, rain, grass, snow, hoar frost, and peace on our borders.

The verse that tells me to thank God for sending the rain reminds me of my son Kris. We taught our children to thank God for simple everyday things like rain. Kris was just three and we were still living in Africa. We were all in bed. It was dark in the house, and then a tropical rainstorm broke out. We had a tin roof, so the rain made a loud sound. The rain would come in a short burst and then let up for a bit, and then another burst followed by another brief silence. After a while, Kris said in the darkness, "Daddy, why doesn't God get a bigger cup?"

In the Bad Times?

It's easy to give thanks to God when things are going well. I suppose it's easy to give thanks for things like good food and rain if we would just remember to stop and think about it. But how can we give thanks when life is just the pits? There is a saying: "They say that life is a bowl of cherries, but all I got was the pits!"

Someone once said to me, "Don, cheer up, things could get worse." And they were right. I cheered up, and sure enough, things did get worse. I cannot guarantee you much in life, but there are two things that I can guarantee. The first one is that you will have trouble in life. The second one is that you can always find something to be thankful for.

"Always be joyful. Keep on praying. Be thankful in all circumstances, for this is God's will for you who belong to Christ Jesus" (1 Thessalonians 5:16-18). Be thankful in all circumstances, or as some translations say, "no matter what happens to me."

Is Scripture saying that I am even supposed to thank God for flat tires? No, it doesn't say, "for" all circumstances. Somethings are not from God. Some things come to us as the result of evil and sin. 1 Corinthians 14:33 says, "God is not a God of [the author of] disorder [confusion, tumult, unquietness] but of peace." The words in parentheses are found in a variety of translations. I have made this point quite clear already. Because we live in a fallen world, and because of the freedom we have, bad things will happen. But we must look around at the bigger picture. There are always things we can be thankful for.

I was not thanking God for those flat tires on those hot days. I can look back now, however, and be thankful for so many things that didn't go bad that could have gone bad. There could have been bandits. There could have been venomous snakes. We saw plenty of snakes during our time in Africa. But if it weren't for having so many flat tires, I would not have found that Baptist mission, who had the tires we needed all ready for us to pick up. Those twelve-ply, fifteen-inch tires could not be found anywhere in Tanzania, as far as we had searched.

During one summer when I was in college, I landed a construction job framing houses outside the city. A couple of co-workers there seemed to be in competition about who could put the most swear words into one sentence. I'd never had a problem with cursing and swearing as a youth, but I didn't know how closely I was being watched at this construction job. One day, I put a wall together backward, according to the blueprints. I threw my hammer down on the floor and made an expression that I call "vegetarian" swearing.

One of these guys, who was upwind of me, thought I'd said something else and immediately began to yell, "He swore. He actually swore!"

Fortunately, the other guy, who was downwind, stuck up for me and said, "No, he actually didn't swear."

On our way back to the city after work, these two interrogated me about my beliefs. I thought about it later, and studied Scripture. I now believe that by throwing down my hammer and spouting off a "vegetarian" swear word, I really had been swearing at heart. My spirit was anything but grateful at the time.

"No matter what happens, always be thankful." I didn't have to be thankful for my mistake, but I could be grateful for an understanding boss and a good job.

In the early seventies, a retired pastor came to our church community and taught us that when something goes wrong, try shouting, "Praise the Lord," and see what that did. Right at that time, Nellie and I lived in a two-room shack with no indoor toilet. We called it the honeymoon shack because it was our first year of marriage.

Be thankful in all circumstances, not for all circumstances.

I went out late one night to fill a bucket of stove oil for our heater. It was a long way to the oil tank because there was no driveway into our place. It was a frigid, clear night, and I was carefully carrying a full, open bucket of heating oil back to the house. Then I slipped on the ice and landed on my back, the bucket of oil spilling all over me. I spontaneously yelled, "Praise the Lord." The next thing I knew, I was laughing hilariously. I thought, what would someone say if they saw me and heard me now? But since I was already on my back, I continued to lie there, looking up at the star-filled sky. It was beautiful. Then I thought, what good would it have done to start cursing and swearing? It certainly wouldn't have helped, and it probably would have made me feel worse. Instead, I continued now to laugh at myself. When I entered the house, Nellie and I had a big laugh about it together. I wasn't thankful for ruining my winter coat. But praising God regardless of the disaster had smoothed over the experience. Thank God for those beautiful stars visible on a crisp winter night.

"I will offer you a sacrifice of thanksgiving" (Psalm 116:17). Several times Scripture speaks of a sacrifice of praise or a sacrifice of thanksgiving. It seems like an oxymoron, like hot ice. When you are in the middle of trouble, the last thing you feel like doing is praising God. As I now think of it, I believe that sometimes it feels like a sacrifice to praise God. It is difficult to thank God when everything is going wrong, and there is seemingly nothing for which to give thanks.

Reasons to Be Grateful

Why should I thank God anyway when I am irritated about what is happening or in times of trouble? Let me give you four reasons.

Reason #1 – Give thanks anyway because God is bigger than any irritation. Psalm 136 repeats, "Thank God, for his steadfast love endures forever," twenty-six times. Nothing can happen to us that can separate us from God's love. His love endures forever. God is bigger than any irritation.

Reason #2 – Give thanks anyway because it keeps us objective enough to be open for character growth. Trials and problems are the stuff of life that can refine our character, and act as chisels that cut raw diamonds into jewellery. If you are swearing, cursing, or blaming someone for your misfortune, you will be in no frame of mind to learn and grow. I have a T-shirt that says, "Crisis or Opportunity?" Anything bad that comes our way can be seen either as a crisis or an opportunity. How you choose to see it will make all the difference in how you go through it.

I heard someone tell of when he was learning to praise God, no matter how irritating the experience. One time, he was driving along when he felt a tire go flat. So, as he was pulling over (already late), he just said, "Praise the Lord." He looked out his car window. It was pouring rain. He just said, "Praise the Lord." He got out, and since he had no coat, he just said, "Praise the Lord." He discovered that his jack was broken, and he was now all muddy from trying to use it. He just said, "Praise the Lord." A car stopped to help, and all he could say was, "Praise the Lord." After the gentleman helped this stranger out, he made a comment on how calm the man had been in such lousy circumstances. They ended up sitting together in his car, talking about this. The man ended up sharing Christ with this gentleman right there in the car. He later concluded that if he had not practiced thanking God in all circumstances, he never would've been in a mood that could have led to this outcome.

Reason #3 – Give thanks anyway because an attitude of gratitude produces endorphins in the brain that make you feel better and create better physical health. Gratitude will help you sleep better, give you more energy, help you manage stress more effectively, help you have fewer aches and pains, and improve your ability to focus and pay attention. That is the science of gratitude.

Reason #4 – Give thanks anyway because we might be people's only picture of God. "Be careful how you live among your unbelieving neighbors. Even if they accuse you of doing wrong, they will see your honorable behavior, and they will believe and give honor to God when he comes to judge the world" (1 Peter 2:12).

Quite a few of those flat tires on that African trip our family took drew a large crowd of people, who just stood there watching me work. I was hot, thirsty, dirty, and irritated. I could have easily been in a mood to kick the tires and say a few English swear words that they wouldn't have understood, though they would have understood my disposition. In fact, my own children were learning a lot from how I handled each flat tire. Though by the time I had flat tire number eleven, I had plenty of reason for cursing.

Methods to Praise God

Scripture doesn't just tell us to thank God in all circumstances; it also gives us examples of ways that we can give thanks to God. As we saw in Ephesians, we can thank God with psalms, hymns, spiritual songs, and making melody in our hearts. Psalm 150 says we can praise God with all kinds of musical instruments. It lists trumpets, lutes, harps, tambourines, and cymbals—loud clashing cymbals no less.

The leper who was healed and returned to say, "Thank you," had said it with a loud voice and had fallen on his face. Psalm 63 tells us to praise God with our lips and by lifting up our hands. Psalm 149:3 says we can thank God by dancing. Psalm 149 tells us to praise the Lord in the assembly of the faithful (in other words—in church!).

Sometimes it's a sacrifice to express praise and thanksgiving to God by raising our voice or our hands in church. I remember how I'd wanted in my heart to just feel free to raise my hands to God; I was just so filled with thankfulness that words were not enough. But in the subculture I grew up in, raising hands in church was frowned upon. One time, though my hands felt like fifty-pound weights, I decided that if I wanted to praise God this way, with my body as well as my voice, I was going to go for it. It was really freeing to be able to do that. It was sort of like one's first kiss. I remember how I'd wanted to plant that first kiss on my girlfriend's lips to show my love, but it was so hard. But after that, it was freeing to be able to express my love to her. We certainly shouldn't be afraid of getting emotional in our expressions of love with our spouse. Why should we fear emotion in our love for God? Have I said anything yet about how we have so much to be grateful for?

Post Script

Juanita was the first person to read each chapter of this book. I valued her perspective. Through the years, she heard me share a few stories about my experiences in Africa. But she'd never really learned the details about that part of my life until reading this book. After this chapter, she came to me with a few comments. "First," she said, "I want you to know that it is very good, but I need to ask, why in the world would you take four children to this place?"

The truth is I have asked myself that a few times. The answer always comes out the same. I was young, full of life and energy. Nellie was almost seven years older than me. Before we met, she had served as a missionary nurse on the island of Guam. But her childhood dream was to be a missionary nurse in Africa. She is the one who wanted to apply for a mission assignment.

Our application was submitted before our first child was born. The call came the day Nellie was released from the hospital, having just given birth to our fourth and youngest child. On our way home, the two of us and the baby went for pizza. When I told Nellie about the call, she never missed a beat, saying, "Let's do it." Nine months later, we were in Africa. She would often say, "The safest place on earth is where God wanted us to be." I now look at that belief through the eyes of the law of love and freedom, and I see it differently. I really didn't see ourselves in any more danger there than at home in Canada. God is with us wherever we choose to go, but it is always our choice to go.

I treasure my memories and experiences of those years in Africa. In many ways, it made me who I am today. I'm not thankful, of course, that Nellie died in Africa. I am grateful, however, that she had the opportunity to live her dream. Her grave marker says, "Nellie Wren Straub, who loved her African friends – She who believes in me, though she dies, yet shall she live. John 11:25."

On my bucket list, I have a dream of returning to Africa for my last time to visit her grave with my four children, and, hopefully, some of my grandchildren.

Gratitude is a bridge to freedom. Be free!

10

Speak Life to Yourself
Healthy Self-Talk—A Bridge to Freedom

"You're so skinny, you have to run around in a shower to get wet." This was one of many teasing comments thrown at me by my best friend in high school.

"Nincompoop!" (a word that means stupid) was my dad's favorite expression when he was angry with me.

"You have a face only a mother could love." This was a comment often made to me because of my huge problem with acne in high school.

"Why do you have to be such a stick in the mud?!" There were many things that I couldn't participate in because of my religious beliefs.

"Mary had a little lamb, little lamb, little lamb . . ." The upper-grade girls sang that to me. They were huddled in a tight circle surrounding me, looking down on me while I was lying on my back on the skating rink ice. I was just learning to skate, much later than the typical Canadian.

These are only a sample of the words that caused me personal hurt during my growing up years.

"Sticks and stones may break my bones, but words will never hurt me." I said it earlier, but I need to state it again. This is the biggest lie ever told. Words do wound and damage a person. My mother meant well when she taught me those words. She was trying to help me ignore what other kids said to me. But their words still wounded me.

> One of the biggest lies ever told is that
> "words will never hurt you."

Parents will never be able to completely shelter their children from these kinds of experiences. The key is to help your children understand that this is not an appropriate kind of behavior. Parents need to model healthy communication with their children. A wound by the words of a parent goes the deepest.

"Speak Life" is a great song, especially the video version, sung by Toby Mac (written by Toby McKeehan, Ryan Stevenson and Jamie Moore, 2012). It beautifully addresses this issue of how our words affect others. Here are some selected lines from the lyrics:

It's crazy, amazing
We can turn our heart through the words we say
Mountains crumble with every syllable
Hope can live or die
So speak life, speak life . . .

Look into the eyes of the broken hearted
Watch them come alive as soon as you speak hope
You speak love, you speak life

Some days the tongue gets twisted
Other days my thoughts just fall apart . . .

Raise your thoughts a little higher
Use your words to inspire
Joy will fall like rain
when you speak life with the things you say

In this chapter, I won't be emphasizing how we speak to other people or how others talk to us. My emphasis will be on how we speak to ourselves—our own self-talk. The words of Toby's song can be interpreted this way if we think about it. We all self-talk about 50,000 words a day. Most of them are benign, but many of them wound. We wound ourselves over and over by this bad habit. A self-talk wound perpetuates and amplifies the wounds from others. Keep this in mind as you continue to read.

The Power of Our Thoughts

If I think the way I have always thought
I will feel the way I have always felt
If I feel the way I have always felt
I will do what I have always done
If I do what I have always done
I will get what I have always gotten
If nothing changes then nothing changes

These words, written by "Anonymous," are one of the biggest truths that has ever been told. Notice where it starts: *If I think the way I have always thought.*

Based on how the brain works, I don't believe that my mind creates many truly original thoughts. My mind either adopts or rejects things I hear from others. It may not fully adopt or reject another person's words. It may modify them to some degree to fit what major premises I've come to adopt as truth. Recall the filter your brain has that I explained in an earlier chapter. The time in our life when we are most susceptible to adopting ideas as being true is before the age of six. I explained why in the chapter, "We have Two Brains." This is the reason why the most powerful influencers of our thoughts are our parents.

As I also said earlier, as children, we formulate our thoughts about who God is by observing our parents. This is the reason why it's not who God thinks I am that matters, but who I think God thinks I am that matters. In fact, I could say it another way for anyone who doesn't believe in God. It's not who you really are that matters, but who you think you are that matters. I believe that those who believe in an accepting, loving, nonjudgmental God have a great advantage in this area of healthy self-talk. Christians have the answer key to the question, "Who am I?" I am not an accident that happened between molecules in a mud soup. I am created in the image of God. I am God's child. I am worthy and valuable.

> If nothing changes then nothing changes.

God said, "Let there be light," and light appeared. "Let there be . . ." and whatever God said, it appeared. There is power in God's word. We are created in God's image. He made us procreative. He told us to multiply and fill the earth. He made us creative. We can create and invent. He commanded us to use our creative abilities to subdue the earth, or in other words, take care of the earth. He also created us to be free beings. We can choose to protect the earth or destroy it.

A New Way to Pray

Almost fifty years ago, a retired pastor came to my church and taught us to thank God in all circumstances. He also taught us other ways to pray more effectively. He told us to stop begging God or trying to twist God's arm. Instead, we're to come with a prayerful attitude of, "Your will be done instead of mine." But we can pray for anything that we know is God's will as if it has already happened. In other words, pray like you have already received it.

"But if we confess our sins to him, he is faithful and just to forgive us and to cleanse us from every wrong" (1 John 1:9). "Therefore, I say to you, any sin and blasphemy will be forgiven men, but the blasphemy against the Spirit will not be forgiven men" (Matthew 12:31 NKJV). And in speaking about the Spirit, "And when he comes, he will convict the world of sin, and of righteousness, and of judgment" (John 16:8 NKJV). Put these three thoughts together, and it becomes easy to understand. Any sin will be forgiven except one: it is a sin that we do not ask to be forgiven; not asking for forgiveness is resisting the Spirit's conviction to confess and repent.

We know that it is God's will to forgive our sins, so we don't have to beg him to forgive. We don't have to ask him to love and accept us either. We just have to receive his forgiveness, and thank him for his unconditional love and acceptance. "Lord, thank you for accepting me just as I am. Thank you for your amazing grace and forgiveness." It would not be suitable to end with, "but your will be done."

We also know that God promises to be with us through both good and bad times. "Have I not commanded you? Be strong and courageous. Do not be afraid; do not be dismayed, for the Lord your God is with you wherever you go. (Joshua 1:9 NIV). There are many more verses like this one that could be quoted. We do not have to ask God to be with us when we are going through troublesome times. We can pray, "Thank you for being with me. Thank you for carrying me through this."

We don't need to ask God for anything
he has already promised us.

There are times where we must ask, and then let go of the outcome. We must realize that in the end, it is God's decision to work a miracle. When someone is sick, ask God for healing using the words, "but your will be done." At the same time, remember that it's not God's will if healing doesn't happen. God's ultimate will for the universe is freedom because there is no love without freedom. Therefore, knowing that God is love and sickness is NOT God's will, we come with an attitude of submission when his choice is not to work a miracle of healing. The greater prayer is praying, "Lord, if you choose not to heal, I will love and trust you anyway." "Thank you for being with me and keeping me strong through it all." "Thank you for the gift of freedom." Remember, even though freedom results in pain at times, freedom is a blessing because there is no love without freedom.

The words we speak in self-talk hold power in no small degree. The power may not be making a dead person rise from the grave, or a lame person to get up and walk. The power lies in that our words (thoughts) produce a better attitude and inner strength to walk through the ordeal in peace and trust in God. In this respect, our thoughts (self-talk) manifest themselves in the outcome.

Questions We Ask Ourselves

An important part of our self-talk is the questions we ask. What questions are you asking yourself? Our brain is a powerful computer, like no other computer invented by humans. When we ask ourselves a question, our brain goes to work attempting to find an answer, and it will eventually.

Jewish prisoner, Stanislavsky Lech, felt like he could not live any longer in the prison labor camp. He began to ask himself, "How can I escape?" Every time he posed this question to another prisoner, he was scoffed at because it was "impossible." Nevertheless, he kept asking himself the question. Then the answer came. On his way back from working at the end of one day, he saw it. It was a truck load of dead, naked bodies. He stripped off his clothing and wiggled his way into the pile. He was there for quite a few days. It was not easy, as you can only imagine, but then one day, the truck started and drove out of the camp. He was dumped into a ditch where he was able to sneak out unnoticed, and lived to tell the story (Robbins 1991).

Notice the type of question Lech asked himself. How? He could have asked, "Why am I here?" Most of the time, "why?" questions either lead to a dead end or an answer that casts blame on others or shame on yourself. "How?" questions invite a productive answer, a solution (Robbins 1991). Ask yourself more "how?" questions. "How can I have a better relationship?" "How can I advance in my job?" "How can I overcome my bad habit?"

How Our Thoughts Hold Power

Imagine a freshly picked rose. What if you have the thought, "What an ugly rose!" Does that thought make the rose ugly? No. If you believe that thought, however, you will most likely throw the rose in the trash. Let's say that someone comes to you and says, "Your good friend, so and so, was just killed in a car accident." How would you immediately feel and act? You'd most likely feel shock, pain, or sadness. But what if that person who was supposedly killed was, at that moment, sitting in the same room with you? How would you feel and act then? You might possibly laugh, knowing that it wasn't true. The power of a thought is in whether you believe the thought, even if the thought is a lie.

Referring to the devil, Jesus said, "There is no truth in him. When he lies, it is consistent with his character; for he is a liar and the father of lies" (John 8:44). Satan's most powerful weapon is the lie. If he can get us to believe that God does not love all the time, he has us in his grasp. If he can get us to believe that we are a piece of trash, never enough, a failure, a loser, stupid, worthless, or whatever, we are vulnerable to his temptations.

Let me give you a lesson in psychology. I call it Psychology 101 (if you have been to college, you know that 101 courses are basic, level-entry classes). **A** is what happens to you. **C** is your response—first your feelings, and then your behaviors.

A	**C**
What Happens	**Your Response**
	Your Feelings
	Your Behaviors

I spend about half my counseling hours working with groups. I like groups because I can illustrate this process by going around the group, asking each person to tell me how they would feel and how they would act when **A** happens. Let's say that **A** is someone saying, "You're so stupid." Each person in the group has a slightly different answer. The most common answers are: 1) Feel angry and swear at the person, or tell the person off. 2) Feel angry and shut down or walk away. 3) Laugh, and then ask the person why they said it. Of course, there are variations of each of these three general types of reactions.

If I drop something, it always falls to the ground. This is because gravity causes it to fall. Unlike the law of gravity, **A** does not cause **C**. We know **A** does not cause **C** because **C** will be different for different people. The feelings and behaviors will be different for different people. A person can have different feelings and behaviors depending on who does **A**.

A does not cause **C**.

B causes **C**.

B stands for beliefs and baggage from your past.

A   **B**   **C**

What you believe
(Your interpretation of A)
(Your belief about yourself)

B stands for what you believe about what is happening (**A**), or what you believe about the person who is making **A** happen. It also stands for what you believe about yourself at that moment.

If you believe—on an implicit, emotional level—that you are stupid because of your baggage from the past, **C** will probably be anger with an aggressive, passive/aggressive, or passive response. All these are unhealthy, inappropriate responses. I say more about this in the chapter on anger.

If you believe that you are smart or capable because you carry no baggage from the past, you will probably laugh and be curious about the comment. This is a healthy, appropriate response.

Again, **A** does not cause **C**. No one can make you respond in a certain way. Your own past experiences (baggage) may trigger your reaction. If you have no negative previous experience with being called stupid and a strong experience of doing well in school, you will most likely respond calmly and with curiosity.

In group therapy, I first ask people to listen to their body when I say, "You're stupid!" Then I ask them to do the same for, "You're an apple!" The difference those two different comments made in their bodies were usually quite noticeable.

> It's not what happens to you but your interpretation of what happens to you that determines your response.

In general, most of the group felt uncomfortable being called stupid, but there was no painful feeling in being called an apple. People felt either neutral or found it funny. Then one day I got a different reaction from a participant. That person got the same uncomfortable feeling in their body with the word *apple* as with the word *stupid*. I asked the participant why that was. The person disclosed that, as a First Nation's Canadian (Native American), being called an apple was derogatory because it meant they were "red on the outside and white on the inside." So, I switched to the word *banana*. But then one day an Asian participant had the same experience. In some Asian circles, a banana means "yellow on the outside and white on the inside." Now I use the word *pineapple*. "You are a pineapple!" So far, I've had only one person who had an adverse reaction to *pineapple*. It was because that person had experienced a workplace where they called new employees "pineapples." Because there were no racial or cultural connections, I still use *pineapple* for this exercise in groups.

This **ABC** principle was first written down by a Greek philosopher, Epictetus, almost 2,000 years ago. Epictetus is famous for saying, "Men are disturbed [**C**] not by things [**A**], but by the view which they take of them [**B**]." I, of course, added the **A**, **B** & **C** into the quote.

Another illustration I like to use is my **BFT** sandwich. **B** stands for behavior, **F** stands for feelings, and **T** stands for thoughts.

B

F

T

A thought (cognition) creates a feeling. A feeling drives a behavior. A negative thought I have about myself creates an uncomfortable feeling, and then that uncomfortable feeling drives a negative behavior. A positive, truthful thought I have about myself creates a comfortable feeling, and then that comfortable feeling drives a positive behavior.

It works from the top-down as well. Behaving in a negative, hurtful way creates an uncomfortable feeling, and then that uncomfortable feeling drives a negative thought I have about myself. Behaving in a positive, kind way creates a comfortable feeling, and then that comfortable feeling drives a truthful, positive thought I have about myself.

Stinking Thinking

The word cognitive means thinking or thought. Most people are familiar with the phrase, cognitive behavioral therapy (CBT). This is one of the most common types of therapy used by counselors. It is as biblical as your Bible.

"Don't worry about anything; instead, pray about everything. Tell God what you need, and thank him for all he has done. If you do this, you will experience God's peace, which is far more wonderful than the human mind can understand. His peace will guard your hearts and minds as you live in Christ Jesus. And now, dear brothers and sisters, let me say one more thing as I close this letter. Fix your thoughts on what is true and honorable and right. Think about things that are pure and lovely and admirable. Think about things that are excellent and worthy of praise. Keep putting into practice all you learned from me and heard from me and saw me doing, and the God of peace will be with you" (Philippians 4:6-9).

I'm not a fan of the term *positive thinking*. A positive thought may be a lie. "I'm God." "I am the most brilliant person in the world." These are positive, but your logical brain probably knows that they're not true. If it doesn't, you're in trouble! I believe in truthful thinking that is positive. I believe in looking for something truthfully good in everyone, including myself. "The truth will set you free" (John 8:32b).

"We demolish arguments and every pretension that sets itself up against the knowledge of God, and we take captive every thought to make it obedient to Christ" (2 Corinthians 10:5 NIV). Let's return the term mindfulness. Use your mind to be mindful of your thoughts. When you become mindful of a thought (self-talk) that's untrue or unhealthy, capture it. In other words, call it what it is—stinking thinking or a lie. Then change it to a new, truthful thought. Don't allow yourself to put yourself down.

Another source of our thoughts is the voices of the Holy Spirit and the Devil. It's important to ground ourselves in Scripture so we can be mindful as to which voice we are hearing. I've come across so many people who say things like, "I just know that God sent this person into my life." Then months or years later, they get divorced. Just because we get a feeling in our body that this is the right person or the right thing to do, does not mean that it is. We must test everything by the Word of God.

The Will of God

I have concluded that there are three aspects to God's will and knowing what God's will is.

The first aspect is God's sovereign will. This consists of the big things that Scripture informs us about. It is God's will that He will one day return and make a new heaven and earth. It is God's will that everyone repents and comes to salvation. This doesn't mean that everyone will choose life because of the gift of freedom. These are some examples of God's sovereign will.

The second aspect is God's moral will—the Ten Commandments. One of my theology teachers said, "If someone tries to tell you that there is more than one law, find another church." He meant that the law of love is the only law. Of course, Jesus broke love down into two laws: love God and love your neighbor. "'Teacher, which is the most important commandment in the law of Moses?' Jesus replied, 'You must love the Lord your God with all your heart, all your soul, and all your mind. This is the first and greatest commandment. A second is equally important: Love your neighbor as yourself. All the other commandments and all the demands of the prophets are based on these two commandments'" (Matthew 22:36-40).

The third aspect of God's will is the one that most people struggle with. To find out the details of the first two aspects of God's will, we go to the Scriptures. The third aspect of God's will is his will for us as individuals. What career path should I follow? What person shall I marry? How should I spend my money? What house should I buy? What career should I pursue? What university should I attend?

I see this aspect of God's will more like a large circle rather than a specific point. God gives us the freedom to decide for ourselves by considering our personality, likes and dislikes, and signature strengths. Also, we can draw on the second aspect of God's will to be sure that we stay inside the circle of choices that are not contradictory to God's moral will. I have many people come to me for counseling on some of these matters. When they do, it's usually because they are stuck. They can't seem to know what God wants them to do. It's freeing to know that God created us in his image, and gave us the power to choose and create our future within the boundaries of his moral will.

What Would Jesus Think?

Years ago, there was a fad among young Christians. We wore bracelets with WWJD on them, "What Would Jesus Do?" I would like to suggest that perhaps more importantly, "What Would Jesus Think?"

More than ten years ago, I had the honor of playing the role of Jesus in a passion play at Easter. Several churches and a Christian school worked together on it. It started when my church sent me, as a pastor, to a Christian university in Tennessee to check out their program called "Son Rise." I was amazed. They gave me permission to use their script and ideas in Canada.

We did about four or five shows each year for three years. It required more than 250 actors and technicians behind the scenes to make it happen. We used both the inside of a school gymnasium and a huge field behind the school for the stages. The audience would move from stage to stage for each succeeding scene.

First was a market place where Jesus entered on a donkey. After dismounting, he healed people and played games with the children. Next was a platform where Jesus ate the last supper and washed the disciples' feet. Then it was the Garden of Gethsemane, where an actor played the part of Satan attempting to get Jesus to change his mind. After that, the school rooftop became Pilot's judgment hall with actors in costume mingled in the audience shouting, "Crucify him!" From there, Jesus carried the cross to the opposite side of the school field for the crucifixion. Again, actors among the audience would either be mocking or weeping. It made it very emotional and real to the audience. It ended with Jesus' body being carried into the gym for the burial, resurrection, and the ascension of Jesus up and out of sight by invisible airplane wire. The song, "Arise My Love," by NewSong, played during the resurrection and ascension. It brought the audience to their feet in applause and even whistling and cheering. It still gives me chills, remembering it from my point of view as Jesus.

It's not who we are that matters but who we think we are.

Thousands came to experience the passion play. The actors themselves were moved by it. There are no words to describe what it was like to play the role of Jesus. I was "crucified" and "resurrected" at least a dozen times over those three years. It was painful enough to fake the crucifixion, considering some of the cold spring days that I was "hanging" on the cross almost naked. I discovered that I'd never have been able to endure the actual pain of going through what Jesus went through. I discovered that I was such a wimp. To act it with integrity, I had to start with getting my mind in touch with the mind of Jesus. What would Jesus think? While I looked down from the cross into the faces of people, I saw some actors in costume weeping and others mocking me. I also saw many in the audience openly crying. I tried my best to see them as Jesus saw them.

It broke Jesus' heart. He died of a broken heart! "Father, forgive these people, because they don't know what they are doing" (Luke 23:34). The experience of playing Jesus affected and changed me profoundly.

What would Jesus think? In fact, what does God think about you? God thinks you are worthy. "He will rejoice over you with great gladness. With his love, he will calm all your fears. He will exult over you by singing a happy song" (Zephaniah 3:17). God thinks of you as his very own child, "See how very much our heavenly Father loves us, for he allows us to be called his children, and we really are!" (John 3:1).

You're not a worm, you're the apple of God's eye.

Are you familiar with John Newton's song, "Amazing grace, how sweet the sound, that saved a **wretch** like me."? Isaac Watts, in another song, penned the words, "Alas! and did my Savior bleed, And did my Sovereign die? Would He devote that sacred head, For such a **worm** as I?" This reference to being a worm may have come from Psalm 22:6: "But I am a worm and not a man." The idea that we are wretched or worms are not the thoughts that God has toward us. They are the expressions of humans who are feeling shame. The truth is, "For this is what the Lord Almighty says: 'After the Glorious One has sent me against the nations that have plundered you—for whoever touches you touches the apple of his eye'" (Zechariah 2:8 NIV). Another translation says, "After a period of glory, the LORD of Heaven's Armies sent me against the nations who plundered you. For he said, 'Anyone who harms you harms my most precious possession'" (Zechariah 2:8).

You are not wretched. You are not a worm. You are the apple! In fact, you are God's most precious possession. You are worthy and valuable, even priceless!

Our words either drain life or speak life into others. More importantly, our self-talk either drains us or speaks life into us. Don't let a day go by without saying to yourself, "I am a child of God! I am worthy and valuable! I am the apple of God's eye!" With words like these, you speak life to yourself!

Healthy self-talk is a bridge to freedom. Be free!

Pictures above are of myself, playing the role of Jesus in *Son Rise.*

11

In the Hands of an Angry God
Assertiveness—A Bridge to Freedom

I shoved the car into reverse, stepped on the gas pedal, and "bang!" I practically ripped off the car door. It was folded back, and the garage door was severely wounded. I was so angry! My son had brought home his report card, and on it was a failing grade in math. I'd told the teacher to communicate with me if Kris was having a problem with anything. After wrecking the car door, I had to figure something else out because I couldn't drive anywhere in my car. I was supposed to be the platform chairperson at an evangelistic meeting at my church that night. How ironic.

Being that angry is like being drunk. Like the first effects of alcohol on the brain, our frontal lobe shuts down. It's like driving a car without brakes. We have no control at that moment because we are in a fight, flight, or freeze response.

My ninth-grade teacher told my parents that I was a very angry boy, but I just didn't show it. He said that after my parents complained to him for striking me behind my knees with double yardsticks. My parents laughed about it when they told me, and transferred me to another school. I now know, however, that it is possible to be angry and not show it. I'm just not sure that was the case in ninth grade. Having said that, I did discover later in life that a passive expression of anger has been my general method of operating.

God's Anger

There are more than forty references to God's anger (wrath) in Scripture. "Remember how angry you made the Lord at Mount Sinai, where he was ready to destroy you" (Deuteronomy 9:8). "Therefore, go and say these words to Israel, 'This is what the Lord says: O Israel, my faithless people, come home to me again, for I am merciful. I will not be angry with you forever'" (Jeremiah 3:12).

In the previous chapter, I wrote about how God thinks of us. We are his children, his most precious possession, the apple of his eye. Pastor Jonathan Edwards first preached his famous sermon, "Sinners in the Hands of an Angry God" on July 8, 1741. Edwards says that God abhors you, looks on you like you are unworthy of anything, and to God you are worse than hateful poisonous snakes. Then he proceeds to describe hell fire, using descriptive words never found in Scripture. Edwards won many "converts" with this sermon, but fear is the opposite of love and a poor motivator for seeking a relationship with God.

I agree with Zahnd (2017) that this famous sermon regrettably shaped American Christians' image of God. The reason this is such a tragedy is that Christians behave in the way they think God is like. Our thoughts (if believed) create our behaviors. Jesus said that our lives are to be like salt, making people thirsty for God. "In the same way, let your good deeds shine out for all to see so that everyone will praise your heavenly Father" (Matthew 5:16).

I work with so many people every day that have no use for religion, especially Christianity. Their conclusions have been made by observing angry, judgmental, intolerant people who claim to be born again. Every so often, I get a fundamentalist Christian in my therapy group. Unfortunately, the person outwardly appears to be the most dysfunctional one of them all. I see them through the lens of mental illness, but others see them through the lens of their claim to be a Christian.

What is Anger?

Anger is an emotion. It's an appropriate emotion when there is an injustice. A person who does not feel angry in the face of injustice could be labeled a psychopath. Anger itself is not a problem. How we express anger is the issue to be concerned about. There are both healthy and unhealthy ways of expressing anger.

"And don't sin by letting anger gain control over you. Don't let the sun go down while you are still angry, for anger gives a mighty foothold to the Devil" (Ephesians 4:26). The King James Version says it like this, "Be angry, and sin not: let not the sun go down upon your wrath." Anger is not a sin! How you express anger may be a sin.

Anger is an appropriate emotion when there is injustice.

Like all the emotions, anger serves a purpose. Anger is an action signal to protect yourself and those you love from injustice. If you witness racism, it's not productive to take injustice into your own hands and knock some heads together. That response will only get you into trouble. Instead, channel the anger into something constructive, such as writing a letter to the editor of the local newspaper. If people never got angry at racism, blacks and whites would still be living with separate restrooms, separate schools, and using separate drinking fountains. Nothing changes until people get angry enough to make changes. If someone did not get angry at diseases that kill, we would not have invented cures.

Below is a continuum of ways of expressing anger. The extreme left is very passive, and the extreme right is very aggressive.

Hidden Passive Assertive Aggressive Rage

Most people use a few, if not all, of these styles in their everyday communication. **Hidden** represents the MOST passive style, and **Rage** represents the MOST aggressive style. **Passive** and **Aggressive** could represent a passive-aggressive style. It is a continuum, so **Passive** represents a more passive passive-aggressive style. Gossiping is an example. **Aggressive** represents a more aggressive, passive-aggressive style. Secretly letting the air out of someone's tires is an example. **Assertive** represents an appropriate style of expressing anger.

Regardless of which unhealthy style we choose to use in any given situation, the ultimate goal is usually to get what we want. It's about being in control. We can get very good at switching methods depending who it is that we're attempting to manipulate.

Assertiveness is the preferred style of communication. There are occasions, however, when a passive style is best. For example, if someone threatens to harm you physically if you don't hand over your wallet, be passive and hand it over. There are occasions when the aggressive style may be appropriate. For example, if a building is on fire and some people are not moving, raise your voice and demand that they leave immediately.

Aggressive Style

Aggression is more the thunder and lightning style of expressing anger. It can be expressed by raising the volume of your voice, yelling, screaming, swearing, name-calling, destroying things, or punching people. A subtle expression of the aggressive style is not allowing another person to hold an opposing opinion. A person using this style keeps on pushing to get their points across without listening to the other side and validating other opinions. The aggressive expression of anger destroys relationships. But when a person destroys relationships, they suffer too. Aggressive people only respect themselves, not others. Of course, it is a false sense of self-respect. Aggressive people lose the respect of others very quickly.

Some people adopt the aggressive style because it was modeled by a parent. Others reject this model for the same reason. We don't always copy a parent's style, even if we had only one parent. It has to do with our interpretation of what we've witnessed. Often, the aggressive style is adopted because we discover by personal experience that it's how we can get what we want, or we observed one of our parents getting what they wanted by being aggressive. If parents don't set boundaries and give in to aggressiveness by rewarding it, the child may adopt it as a preferred style. Aggressive employers or managers may continue this style because it gets things done. Most of the time, they have no idea that their employees are complaining about them behind their backs.

It is vital to become mindful of the actual results of having an aggressive style. We need to be brutally honest with ourselves, and be mindful of other peoples' responses and comments. It's easy to live in denial about these things. It's easy to justify aggressive behavior with many rationalizations. The aggressive style can give a person a sense of power. The adrenaline rush can be both intoxicating and addictive.

Which of these statements describe you? These are examples of the aggressive style.

- I scream at people when I am angry.
- When someone makes me angry, I let them have it.
- I can't control myself when I am angry.
- When discussing a controversial topic, my tone of voice can become elevated.
- I have been known to speak rudely or insensitively.
- I can take an "I don't care" attitude toward the needs of others.
- I am uptight and irritable much of the time.
- I don't tell people that I'm mad at them, but I get back at them in other ways.
- I joke about sensitive topics with people I don't like.
- I do nasty things to people.
- I have many critical thoughts.
- I am very impatient with people.
- I love to hear that people I don't like are having troubles.
- I blow up quickly.
- Even though I feel guilty when I yell at others, I don't apologize.
- I don't give up defending my opinion about things when others disagree.
- I have a history of bickering with family members.
- I find it hard to keep my thoughts to myself when it's evident that someone else is wrong.
- I tend to give advice, even when not asked for it.
- I can be blunt and forceful when someone does something that I don't like.

Passive Style

Passive people believe that other people are more important than they are. They don't respect themselves, just others. They think that other people are entitled to have control over their own lives, but they are not. They usually play the role of the servant. They don't believe that they can do anything as effectively as others can. Passive people have a profound fear of rejection. They believe that if they don't do what others want or expect them to do, they will not be liked. There are a lot of feelings of helplessness and frustration at not being in control of their own lives. After a time, they can feel resentful, bitter, unappreciated, and used.

Those who adopt the passive style may have grown up in extremely considerate families. These families never say "no" when asked to do something for someone, and never ask for help when help is needed. This was my do-it-myself dad. Right up to his late eighties, he would move things far too heavy all by himself, even though the family would warn him not to. This is how I became someone who will try to fix or move anything all by myself. I can't say how many times I've hurt myself in the process. People often adopt passiveness when they grow up in homes that demand perfection and/or where they did not see the assertiveness style modeled.

Which of these statements describe you? These are examples of the passive style.

- I try my best never to get angry.
- I don't like others to know my problems.
- I have a tendency to be depressed.
- Sometimes I get paralyzed when being in unwanted situations.
- I rarely get angry at others, but I am often angry at myself.

- I usually blame myself when there is anger involved.
- I cut myself, take pills, drink too much alcohol, use illicit drugs, or binge eat.
- I am not inclined to initiate a conversation about a controversial topic.
- I have a lot of physical complaints that don't seem to have any source (headaches, sleep problems, or stomach ailments).
- Even when I am flustered, I present that everything is fine.
- If someone upsets me, I can go for days without discussing it, and perhaps I will never discuss it at all.
- I often doubt the validity of my opinions.

Passive-aggressive Style

This style is a mixture of both aggressive and passive styles. Some believe it's the "best" of both worlds. Regardless, it is still one of the three unhealthy styles of expressing anger. From my experience of assessing hundreds of clients, using both formal assessments and informal interviewing, the passive-aggressive style is the most common. Passive-aggressive is generally performed anonymously. Sarcasm is passive-aggressive because we hide behind the so-called humor that is intended to hurt. Rather than speaking directly to a person, sometimes people will speak out loud about someone or something, knowing the person they want to hurt will overhear it. This is not necessarily anonymous but is very much passive-aggressive in style.

Which of these statements describes you? These are examples of the passive-aggressive style.

- I become silent when I get frustrated, and I know that the silent treatment bothers other people.
- I tend to pout or sulk.
- I can give someone the cold shoulder.
- I never say anything to people I'm angry with, but I enjoy frustrating them in return.
- When someone points out my problems, I'll say what they want to hear but then not change.
- I sometimes approach tasks I don't like by doing them half-heartedly.
- I procrastinate doing things for people I don't like.
- I gossip or complain about people who are not doing things right or properly.
- I sometimes get involved with hidden misbehaviors.
- I might say that I will do someone a favor, but then not follow through with it as a way to let them know I didn't want to do it in the first place.

Assertive Style

Assertiveness is a healthy style of expressing anger. It's when we respect ourselves and others equally. Assertiveness does not fear conflict or criticism. It's about being visible and having a voice. We believe that it's okay to be flawed. We're able to hold differing opinions, and have wishes of our own. Assertiveness is being okay with others' opinions when they differ from ours. It is respectfully asking for what we want, and letting go of the outcome by not forcing what we want. This last point only applies to a relationship between two people on the same level of power. Assertiveness may include communicating and honoring the boundaries we place on ourselves to protect ourselves from harm.

Assertive people do not believe that it is important to get their own way. It also allows other people to be in charge of their own lives because people have a right to be themselves. Being assertive acknowledges that we are not always right or that we always know the best way to do things.

> An assertive person respects both
> themselves and others equally.

Assertiveness is about taking off the disguises or masks that we wear to hide our true selves. It isn't concerned about trying to impress other people. It's about being present and real. Those who are comfortable in their own skin can be assertive. Those who struggle with self-esteem or insecurities also struggle with being assertive.

Which of these statements describe you? These are examples of the assertive style.

- I do not attempt to manipulate or control anyone.
- I do not insist on doing things my way.
- I can speak my truth on whatever subject and allow others to do the same, even if they disagree with me.
- If I choose to go along with others, it's out of love, and I make it my own choice at that moment.
- I can ask for what I want and let go of the outcome.
- I can set reasonable boundaries on myself, communicate them respectfully, and honor them when I need to protect myself.
- When I disagree with someone, there's no raised volume or angry tone to my voice.
- I have a genuine love for myself as well as my neighbor.

Many of the above principles apply when there is no power difference in a relationship. This includes married couples, friends, coworkers, and church members. But sometimes there is a power difference in a relationship, such as parent-child, teacher-student, or police officer-citizen. The rules change somewhat in these situations. Parents, teachers, employers, and police can put boundaries on other people. They have a duty to manage and control those under them (within specific parameters). Assertiveness in these relationships is revealed through a respectful volume of voice, tone of voice, and other nonverbal forms of communication.

The Wrath of God

There are occasions in Scripture when God appears to have an aggressive style of anger. Most experts on communication claim that much of our communication is nonverbal—from seventy to eighty percent of it. Nonverbal communication includes the volume and tone of our voice, facial expressions, and our body language. Sometimes it includes audible sounds that aren't words, or are just one word, such as "really," "good," and "wow." The implications of this fact tell us that only reading words in Scripture is not enough information to precisely know the style of God's anger.

When I read about Jesus clearing the temple by knocking over tables, I imagine tears running down his cheeks and deep sadness in his voice. I'm not saying I'm right, but who's to say it wasn't that way, especially considering his character of love. Jesus said, "The Scriptures declare, 'My temple will be called a place of prayer,' but you have turned it into a den of thieves!'" (Matthew 21:13). The children who were there must not have been disturbed by it all because they stayed by to watch and proclaimed, "Praise God for the Son of David" (Matthew 21:15).

I've already stated that there are occasions when an aggressive raising of the voice is appropriate. I see God in the Old Testament, raising his voice at times just to get the people's attention. The "children of Israel" were more like children than mature adults. They had become so depraved while living in Egypt. After their exodus to the desert, God had to treat them like children at times in order to keep them alive in such a dangerous environment. This is not to say that adults are justified for yelling at children. The fear of loud noises is the one fear we are born with.

The Old Testament depicts the Israelites in a brutal battle against the pagan tribes. This was not God's preferred method. "I will send the hornet ahead of you to drive the Hivites, Canaanites, and Hittites out of your way" (Exodus 23:38 NIV). Recall how he armed Gideon and only three-hundred brave men to drive out the enemy with just trumpets, clay jars, and torches. The Israelites, however, started to scrap with these tribes, and God let them have their own way. In Scripture, what God doesn't prevent reads like he causes it. God wanted to be the only king of Israel, but the people demanded a human king like the other nations, so God allowed it. You can read about this in 1 Samuel 8. God is about giving us the freedom to choose our own path. Still, now and again, God raises his voice like on Mount Sinai.

As a parent, I had to "lay down the law," so to speak to keep my children alive. "If you play on the road, you will be grounded." "If you horseplay near the campfire, you will go to your tent." I didn't have to say it abusively, but with a strength that convinced them I meant exactly what I said.

> God's anger is best seen when he gives us
> over to our own choices and the natural
> consequences of that freedom to choose.

I heard an insightful story from a co-worker years ago. It may not use today's politically correct language, but it conveys a timeless truth about natural consequences versus artificial punishment. An Indian father says, "White father crazy. White son reach out to touch fire. White father slap white son's hand. White son hate father. Indian son reach out to touch fire. Indian son burn hand. Indian son hate fire." I have traveled around the world and lived in many different cultures. I must say that my own European culture has a lot to learn about these matters from other cultures.

Jesus told us, "I no longer call you servants because a master doesn't confide in his servants. Now you are my friends since I have told you everything the Father told me" (John 15:15). Here Jesus is communicating his desire to treat us like we are in a relationship with no power differential. Even though God has a right to treat us as servants, he chooses not to. He gives us freedom because he loves us.

"But God shows his anger from heaven against all sinful, wicked people who push the truth away from themselves" (Romans 1:18). Then Paul goes on to explain how God expresses his anger. After pointing out certain sins, he proclaims, "So God let them go ahead and do whatever shameful things their hearts desired" (Romans 1:24). "That is why God abandoned them to their shameful desires" (Romans 1:26). "When they refused to acknowledge God, he abandoned them to their evil minds and let them do things that should never be done" (Romans 1:28). This is how God shows his anger. He allows people to carry on and receive the natural consequences of their lifestyle choices. Once again, we see a God of love giving freedom. I am personally opposed to forcing my Christian values on nonbelievers. In my world view, the law of love and freedom wins in the end. We must be patient and wait for that to take place through a clear demonstration of God's love through his church.

Practical Applications for Parents

This doesn't mean that I can't be assertive and speak my truth. But, after that, I must let go of the outcome and place a boundary on myself and my children to protect us from any harm. This may mean homeschooling or enrolling my children in a Christian school to protect them.

The best form of discipline is giving people over to the natural consequences of sin. As I've mentioned already, however, there are some boundaries that I must place on my younger children to protect them. I must keep my children alive long enough for them to be able to reason for themselves and make their own choices. A rule of thumb that I used when raising my children was to allow them to choose whenever they were mature enough to endure the natural consequences of their choices.

I believe that when a parent gives freedom, the parent must also give full responsibility for that freedom. For example, allowing one of my children to borrow the car meant that they were responsible for paying for damages done or increased insurance premiums if they were at fault in an accident. Children must be taught and guided from childhood to responsible adulthood. They don't naturally grow from being one hundred percent dependent on their parents to being fully independent adults. This requires proper nurturing and teaching every step of the way.

In contrast to Jonathan Edward's view of how God sees us, Scripture says, "Is not Israel still my son, my darling child?" "I had to punish him, but I still love him." "How long will you wander, my wayward daughter?" (parts of Jeremiah 31:20, 22). These words are spoken to Israel at one of its lowest points in history. They had temple prostitutes and were sacrificing their own children to other gods.

I consider the scriptural word "punishment" to be equal to the English word, discipline. Discipline means to teach for the purpose of changing behavior. "Because the LORD disciplines those he loves, as a father, the son he delights in" (Proverbs 3:2 NIV). Other translations use the word *corrects* or *reproves* in place of the word *disciplines.*

In the field of psychology, there are different types of punishment. Positive punishment involves giving an immediate stimulus that hurts, such as spanking or scolding. Negative punishment involves the removal of something that results in some type of pain, such as missing a favorite TV show. There is a debate as to the effectiveness of punishment. For example, research shows that jail time does not stop people from committing crimes (Cherry 2019). I see imprisonment to be valuable in that it protects society, but most prisons are not very rehabilitative. Some private prisons follow radically different methods and are rehabilitative in nature.

Kendra Cherry (2019) summarizes the research showing what factors increase the effectiveness of punishment:

- Punishment is more effective if it comes immediately after the behavior.
- Punishment is more effective when it is consistently applied.

If you've been a parent or a teacher, you know that both the above factors are difficult to apply. Not only that but even when the above two principles are applied, there are three significant drawbacks:

1. Changes resulting from punishment are very temporary.
2. The recipients are not learning anything.
3. There are usually unintended and undesirable long-term consequences.

I am more concerned about this last one. Harsh emotional or physical punishment can result in antisocial behavior, aggressiveness, and delinquency (Cherry 2019).

A rule that I learned too late in life is to never discipline children when I am flooded. When we are in an angry, flooded state, we do not see or hear everything, and we are likely to be aggressive in our approach to discipline.

The Role of Shame in Anger Styles

Refer back to the iceberg model in chapter three. Unhealthy styles of anger come from unhealthy beliefs we have about ourselves. In other words, stinking thinking self-talk produces unhealthy ways of expressing anger. Negative self-beliefs such as "I'm not enough," "I'm not smart enough," and "I'm not whatever enough" create feelings of shame or false guilt. Whenever there is shame, which is a primary emotion, anger becomes a secondary emotion and becomes expressed in unhealthy behaviors. It comes out as aggressive, passive-aggressive, or passive expressions. These are all self-defeating behaviors because shame is involved.

If anger is not rooted in an inner sense of shame, it can be expressed assertively. When there is shame and insecurity, we get triggered and move into fight, flight, or freeze. We need to be using our logical, rational brain to apply the rules of good assertive communication. When we are in a flooded state, our emotional brain takes control, and we react in a fight (aggressive or passive aggressive), flight (passive), or freeze (extremely passive) response. Remember that passive-aggressive is a mixture of aggressive and passive styles. In a triggered or flooded state, we impulsively make wrong behavior choices in the moment, which we regret later.

This is the reason why it's not wise to discipline in a flooded state. Neither should we continue arguing or fighting in a flooded state. Gottman (2006) points out that there is a link between arguing while in a flooded state and high rates of divorce. He recommends that couples learn to take breaks when they are flooded. I teach married couples to be mindful of their anger. Be mindful of when you feel yourself becoming angry and flooded, or you see your partner becoming angry or flooded. When this occurs, stop talking, make the time out signal (hands forming the capital letter T), and just wait for the other person to stop talking. If the other person is flooded, it may take some time for them to see the signal, but just wait without saying anything.

> When anger arises out of shame, it is
> expressed inappropriately.

It works best when both people agree to this method and understand ahead of time what the time out signal means.

1. It means, "we are flooded." The emphasis is on "we" because when one is flooded, we are flooded. It does no good to blame anyone.
2. It means, "I love you."

3. It means, "I want to have this conversation, but right now, we need some time out."

Then go into separate rooms for some time out and return in twenty to thirty minutes. Make sure your heart rate is back to normal before coming back together again.

At that point, if it is too late to continue the discussion or a bad time or place to have this conversation, then pick a later time and place to continue. Do not try to postpone the conversation before calming down. When it's a good time to continue, start up again using good assertive communication skills. Repeat the time out as many times as you need to. Remember, it is not only useless to argue when you are flooded, it's damaging to the relationship as well. If one of the two of you just walks out in the middle of the conversation, that is being passive instead of assertive. Walking out on a partner can be like pouring gasoline on a fire.

Our View of God Counts

A great book, *How God Changes Your Brain: Breakthrough Findings from a Leading Neuroscientist,* highlights research that shows those who believe in an accepting, nonjudgement god have better mental health than the average population. Those who believe in a harsh, vindictive god, along with having a lot of fear of judgment and punishment, have much worse mental health (Newberg and Waldman 2009). There is no specific religion that one can identify as being more harmful than others. Instead, there are people or sects within any religion, from Christianity to Islam, who believe in a harsh, vindictive god. The problem generally comes when individuals use their religion to justify their angry feelings toward others. These individuals sometimes become hostile and militant (Newberg and Waldman 2009).

Our brains have mirror neurons. When we see someone take a drink of water, our mirror neurons fire. Suddenly, we may get thirsty ourselves. When we're on our way to the gym and are thinking about going swimming, our mirror neurons fire. Mirror neurons are the same neurons that fire when we actually do drink water or swim. Knowing this can benefit athletes. Those who not only practice on the court, skating rink, or ski hill, but also spend time visualizing themselves successfully shooting hoops, swimming fast, or skiing, do better than those who only practice physically.

Newberg and Waldman (2009) point out research that shows any exposure to any form of aggressive anger (visual or audio expressions) is hazardous, not only to the health of an individual but to society as well. When people are exposed to preaching with an angry tone, angry speeches at a political rally, a harsh, angry face in a picture, watching violence on the news or in a movie, playing violent video games, or listening to music with hostile lyrics, their mirror neurons fire and their amygdala lights up. People feel more angry, aggressive, negative, and powerless, and this can have a negative effect on society in general when many people are exposed to anger in these ways.

Letting Go

Anger is an acid that corrodes the vessel that holds it.

Anger is an appropriate emotion when there is an injustice. Therefore, why wouldn't God get angry? He sees more injustice going on at any given time than any of us. But God doesn't have fear like we do, and indeed he has no shame, so God can be assertive. God is always in control of himself.

Practically every day, I walked by a poster outside the headmaster's office where I taught in Africa. The poster said, "Anger is an acid that corrodes the vessel that holds it." This is not to say that the emotion of anger is bad. It's how much and how long we hold the anger, and how we express it that counts. There must be room for tolerance and grace in this world. Grace and tolerance start with individuals practicing it. But it works best when individuals have discovered God's grace, or at least God's grace revealed through the life of someone who has been changed by God's grace.

As we will see in the next chapter on forgiveness, anger is a healthy emotion at a time of injustice. But when we hold on to it chronically, it destroys us. We need to find a way to let go of our anger after it has lost its immediate use. This is done through forgiveness. God is a forgiving God. It is the character of God to be forgiving. Even while being nailed to the cross, he said, "Father, forgive these people for they don't know what they are doing" (Luke 23:34).

On the cross, God took full responsibility for our sins. He acts like he is the one who committed them. The wrath of God is not an angry father torturing his son for our sins. "No!" A thousand times, "No!" "For God was in Christ, reconciling the world to himself, no longer counting people's sins against them. And he gave us this wonderful message of reconciliation. So we are Christ's ambassadors; God is making his appeal through us. We speak for Christ when we plead, 'Come back to God!'" (2 Corinthians 5:19-20).

Are we in the hands of an angry God? A thousand times, "No!" We are in the hands of a loving God!

Assertiveness is a bridge to freedom. Be free!

12

Letting Go of Deep Hurt
Forgiveness—A Bridge to Freedom

"Don, the board of directors voted to give your church a full-time pastor as long as it isn't Don Straub!" Juanita and I gasped, out of complete shock. We were in a private meeting with two officials of our church organization. We were waiting for the decision on whether our church would employ me full time instead of the half time position that I'd held for almost ten years.

My local church would have to come up with enough money to pay the other half of my salary, or receive a full-salaried pastor paid by the larger organization. I'd already resigned from my teaching position because of the burnout that caused me to go on stress leave for several months. I knew that I could never return to both half-time positions because they both felt like full-time positions. The organization offered me either a full time pastoral or teaching position somewhere else. Due to personal family circumstances, however, that was not a possibility for us.

I had not expected this pronouncement. I was given the impression that getting the full-time pastor's salary was a shoo-in.

But no one had guessed what a board of directors would do. I felt betrayed and caught between a rock and a hard place, so I resigned.

My life would never be the same from that point on. Although I could have continued in full time employment somewhere else, it felt like I had been fired. I had been a part of this new church almost from day one. It felt like I'd lost a part of myself. The floor dropped from beneath me. I was in shock. Whatever pain I felt, Juanita felt it ten times more. How could I deal with such deep hurt?

It took me a long time before I could even attend church again. Later, I received a sincere and full apology face-to-face on behalf of the organization for the unfair decision that had been made. At that same time, I was invited to do a week-long workshop at a major province-wide church gathering. It helped in my own personal healing, but much more personal work was needed for me to complete my own journey out of the pain of what felt like rejection. That journey was a journey of forgiveness.

I was finally able to own my role in how it had all gone down. As pastor, I caused others pain by my decision to resign. Today, however, I speak regularly at the same church, and I present workshops throughout the province. I have no resentment towards the organization. I now have a much wider circle of influence in my city. I speak at several churches and to people of different denominations who attend my "Bridges to Freedom" weekends and marriage workshops. I consider my work as a counselor in a not-for-profit, government-funded addictions treatment center to be my "mission field." I have more opportunities to share the grace and love of God in the secular community. Without having the title of "Pastor," an immediate barrier is removed for many people. As I look back now, I would never have been able to take a Master of Arts Degree in Professional Counseling if I had not been given the gift of time. Like I've already stated, God does not cause these painful events in our lives—we do, by the choices we make. But God can bring good out of it if we keep trusting in him (see Romans 8:28).

I was without a job, so I made the decision to start my own business. I called it "Koinonia Services." *Koinonia* is a Greek word for community. My plan was to live by trusting God to provide. I advertised myself to do odd jobs like tutoring, painting, pulling weeds, or whatever I could do to help. I chose not to charge any set fee. I would allow people to pay me whatever they could afford. To this day, I still do the same in my private counseling practice and workshops. I never want money to be a barrier to people obtaining my services.

God has always provided generously. During the months after leaving the role of a pastor, finances were tight. Juanita had her own business as a graphic artist, but it was not nearly enough to keep us afloat. Some months we didn't know how we were going to balance the budget. We had recently changed our house mortgage to a company that allowed us to pay interest only if we needed to. This was a timely miracle that helped. We never told people about any of this. We just prayed, and when we needed something to make it through the month, an envelope with a few one hundred dollar bills would appear under our welcome mat at the front door. It was always just the amount we needed at the time. To this day, we have no idea who was doing this and how they knew the exact amount we needed.

Then, miraculously, I awoke at three in the morning one day with the strange compulsion to investigate my retirement information package. I discovered that it was just a few days before a cut-off date, after which I would not be eligible for a huge cash payout and a supplementary monthly income on top of my regular pension. If I had waited until the age of sixty-five, rather than retiring after quitting, I would have lost it. I immediately called the conference treasurer to verify my findings. Even he was not aware of such a clause in the contract. After doing some investigation himself, he confirmed that what I'd discovered was correct. I had only a couple of more days to apply for retirement before I would have lost it. Because of early retirement, I not only had the time but the financial ability to pay for my master's degree. I chose a university in the US because it was both Christian and accredited with American and Canadian counseling associations. This ensured my required certification upon graduation.

It was in my studies at university that I came upon some research on the far-reaching benefits of forgiveness. This led me to dig deeper into the topic of forgiveness, and to write a paper on the topic of self-forgiveness. What I learned about forgiveness on both a spiritual and psychological level greatly helped me on my own journey out of deep hurt. Forgiveness is both simple and more complicated than many understand, especially when the hurt is so deep. Forgiveness is a process, a lifelong process.

Forgiveness Therapy

Why is public speaking one of the top three fears of humankind? It's because our greatest fear is rejection, and our greatest need is acceptance. The greatest rejection comes from being hurt by the people we most love and trust. This generally means close family members and those who, by their position, we expect to be fair and trustworthy. I have now learned to have no expectations of anyone. We live in a fallen world, and people, regardless of title, are all sinful by nature. Having expectations sets us up for disappointment and for becoming a victim. A victim is someone without power. Having expectations sets us up to give away our power. A person without power allows the fight, flight, and freeze reaction to hijack rational decisions and behaviors. This is what I did when I resigned from my position as pastor. I'd had expectations, and they were not met.

In my research on the topic of forgiveness, I came across an author by the name of Robert Enright. He is a professor of educational psychology and a licensed psychologist. He is also an author of seven books on forgiveness, and a founding board member of the International Forgiveness Institute, Inc. I'd never thought there was such a thing as an organization that holds national conferences on forgiveness.

I have learned how to do forgiveness therapy from Enright's book for counselors, *Helping Clients Forgive: An Empirical Guide for Resolving Anger and Restoring Hope* (Enright and Fitzgibbons 2000). I use his book, *Forgiveness is a Choice: A Step-by-Step Guide for Resolving Anger and Restoring Hope* (Enright 2001) in group therapy on forgiveness. Each person in the group purchases a copy and individually works through it, complete with guided journaling. We then meet weekly to share and discuss that chapter in the book.

Perhaps it seems strange to talk about forgiveness in the context of psychotherapy. After all, isn't forgiveness a spiritual thing? Isn't forgiveness just a simple act? God forgives us, and then we forgive others. Why does it have to be so complicated? I didn't know that is was until I was deeply hurt. At that point, I did not want to forgive! At one point, I didn't know how I could forgive. After being a counselor for a while, I discovered that there are many people, both Christians and non-Christians alike, that carry the same resistance to forgive. It helps to understand what forgiveness is and what it is not.

Why Forgive?

"Then Peter came to him and asked, 'Lord, how often should I forgive someone who sins against me? Seven times?' 'No!' Jesus replied, 'Seventy times seven!'" (Matthew 18:21-22). These verses are followed by the parable I shared in a previous chapter of the king who demands that the people he forgives must, in turn, pass the forgiveness on to others who have offended them.

"But when you are praying, first forgive anyone you are holding a grudge against, so that your Father in heaven will forgive your sins, too" (Mark 11:25). Jesus taught us to pray, "forgive us our sins, just as we have forgiven those who have sinned against us" (Matthew 6:12).

It sounds like Jesus is commanding forgiveness. It even seems like Jesus is conditioning his forgiveness towards us on our forgiveness of others. Did he condition his forgiveness from the cross? "Father, forgive these people because they don't know what they are doing" (Luke 23:34). How does putting conditions on forgiveness fit with the law of love and freedom? As I have explained before, I believe that we cannot break the law of love. Whenever we choose not to love, we will experience the natural consequences of that choice. Even science has discovered the negative impacts of not forgiving others.

Before we go into that further, however, consider this illustration. Let's pretend that I am carrying a huge armful of firewood. You come to me with several valuable gifts. As you offer me these gifts, you tell me to drop the wood so that I can take the gifts. Likewise, if my arms are full of bitterness, anger, hatred, and condemnation, I cannot receive all the gifts God has for me like peace, joy, and contentment. Jesus says, "My yoke is easy, and my burden is light" (Matthew 11:30 NIV). Life is easier if you forgive than if you don't forgive! Most people describe their inability to forgive as being locked up in an emotional prison. We each hold the key to our own emotional prison—forgiveness.

Forgiveness is a component of all world religions. Enright believes that his fifteen years of scientific research has found sufficient evidence that forgiveness has positive effects on mental health (Enright 2001). Examples of mental health problems helped by forgiveness therapy include anxiety, depression, anger management, paranoia, emotional immaturity, intense fears, lack of assertiveness, and relationship problems (Enright 2001). Reconciliation takes two people working in cooperation. Forgiveness must happen before reconciliation can occur. When we consider the harmful physical effects of suppressed anger, discussed in a previous chapter on emotions, we can understand that forgiveness will help alleviate those as well. This is more understandable as we learn what forgiveness is and what it is not.

Why is Forgiveness So Difficult?

Change is always a difficult process. Some people have held onto their anger for so long that it feels like a comfortable pair of shoes. Anger is an anesthetic to pain, so letting go of anger may bring more pain in the short term. Some people think that having anger towards someone who hurt them is a way to control that person and a way to feel dominant over that person. Of course, neither of these ideas is true. To some, forgiveness feels like you are letting the other person off the hook. Forgiveness is not saying that what the person did had no significance, is excusable, or could be condoned (Colier 2018). The past cannot be undone.

Don't forget that, for some, forgiveness is about forgiving someone who lied to them, stole from them, insulted them, or embarrassed them. As a counselor, I have often asked clients to forgive people who raped them, had an affair on them, killed a loved one, or molested their child. The worst offense that I have ever personally experienced pales in comparison with the things I hear almost every day as a counselor. The atrocities that I hear in my counseling office have, on occasion, sent me to my own counselor for help with the secondary trauma that I've experienced. Forgiveness of this magnitude is not an easy thing to ask people to do. If I did not wholeheartedly believe that forgiveness benefitted the forgiver and not the offender, I could not ask such a thing from people.

What is Forgiveness?

Scientists strive to find operational definitions so things can be measured for research purposes. Enright and Fitzgibbons (2000) created an operational definition of forgiveness. Using this definition of forgiveness, researchers could measure a person's level of forgiveness before and after forgiveness therapy. The instrument is called the "Enright Forgiveness Scale." It measures the healthiness of thoughts, emotions, and behaviors toward the offender. Here is their operational definition of forgiveness in simpler terms and using my own words to make it more understandable: *Forgiveness is moving away from anger and towards love and compassion. A person willingly chooses to do this even though they have a right to be angry, and even though the wrongdoer does not deserve love and compassion.*

You might be able to understand by now that forgiveness is not necessarily a one-step event. Condemnation and forgiveness are not merely black or white. There are many degrees of forgiveness between being in a state of anger and in a state of love and compassion. Forgiveness is a continuum. It's a process that requires work over time. The deeper the hurt, the more difficult it is to move across the continuum.

Unforgiveness ------→-------→------→ **Forgiveness**
(Anger)   **(Love)**

This may surprise Christians, but we need to remember that we are not God. God is love, perfect love. God perfectly forgives us. This chapter is not about God's forgiveness. It's about our forgiveness of other people and of ourselves. Humans do not perfectly love. Becoming like Jesus is a process. No one is perfect, so no one has forgiven perfectly either. Forgiveness is a choice, but it is a continual choosing to forgive. Forgiveness can be superficial or deep, the quality may vary, and it is not always clear along the way (Enright and Fitzgibbons 2000).

What Forgiveness is NOT

First, and probably most importantly, forgiveness is NOT condoning, justifying, or excusing someone's wrong behavior. If it were, there would be no need to forgive. The very word implies that guilt, wrongdoing, hurt, and sin are involved.

Second, forgiveness is NOT mercy, leniency, or pardon (Enright and Fitzgibbons 2000). These may be included when God says, "I forgive you." Humans, however, may have to exercise justice to keep society safe from certain people. We may be relieved if someone goes to prison for murder or rape because they can't hurt more people, but there can still be forgiveness. Sometimes people can exercise mercy, leniency, or pardon on top of forgiveness, but it depends on the circumstances.

Third, forgiveness is NOT forgetting, because we can't forget. In Scripture, God speaks like he forgets our sins once they have been forgiven. "And I will forgive their wickedness, and I will never again remember their sins" (Hebrews 8:12). God is omniscient (all-knowing), so he cannot literally forget. But just as if he has forgotten, God chooses to treat us as if we'd never sinned. Someone once shared something that helps me remember what the word justification means. When I am justified, God treats me, "just if I'd never sinned." This is how perfect God's forgiveness is. Humans have a challenging time doing this.

Fourth, forgiveness is NOT trusting someone. Trusting someone is another thing altogether. People need to show they are trustworthy before you can trust them. I tend to trust people even when I only know them a bit, but I am cautious as to how much trust I have for them. The more I experience them as being trustworthy, the more I will trust them. It's unnatural to trust someone who is untrustworthy, but we can forgive them.

Fifth, forgiveness is NOT reconciling. Reconciliation is a beautiful thing, but it is not always necessary or possible. Some people are too toxic and dangerous to be in a relationship with. Others may be dead or living far away. Regardless, reconciliation requires work by both parties who are at odds with each other. One person can forgive, but it takes two to reconcile.

Forgiveness must precede reconciliation in any relationship. God is the one who forgives us even before we ask. "But God showed his great love for us by sending Christ to die for us while we were still sinners" (Romans 5:8). "Father, forgive these people, for they don't know what they are doing" (Luke 23:34). "For God was in Christ, reconciling the world to himself, no longer counting people's sins against them. And he gave us this wonderful message of reconciliation" (2 Corinthians 5:19). God initiated reconciliation. Our part is to receive this invitation and play our role in the process, or there is no reconciliation.

The Power of Forgiveness

Over the years, I have collected quotes from a variety of fellow counselors and sometimes clients. I don't know the origins of these quotes, but, regardless, they are powerful thoughts on forgiveness. They are in harmony with both science and Scripture.

- Forgiveness means seeing value in everyone—regardless of their behavior.
- Jesus said, "Love your enemies."
- The happiest relationships happen when forgiveness is routine.
- Forgiveness in a relationship is like hitting the reset button on a computer. It puts it back to the manufacturer's specifications.
- To NOT forgive is a decision to suffer.
- Forgiveness is the most powerful healer of all.
- Forgiveness is letting go of all hopes for a better past.
- Forgiveness is a process, so we continue to forgive.
- Forgiveness is easier when we let go of being a victim.
- Not forgiving is like drinking poison and waiting for the offender to die.
- Not forgiving is an acid that corrodes the vessel that holds it.
- We are responsible for our own happiness.

I have witnessed the power of forgiveness in myself and the lives of so many of my clients over the years. Matthew West sings a song called "Forgiveness." He states that his song was inspired by a woman who forgave the drunk driver who killed her daughter. His song's perspective of forgiveness is dead-on, according to both science and Scripture. He says that there is no end to what the power of forgiveness can do. It can even set a prisoner free, but the prisoner that it really frees is the one who forgives. You can find his song and this story on YouTube.

> Not forgiving is like drinking poison and
> waiting for the offender to die.

How Do I Forgive Someone?

It starts with willingness, a choice, a decision to forgive. It may help, however, to do some reflection beforehand. Robert Enright outlines tools for the journey of forgiveness in his book, *Forgiveness is a Choice* (Enright 2001).

You may first need to do some introspection on your own anger and shame. You may need to ask yourself some tough questions and look for sincere, honest answers. What are you pretending not to know? What has your anger and shame over the offense cost you? Has it affected your spiritual, mental, or physical health? Has it changed the way you look at the world in general? Has it caused some permanent damage to your life?

You may need to come to the place where you feel that your anger has cost you too much. Is it still taking too big of a toll on your life? You may have tried all kinds of things to suppress your anger or deny your anger, but nothing works. We call this hitting bottom. This is the place you might have to arrive at to finally make the decision to forgive.

You must understand what forgiveness is and what it is not. You need to fully grasp that forgiveness is for you, not the other person. There can be no strings attached to forgiveness. In other words, give up waiting for the other person to apologize or make amends. It may never happen. They may not even have a clue as to the magnitude of the hurt they've caused you. If you need to wait for any conditions to be met, you are the one who suffers longer and may never find the relief you are looking for.

Also, there is no need to communicate your choice to forgive with the offender. You would only do this if the person really desires your forgiveness. If it is a parent that you are forgiving, it may cause them unnecessary pain to bring things up to them. Parents do the best they can with the tools that they have. They may not understand what you're trying to say. Just forgive. If you really wish to have some tangible way of finding closure, however, try writing a letter. But don't deliver it. Burn it.

I recommend four parts to a letter of forgiveness. The first part is to apologize, ask forgiveness, and make amends for whatever you have done wrong. However, if you were below the age of twelve when this person hurt you, skip this part of the letter. You were only a child and not accountable. The offender was the adult and the one responsible. But in adult-adult relationships, each person probably played a negative role. Own your part, even if it was only a fraction of the wrongdoing.

In the second part of the letter, be specific on how the person hurt you. Talk about specific words said or actions taken. In the third part, tell the person the good things that you appreciate about them. And in the fourth and final part, summarize how you are moving forward. Let them know that you are letting go of all your anger, resentment, and bitterness toward them and moving on in your life to a higher place of love and compassion.

Perhaps end your letter with the sentence, "I am choosing not to be a victim of my anger and past hurts any longer. I embrace my personal power and choose to forgive and let go of my pain."

> Forgiveness is a choice to let go of my anger
> toward the person who has hurt me.

Some people have been so long ingrained in the wrong definition of forgiveness that they trip over the word *forgiveness*. If you carry that much baggage about this word and it prevents you from forgiving, then substitute the phrase *letting go* for the word *forgiveness*. Essentially, that is what you are doing when you forgive. It's like the grieving process. You find acceptance by letting go of the past because you cannot change it. In the forgiveness process, you cannot change what has happened. You first accept the pain of what has happened because you cannot change it. Then let it go. If you can't let go, you can't move forward. The past becomes a ball and chain, keeping you back from all the good things God has for you in the future.

Enright also gives some tools on how to work on the process of forgiveness. For example, it may help to get some understanding of the offender. This could mean trying to understand what life was like for this person as a child. Remember that hurt people hurt people. It may also be helpful to learn what life was like for that person at the time of the offense (Enright 2001).

This is what helped me in my own forgiveness of my parents. I heard my dad tell stories of his dad. If one of the kids left a gate open and the cows escaped, they would all hide out in the barn at night. They were terrified of their father's anger. From what I could glean, my dad was a better father than his dad had been. I like to think that I did a better job of parenting than my parents. My parents' generation had very little knowledge of parenting skills compared with what we have today. I have seen my sons and daughters doing a much better job of parenting than I did. Forgiveness can break the generational cycle of hurt people hurting people.

I love it when my son Kris says to his son, "Colton, I want to tell you something very important. I love you!"

One time, I was babysitting two of my grandsons who are cousins. One had an iPad while the other was next to him, watching.

After a while, the one watching attempted to grab the iPad. The one with the iPad pulled it back, set it aside, put his hands gently on each of his cousin's cheeks and calmly said, "I am using the iPad now, but I will let you use it very soon." Where did that method come from? His mom and dad obviously treated him that way.

Remember that understanding does not excuse the person. Understanding helps build compassion for this person as a child of God and a member of the human race. Forgiveness is a process of growing love and compassion towards the person who offended you (Khoddam 2014). "The Lord is like a father to his children, tender and compassionate to those who fear him. For he understands how weak we are; he knows we are only dust" (Psalm 103:14).

The key ingredient is continuing to choose to forgive or let go. Every time you begin to remember the offense, forgive again. Every time you feel angry, forgive again. Just say the words, "I forgive you," or "I let it go." Forgiveness is a process. You are not God. Embrace your imperfection because you may never fully get to the end of the forgiveness process this side of eternity. But there is freedom within the process.

I recall a man I had in group therapy. He knew that the topic of the day was going to be forgiveness. He entered the group room, but, on his way to take a chair, he stopped and faced me. He looked straight at me and said, "Don't even think for a second that you are going to get me to forgive my sister. It isn't going to happen in a million years!" I smiled and went on with the therapy session as usual. I explained forgiveness. At the end of the session, on his way out of the room, he stopped again and faced me. "You got me!" is all he said.

The next day, he allowed me to wash his feet as I played the role of his sister. It was a symbolic way for him to let go of his anger and forgive her. He said that he felt a million pounds lighter.

That is the power of forgiveness. I allow my group members to experience forgiveness in this very tangible way. I let them choose someone that they have previously decided to forgive. Those moments are what make my job as a counselor so gratifying. I have washed many feet in groups, acting as current or ex-partners, parents, siblings, or whomever the client needs me to be at that moment. Their tears say it all as I ask them at the end, "Will you forgive me?" and they say, "Yes, I forgive you."

Forgiving Yourself

Now, what about yourself? In my "Bridges to Freedom" groups, I do an exercise where participants circulate, face each other, place their right on hand each other's left shoulder, and say, "God has forgiven you." Then the other person responds with the words, "God has forgiven me." In the debrief that follows the exercise, I ask, "Which is more difficult to say, 'God has forgiven you' or 'God has forgiven me?'" Almost always, people answer, "God has forgiven me!"

If you cannot truly forgive yourself, how can you truly forgive another? "Love your neighbor as yourself." If you can't forgive yourself, then you are angry at yourself. Being angry at yourself prevents you from fully accepting yourself and moving forward as well. God has forgiven you, so why not forgive yourself as a way of embracing that truth? It is time to let go of your own anger towards yourself, and begin to love yourself in healthy ways.

I ask you now. Are you ready to forgive someone? Are you ready to forgive yourself? What is keeping you from letting go of the pain that you have carried for so long? For what reason do you think you must continue to suffer? What have you got to lose except the pain of your anger, resentment, and bitterness? Set yourself free today. Come out of prison. Remember that freedom may not come all at once because it is a process. But the process begins with a choice to forgive and continues with a choice to forgive.

Forgiveness is a bridge to freedom. Be free!

13

Repairing Your Past
Psychotherapy—A Bridge to Freedom

"Don, I am giving you an assignment. I want you to do something every day children would generally do. Play a game, build a sandcastle on the beach, roll on the lawn, or whatever creative activity you can think of." These were the words of my psychotherapist when I was getting his help for my burnout. Regaining my inner child changed my life. This is an example of psychotherapy.

Let's clear something up, right from the start. Psychotherapy isn't voodoo or some new age mumbo jumbo. Psycho means the mind. Psychotherapy means "therapy of the mind." I go to a medical doctor when I have physical issues with my body. I go to a physiotherapist when I've sprained a join. I go to a chiropractor when my back hurts. I go to my ophthalmologist when my vision is poor. I go to my psychotherapist when my thoughts, emotions, or behaviors are out of control, and the usual spiritual disciplines are not enough.

Choosing a Counselor

I use the words *psychotherapy* and *counseling* interchangeably. I prefer the word *psychotherapy,* but for the purposes of this chapter, I will usually use *counselor.* In our culture, many people call themselves counselors. Not all counselors are the same. Pastors are counselors at times, but few have the expert training for clinical counseling. Canada has an inferior regulatory system for counseling compared with the United States. In most of Canada, it is "buyers beware." When looking for a counselor, find one with a minimum of a Master's degree in counseling, psychology, or social work.

If you want to know if a counselor is a Christian, you may need to ask. Those of us who belong to a credible certifying organization follow a code of ethics. One ethical practice is to be neutral with a client in the arena of spiritual matters. If people ask for a Christian counselor, then we, as licensed clinical counselors, can accommodate them as much as they desire, and we are qualified to do so. I am, therefore, free to quote Scripture with some clients, whereas with others I'm not. It is not ethical for a counselor to attempt to help someone in an area or use methods that they are not trained in. It's their duty, if possible, to refer the client to another counselor who is qualified. Just because a counselor is a Christian does not mean that they're qualified to help with purely spiritual issues and can use Scripture intelligently.

You have a right to shop for a counselor. You can ask the counselor questions before making an appointment. You can also change your mind after visiting with the counselor at any time if you think your needs are not being addressed appropriately. Don't be afraid to ask questions about the counselor's methods. In my practice, I always explain, in easy language, the scientific support for all my methods. I never charge for my initial assessment session. I want people to feel free to decide if they wish to continue after they meet me and learn about my methods. I also want to know whether I can help them. It's not ethical for a counselor to continue if they are not adequately trained to meet the client's specific needs and goals.

> Seek a professional counselor when the usual
> spiritual disciplines are not enough.

Counselors have been educated in different schools of thought. You might want to ask questions about their therapeutic orientation. Orientations such as cognitive, behavioral, narrative, solution-focused, integrative, or wholistic are the most common ones that align with Scripture. Good counselors are eclectic. That means they use a variety of orientations depending on the needs of the client.

Clients come with different needs. Most counselors are trained to help with general disorders such as depression, anxiety, anger, shame, and personality disorders. It's best to find a counselor who is specially trained in trauma counseling or marriage counseling if one of those is your primary need. These counselors are certified specifically for these areas of expertise.

When I was a pastor, I was thrown into situations of helping people with marriage problems or other mental issues. Since I wasn't trained in counseling at the time, I usually encouraged them to find a professional counselor. Pastors who have no clinical training and attempt to be all things to all people are possibly doing more harm than good. After taking a master's degree in professional counseling, I realized how poorly equipped I had been to do any sort of proper counseling.

The Wellness Wheel and Natural Products

I believe in a wholistic approach to health. The only difference between the words *wholistic* and *holistic* is that *holistic* is a more academic term. I prefer the spelling, *wholistic* because in non-academic circles there's some confusion as to whether they mean the same thing, which they actually do.

In my workplace, as a live-in addictions treatment program, we use the wellness wheel to illustrate a wholistic approach. I've seen wellness wheels that have as few as six and as many as twelve components. We use the more simplistic model with six components: physical, emotional, intellectual, occupational, social, and spiritual. Each component affects the others. Overcoming an addiction, treating depression and anxiety, and improving relationships all benefit from balancing these six components of the wellness wheel.

I direct a client to a medical doctor if there is severe depression. I tell them to ask the doctor for a thyroid check, for example. I encourage them to obtain prescription medications if they are at risk of suicide, psychosis (seeing or hearing things that are not there), or doing self-harm, such as cutting or burning. My training has taught me that pharmaceuticals are necessary in these situations. Along with medications, they can do therapy sessions until the drugs are unnecessary. I make sure that they know to reduce their medications only under the direct care of a medical doctor.

If my clients have moderate or mild depression, I encourage a diet of whole grains, vegetables and fruits, and low amounts of refined sugar and carbohydrates. Carbohydrates are "comfort" foods, but, after increasing blood sugar levels sharply, they end up decreasing blood sugar levels and increasing depression (Wilson 2001). I also recommend harmless natural products, such as

PharmaGABA (rather than plain Gaba), a B complex vitamin, B-12, St. John's Wort, or 5 HPT (the amino acid tryptophan found in turkey). Of course, I tell them not to exceed the directions on the bottle. Because depression and anxiety are two sides of the same coin, I recommend the same products for anxiety. When you treat one, you help the other as well.

Dr. Archibald Hart (1999), in his book, *The Anxiety Cure*, goes into depth on all of these aspects when treating anxiety. I like his "Three Rs" approach: Recreation, Relaxation, and Rest.

Recreation means "re-creation." Amusement (video games and movies, for example) may not be a bad thing, but don't confuse these with recreation. Recreation needs to be active, building core muscle and oxygenating the brain and body through vigorous activity.

Relaxation is not "vegging out." Relaxation is an active mental process, such as practicing mindfulness exercises.

Rest is not just sleeping. An average of eight hours of sleep is important and affects all the other aspects of the wellness wheel. But rest is more than sleep. Hart (1999) refers to the biblical concept of sabbath, a word that literally means "rest." He endorses a program of daily, weekly, and longer periods in the year to rest. Daily rest includes small periods to reflect, relax, and practice spiritual disciplines such as prayer and study of Scripture. Weekly rest means taking a day to destress and focus on our relationship with God, family, and friends. Lastly, we need to take longer periods of rest, such as vacations, getaways, and sabbaticals. One of the best things my church did for me as their pastor was to make me take a week off to go away somewhere alone to rest. This was over and above a few weeks for a vacation with my family. I went to a campsite on the west coast of Vancouver Island to read, hike, and reflect. Have you ever come back from a vacation needing a rest from your vacation? My sabbatical was not one of those. I came back truly rested.

Cognitive Behavioral Therapy (CBT)

I explained CBT in a previous chapter. It's the most common type of therapy used by counselors. One of my teachers in university said to think of CBT as a way to teach your clients to be their own counselors. One issue that might come up for some Christians is the balance between human effort and the power of the Holy Spirit in their life. Christians have a range of views on this. If my clients are Christian, I can encourage them and even help them find ways to develop spiritual disciplines, such as prayer and Bible study. If my client is not a Christian, I encourage them to draw on their personal spiritual beliefs and practices. If my client has no spiritual orientation whatsoever, I need to help them with appropriate scientific methods of retraining the brain and behavior modification skills. I believe that a combination of science and spiritual practices is a more wholistic approach. A wholistic approach recognizes that we are bio-psycho-social-spiritual beings.

Depression

Cognitive therapies for depression are straightforward. In his book, *Flourish*, Martin E. P. Seligman (2011) gives a few very practical but well-researched methods of treating depression.

My favorite exercise is quite simple. At the end of each day, write out three things that went well that day. Then, for each of them, tell why you think it went well. If you can take ownership of any part of it, don't be afraid to write that down. This exercise is better than just naming all the things you are thankful for. That gets old and boring because it will most likely be the same list every day. This exercise will usually be different every day.

Gratitude is always good. Think of someone that helped you in the past and ask that person to meet with you at a café. Take some time during the visit to tell the person what you are grateful to them for (Seligman 2011).

I send many of my clients to take the VIA (Values in Action) Character Strengths test at www.authentichappiness.org. The test is free, and you will not be sent any emails from them. The website is from the Pennsylvania School of Positive Psychology. In this inventory, you will discover your signature strengths. They're usually the top five strengths out of the twenty-four listed on your print out. It will help you to be more positive (less depressed) and happy if you can utilize any or all your signature strengths in your everyday life. It's even better if you can find a career that uses your signature strengths (Seligman 2011).

All of the above exercises are practical examples of cognitive-behavioral therapy. If you change your thinking (cognitions) or your behavior, your feelings will change. Recall the BFT (Behavior - Feeling - Thoughts) sandwich.

Grieving a Loss

Loss is much more than having people in your life die. We may need to grieve the loss of a relationship (a separation or a move), loss of a job (being laid off, fired, or retired), loss of a bodily function (through accident, disease, or aging), loss of a childhood that we never had, and much more. Some losses are more significant than others, but this depends on the person too.

Time heals nothing, but work over time heals. There are tasks in grieving. If someone dies, attending a ceremony (funeral, memorial service, or celebration of life) helps to heal. If you missed out for some reason, create your own little ceremony. Invite some friends to join you. Share some pictures, share memories of the person, read a poem or some Scripture, and pray.

Do some introspection. Sit in a quiet place and journal your emotions and thoughts. Write down what you are angry about. Anger is generally a part of the grieving process because death is an injustice. Anger is an appropriate emotion when there is an injustice, at least in the short term. Don't forget to journal the good memories of this person. Focus on how this person influenced you in positive ways. How are you a better person because of this person's life? You can do this in the form of a letter to this person. After writing this letter, write a second letter from this person as a reply to yourself. Put things into this letter that you want or need to hear. This second letter is the most powerful for healing.

Talk about your loss to every person who is willing to listen. Most people hold in their thoughts and emotions. The more you share, the greater the healing. If you do not have many people to talk to, join a small grief group. Most large churches have them. Sometimes funeral homes sponsor them as well. Join a group, even if it isn't your church. You will be welcomed.

Some people believe that to completely heal and not feel any more pain over the loss is disrespectful. I ask these clients to consider what the person who died would want for them now. The answer is always that they would want them to be happy and move on with their life!

There is no set length of time to grieve. Every person is different. Sometimes it drags on because it is complicated grief. Complicated grief is when there is shame or guilt attached to the loss. I find that there is usually a false sense of guilt involved (shame), and my client needs to hear that from someone else to reach acceptance of the loss. True guilt might be attached to the loss of a job or a relationship. In this case, do the work of forgiveness—both towards the offender and yourself. If you begin to feel that you are unable to find acceptance of the loss and cannot return to your usual way of living, seek out a professional counselor for help.

Mindfulness

I want to return to the concept of mindfulness to expand on it. Mindfulness means that your mind is paying close attention to your mind and body. You can be mindful of your thoughts, emotions, bodily sensations, and behaviors. Mindfulness has three components: concentration, sensory clarity, and equanimity (Butina 2014). Everything you do goes better when you can concentrate on what you are doing. When you have sensory clarity, you are not only aware of your emotion in the moment, you are aware of the thoughts connected to the emotion and the behaviors that result. Equanimity is your ability to experience things without being carried away by them. This allows you to regulate your emotions and have greater control over your responses.

You can be mindful of what others around you are experiencing as well. It is quite useful to be mindful of another person's mood. We can empathize and perhaps adjust our behavior accordingly. It takes training and practice to become good at being mindful. When you work out at the gym, you increase strength, endurance, and flexibility. When you practice mindfulness, you increase concentration, sensory clarity, and equanimity. Following are some mindfulness exercises to practice.

Mindfulness Exercises

One mindfulness exercise that is excellent for handling intrusive thoughts, I call the "Empty Room" exercise (Forsyth and Eifert 2007). Just close your eyes, take some deep breaths, and imagine that your mind is a big empty room. There are no windows, pictures, or furniture. There are only two doors on opposite sides of the room. Let your mind wander, and as each new thought comes up, imagine it has entered through one of the doors and hovers in the middle of the room. Then as a new thought enters, imagine that the previous thought leaves through the other door. Begin to label each thought with, "It's just a thought, it's just a thought, it's just a thought." If you get any critical or judgmental thoughts, label those as, "It's just a judgmental thought." Practice this to be able to use it whenever you are actually bothered by disturbing or judgmental thoughts.

As I explained in a previous chapter, if we believe a thought, it can take us away to places we don't want or need to go. Labeling a thought as "just a thought" helps us to detach from it, and reminds us that not all thoughts are truthful or helpful. We don't need to be hijacked by them. "It's just a thought." "It's just a judgmental thought." "Take every thought captive" (2 Corinthians 10:5 NIV).

I remember one of my first clients that I taught this exercise to. She came back to me in a future session, exclaiming how well it had worked. She was at her desk when a co-worker came to her and started criticizing her. As she looked at this co-worker, she was thinking, "in the door and out the door, it's just a judgmental thought, in the door and out the door." She was not buying into the thoughts being created by this co-worker. She remained detached from them. They were just thoughts. This is how to keep from becoming triggered by them.

"Mindful walking" or "mindful eating" are a couple of other mindfulness exercises (Forsyth and Eifert 2007). Pay attention to your body as you walk. Think about the rhythm of it. Notice any bodily sensations in your hips, legs, and feet. Notice how things move and function. Pay attention to the food you are eating. Don't shovel all kinds of foods into your mouth at the same time. Mindfully eat each food separately. Take the time to eat slowly. Notice the texture and flavors of each individual food. These exercises may seem to have no value, but they train your brain to more mindful of the little things in your life of which you are not usually aware.

Mindful breathing is the most common mindfulness exercise. Belly breathing is especially good (Hart 1999). Focus on how you breathe and make each breath intentional. To inhale, lift your rib cage up and out, and then pull your diaphragm down by extending your belly out. This brings into your lungs as much air as possible. Then, suck your belly in and lower your rib cage to squeeze as much air out of your lungs as you can. This is a good exercise for managing anxiety because it brings you out of the future and into the present. It is also good at oxygenating your brain. When we breathe normally, we usually take shallow breaths. This means that we re-breathe the same stale deoxygenated air over and over.

Calm Place with the Butterfly Hug

The exercise I teach every client is the calm place combined with the butterfly hug. Pick a place that you have been where you experienced only good feelings. There were no fights or accidents in this place. Most people pick somewhere they have been by a body of water. If you can't remember any such place, then pick a picture in a magazine and study it. Close your eyes and concentrate on this place. Go through the senses of sight, sound, touch, and smell. Go into detail. Notice what there is in the distance and what is close by. Are there mountains, trees, bushes, small plants, stones, rocks? Get as detailed as possible, first with what you see, then what you hear, feel on your body, and smell.

When you are calm, begin to pay attention to your breathing. It's most likely slow, shallow, and down in the abdomen area. When you are anxious, you either hold your breath, or you breathe rapidly and high up in the chest. Memorize the calm breathing. Next, think of a cue word or phrase to link to this place. It could be the name of the place or a word like *serenity, peace,* or *calm.*

When you need to calm yourself down, you can start by saying the cue word a few times. Next, force yourself to breathe the way you did when you practiced this exercise—slow, shallow, and down in the abdomen. Now go to this place and see, hear, feel, and smell it. You can cycle between these three activities.

Then to really help, use the butterfly hug. Cross your wrists in front of you, palms facing you, keeping your thumbs together and your fingers spread. It should look like a butterfly. Place your thumbs just below your throat on the top of your rib cage, and begin tapping your chest with your fingers—left hand, then right hand, then left hand, etc. This is bilateral stimulation of the brain. The right side of your brain makes your left hand tap your right side of your chest, which sends the tapping feeling to your left side of the brain. This bilateral stimulation of the brain has a very calming effect.

There is a plethora of mindfulness type meditation exercises on YouTube, or you can find a variety of apps for your cell phone. Remember, mindfulness means "mind full." It is not the emptying of the mind like the meditation of the Hindu religion. We can take one text of Scripture and dwell on it intentionally for a while in order to listen and apply what the Holy Spirit is saying to us regarding our current life circumstances. This is mindful reading.

One of my favorite books is *The Anxiety Cure: A Proven Method for Dealing with Worry, Stress, and Panic Attacks* by a Christian author, Dr. Archibald D. Hart (1999). At the time he wrote this book he was a Professor of Psychology at Fuller Theological Seminary. He also has a CD with guided meditations, such as the famous muscle contraction and relaxation exercise for stress. You lie down in a comfortable position. You start at your feet and contract the muscles in your toes, count to ten, and then relax for the count of ten. Then contract your feet and ankle muscles, count to ten, and then relax for the count of ten. Keep contracting different muscles in your body from feet to hands to head in this manner. I also recommend his book *Unmasking Male Depression* (Hart 2001).

Emotional Freedom Technique

Emotional Freedom Technique (EFT) is also called tapping. It reduces anxiety by stimulating the pressure points of the parasympathetic nervous system. Our fight, flight, and freeze response has an on switch, the sympathetic neurons, and an off switch, the parasympathetic neurons. By tapping or massaging on the points of the parasympathetic system while dwelling on your anxiety-creating problem, you are essentially turning the fight, flight, and freeze response off. These pressure points are mainly on the head and face. There's also one below the collar bones, under the armpit, and on the outside edge of your hand.

Instructions on how to tap and guided tapping exercises are readily available on YouTube. Tapping can also be used for changing troublesome negative thoughts.

Trauma Therapy

This is an area where you must tread softly. Be sure that you find a counselor who has specialized training in trauma therapy. Be aware that older counselors may be far behind in newer techniques unless they are continually studying this field. Fortunately, licensing bodies require members to take several upgrading courses to renew a license every two or three years.

Therapy for trauma may involve somatic therapy (being mindful of what is going on in your body and changing your body's position to relieve symptoms). Problems arise when an untrained counselor has the client tell about the traumatic experience in detail. This can cause secondary trauma, reinforcing the original trauma in the body. Clients may become highly dysregulated. Counselors must be sure that clients have the resources to calm themselves down.

EMDR

I have been trained in what most authorities believe is the treatment of choice for trauma and post-traumatic stress disorder (PTSD). It's known as EMDR (Corsini 2001). This is an acronym for Eye Movement Desensitization and Reprocessing. It is supported by practically every psychological association and health authority around the world. Let me summarize from a university textbook. Counseling practitioners using traditional methods think of change as being a slow process. EMDR, however, throws that idea out completely. There is sufficient evidence from controlled studies that show how EMDR can create change in minutes rather than weeks or months (Shapiro and Forrest 1997).

I have done almost 2,000 EMDR sessions, and only about five did not work. These were because of something called dissociation.

When we dissociate, our brains shut down in various ways to keep us from feeling great emotional pain. It is the freeze response at a higher level of intensity.

Regular talk therapy is not only slow but it never really gets to the root of the pain. Neither does it take the pain away completely like EMDR. After I was trained in EMDR, I began to use it on practically every client. I wanted to call up all the clients that I'd had in the years before my training and say, "Come on back and let's finish the job!" I have never had anyone say at the end of a cognitive behavioral therapy (CBT) session, "That was a miracle!" But I get those words or similar expressions quite often after EMDR. "What just happened?" "That was weird!" Recently a client said, "I'm healed! It's gone!" That was after she had processed being raped.

Examples of What EMDR Helps

I have helped many people with the following examples of trauma.

- Sexual molestation, rape, and even gang rape
- Vehicular accidents, those in the vehicle, and those witnessing an accident
- Beatings, muggings, assaults, domestic physical abuse
- Schoolyard bullying
- Emotional abuse by a parent or partner
- First responders to traumatic accidents
- Mining accidents involving explosions
- Parental neglect or abandonment
- A child's trauma resulting from parents' divorce
- Natural disasters, such as flood and fire

- Dismemberment of body parts, both those who lost them and those who witness the accident
- Deaths, including suicides
- The effects of war
- Phobias for bugs, taxidermy, and Styrofoam (I would use it on any type of phobia)
- Contracting a significant disease such as cancer
- Breakups and divorce
- Job-related accidents
- Drug overdoses, both those who overdose, and those who witness an overdose
- Attacks by wild animals and dogs
- General anxiety and depression
- Secondary trauma experienced by a news broadcaster and other counselors
- And more!

Along with desensitization, self-esteem rises, and people feel more positive about life. Here is a typical example of reprocessing. A woman started out saying, "I hate my mother. When I was a baby, I really needed her, but she just stuck me in a playpen and left the room." After EMDR, she said, "My mother was working full time with three children. She needed to make us dinner, so she put me in a playpen to keep me safe." Her negative belief about herself before EMDR (concerning that memory) was, "I am unlovable." After EMDR, she believed, "I am lovable."

During EMDR, a memory opens. Sometimes people consciously remember things that they had forgotten about the incident (such as in the previous example). As the memory opens, however, disturbing emotions can intensify significantly until they go down to being neutral. I have seen big burly men shrink in fear at having to focus on a traumatic memory. Some people have so much pain about their past they refuse to do EMDR. At first, it takes a lot of trust in me to enter the process. After they experience relief from one trauma, they are usually willing to face their fears and do more work with EMDR if it is needed.

What EMDR Therapy Looks Like

Following is a summary of what happens during the EMDR process. The client and I work together to choose a disturbing memory to process. First I do a check to see if there are any underlying, earlier memories that we need to process. The protocol is to do the earliest memory, then the worst memory, before doing the more current memory. We only need to process earlier memories if there are any. There's a phenomenon called clustering that usually takes place in EMDR. For example, a client may have been continuously belittled by a parent throughout childhood. If we process the first disturbing memory (or one sample of them), and then the worst disturbing memory (or one sample of them), the entire cluster of memories usually become processed.

After we decide on the memory to target, I ask a series of questions about the experience. The first question is, "What picture represents the worst part of that experience?" The second question is, "When you think of that picture, what words best express your negative belief about yourself now." Examples are, "I am unlovable," "I'm a loser," "I'm stupid," "I am dirty," "I am weak," "I am unworthy," "I am not good enough," and "I am a bad person." Most people can come up with at least one, but some people need a bit of coaching, with examples that help them find the most fitting negative feeling belief. Recall that we have two brains. The logical brain may know I am strong, but the feeling, implicit brain makes me believe, "I am weak." We must use the feeling belief.

The next question I ask is, "What would you rather believe about yourself when you think of this experience?" Examples of positive beliefs contrasting negative beliefs are, "I am lovable," "I am smart," "I am capable," "I am strong," "I am good enough," "I am worthy," and "I am a caring person."

Then I ask them to focus on the experience and tell me how true those positive words **feel** on a scale of one to seven, where one feels completely false, and seven feels completely true. Interestingly, the positive belief rarely feels even close to true at this point. The answers are often down around one or two.

Next, I ask, "When you think of that experience and those negative words (repeat the negative belief), what emotions do you feel now?" The answers are always uncomfortable emotions such as anger, sadness, anxiety, fear, loneliness, shame, guilt, rejection, and hurt.

Then I ask them to rate the level of disturbance (emotional pain) as a doctor or nurse would do for physical pain. "On a scale of zero to ten, where zero is no disturbance or neutral, and ten is the highest level of disturbance you can imagine feeling, how disturbing does this experience feel now?"

The last thing I ask is, "Where do you feel this disturbance in your body?" I get all kinds of answers, such as the head, eyes, throat, shoulders, chest, midsection, stomach, arms, hands, legs, feet, and even private parts (from rape memories). This is body memory. Recall that our implicit, unconscious brain has three types of memory: emotions, body sensations, and beliefs. As you can see, the above questions tapped into all three types of implicit memory.

After asking all these questions, the client is now consciously aware of the power of a memory on an implicit level. So, we begin the EMDR process of eye movements or other types of bilateral (left-right) brain stimulation. Many therapists use two fingers on one hand to create the left and right eye movements. I use a light bar because I get a tennis elbow type of pain when I do it manually. My light bar also has a couple of paddles that vibrate left and right hands and a set of headphones that make a beeping sound in the left and right ears. All three of these stimuli are coordinated as left and then right to create bilateral stimulation of the brain. After graduation, one of our clients, who was in treatment for alcohol addiction, left the following statement regarding the light bar: "EMDR—the only bar in town that provides true solace."

I read back to the client their words describing the worst picture of the event or, if there is no picture, the worst part of the memory and the negative belief. I ask them to notice their feelings and body sensations, and tell them to follow the light. Then I start the bilateral stimulation with the light bar. During the process, clients do not try to do anything. They relax and let their mind heal itself. I stop the light every so often, and ask them what they are experiencing at that point. They give me a short answer about what their mind is paying attention to, and then we continue. I will forgo giving more details to this process. It might continue for only a few minutes, or, on rare occasions, up to over an hour.

At the outcome of the entire process, the client can honestly say that when they think of that memory now, it evokes a score of zero for the level of disturbance or neutral, with no disturbing bodily sensations (desensitization). They can also honestly say that the positive belief about themselves feels true at a level of six or seven out of seven (this is a part of the reprocessing of the memory). The number of sessions required depends on a few factors: the speed a client processes at, the type of trauma, and the quantity of traumatic experiences.

Other Advantages to EMDR

Another thing that I really appreciate about EMDR is safety, both for the client and the counselor. If a client wishes to process embarrassing experiences, such as a rape, there is no need to disclose any of the details to the counselor. Neither does a client need to give any details about the graphic, gory content of a trauma. The counselor is then spared the possibility of secondary trauma as well. If I know that the memory being processed is sexual or gory in content, instead of asking the client to describe a picture, I ask, "Do you have a picture of the event?" This is a "yes" or "no" answer.

How I wish that more first responders, such as police, firefighters, and ambulance attendants knew about EMDR. This is an amazing process of healing when combined with other modalities, such as CBT. I include this information about EMDR in this book in hopes that many more people can be helped with healing their past. To find a counselor that is trained in EMDR, simply search on the internet for "counselor EMDR name of your city."

In the previous chapter, I spoke about my journey of forgiveness. EMDR played a significant role in that journey. It's one thing to forgive on an intellectual level, but quite another to get rid of triggers and strong emotions associated with the people and places involved. EMDR freed me of these triggers and emotions. That made it possible to go back to church and talk to people again with complete comfort. I've met so many people who, because of being hurt by a church, are no longer able to enter a church due to panic attacks.

There are a few theories about how EMDR works. First, the bilateral stimulation of the brain calms the person, helping the client to process very disturbing memories. Some believe it is like REM (rapid eye movement) sleep. After a good REM sleep, people often feel better about what happened the day before. But we know that it's not the eye movements that cause the healing process. Alternate stimulating of the left and right hands also works. I use only the vibrations on the hands for young children who cannot follow the light. Children process traumas quickly because they haven't had years to ruminate on them. The healing seems to be from the bilateral stimulation of the brain. The left brain controls the right side of the body, and the right brain, the left side. Bilateral stimulation, such as the butterfly hug mentioned earlier, seems to calm the fight, flight, and freeze response.

The main point that I want to make about EMDR is that it changes the implicit brain, or the feeling brain. Cognitive-behavioral therapy works on the explicit brain, or the logical brain. EMDR works on the unconscious brain and CBT on the conscious brain. Remember that it's the unconscious or implicit brain that gets triggered in a fight, flight, or freeze reaction. By desensitizing implicit memories, we reduce the triggers.

There are several books, magazine articles, and websites that expound on the above summary of information. Probably the most complete book on the topic of EMDR is *Eye Movement Desensitization and Reprocessing: Basic Principles, Protocols, and Procedures*, Second Edition, by Francine Shapiro (2001). This is the basic textbook we use in training.

Some Christians are resistant to any type of psychotherapy that's not found in Scripture. They believe that if there are mental or emotional issues, it's only because of a lack of faith. There are many modern techniques of healing the body, such as surgery, that are not found in Scripture. But there are a few fundamentalist Christians that believe that going to a doctor is also a lack of faith. Most people hear about EMDR and are skeptical. It's not hypnosis. It's a therapy that works while you are in a very much conscious state of mind. You can find demonstrations of EMDR sessions on YouTube.

I will say, however, that it is the most boring type of psychotherapy I do from a counselor's perspective. I do a lot of waiting during sets of eye movements, so I pray for the clients during those times. I don't see my work as being any different than my Christian doctor, who said he was praying for me during my surgery. I believe in a combination of Christian spirituality and science when it comes to healing the body or the mind. This is the reason why I titled this book, *Bridges to Freedom: Creating Change through Science and Christian Spirituality.*

Summary

In this chapter, my purpose is to give the reader a general idea about what the science of psychotherapy or clinical counseling is like. To go into detail about the different methods would fill dozens of books. My first hope is that if you have a desire to search deeper into any specific area, you read some of the recommended books listed at the end of this book. My second hope is that you can overcome any barriers that are keeping you from seeking professional help through counseling. I can't say how many times I get a person coming to me for help that tells me their spouse refuses to come for help. Sadly, people are still living in ignorance about these things.

I've never been so fulfilled in my career as I have been since becoming a psychotherapist. I now experience the changes that can come from a more wholistic approach in the arena of emotional health. Nothing can match the experience of being a part of the changes that I see when people improve in their mental health and come alive again.

Psychotherapy is a bridge to freedom. Be Free!

14

Miracle, Science, or Coincidence?

Faith—A Bridge to Freedom

We were stranded high in the mountains at night, and it was freezing cold. Suddenly, a man on a snowmobile drove up.

"Who are you?" I asked.

"I'm the abominable snowman," he answered.

"No, you're not. You're an answer to prayer!"

"You're right. As a matter of fact, I am!"

Have you ever experienced a miracle? I'm talking about a true blue, unexplainable event, an event that could not be explained by science or a coincidence. I have experienced this at least once, though I would like to think it actually happened a few times. Who can really say for sure?

Freedom versus a Miracle

If God is a God of freedom, then why or when would God cause a miracle to happen? I believe that's a fair question, and it deserves an answer. Let me be clear. I believe God performs miracles. I believe the miracles that Jesus did were real and genuine. What I don't believe is that many of what people call miracles are actually miracles. I don't believe that God is primarily in the business of performing miracles. I believe that he prefers people have faith in him. And faith does not need proof. If something can be proved, faith is no longer needed.

I remember as a student in high school, we would ask questions that had no answers. For example, "If God can do anything, then can he make a rock so big that he can't move it?" or "What would happen if an unstoppable object hit an unmovable object? I really don't know why we talked like this, but I believe that there are some things that God cannot do. God cannot do anything that contradicts who God is. God cannot do an evil act. God cannot make someone love him.

I often get requests like, "Please pray that God will bring my rebellious son back to the truth." "Please pray that God will change the heart of my husband and bring us back together." God cannot interfere with the free will of people. That would use force and manipulation, not love. A miracle of this nature would require God to change the neuro connections of a brain, and make people something other than their true selves.

The God of freedom gives people choices and allows them to experience the painful consequences of their choices. When any of my children were making wrong choices, I asked God to help me let go of them. To be at peace, I needed to let go of whatever I had no control over. What happened laid in my children's choices. I knew God loved my children more perfectly than I ever could. I thanked the Holy Spirit for being with them and speaking truth to them.

"And when he comes, he will convict the world of its sin, and of God's righteousness, and of the coming judgment" (John 16:8). There is no need to ask God for this because it is what he does.

Scripture says, "Pray at all times and on every occasion in the power of the Holy Spirit. Stay alert and be persistent in your prayers for all Christians everywhere. And pray for me, too. Ask God to give me the right words as I boldly explain God's secret plan that the Good News is for the Gentiles too" (Ephesians 6:18-19).

God can influence, but so can the devil. More importantly, God can influence people through us if we make the choice, as the above verse says, to speak the best words in any situation. Prayer puts us in the frame of mind to be in tune with the Holy Spirit's voice. In the end, however, it all comes down to a person's freedom to choose.

Let's say a person gets into a car accident, almost dies, and, as a result, turns their life around. Some people will immediately jump to the conclusion that this was the work of God to save the person's soul. Does God cause car accidents? That would not align with the character of God. But this car accident can be used by God to convict a person to turn their life around. The devil, however, can also use the same disaster to influence the person to go more deeply into sin. It all comes down to a choice.

This is how I pray for people like the son or the spouse situations described above. I start by thanking God for his promise to be with that person. I thank God for influencing this person through the Holy Spirit. At the same time, I realize that the devil is also speaking to people, attempting to keep them away from God. I also pray that God sends the right people into this person's path, people who could influence the person I am praying for. It all comes down to influencing a person, but they are free to make their own choice in the end.

"The earnest prayer of a righteous person has great power and produces wonderful results" (James 5:16b). There was a time when I thought of a righteous person as one who perfectly keeps all the commandments. If I could keep all the commandments perfectly, I would be righteous, and then God would answer my prayers. Then I discovered Isaiah 64:6, "We are all infected and impure with sin. When we display our righteous deeds, they are nothing but filthy rags." But then comes the good news, "I no longer count on my own righteousness through obeying the law; rather, I become righteous through faith in Christ. For God's way of making us right with himself depends on faith" (Philippians 3:9).

Having great power when I pray cannot be trying to strong-arm God into doing my bidding. "All of you together are Christ's body, and each of you is a part of it" (1 Corinthians 12:27). I, being a part of the body of Jesus, can play a role in influencing a person to make the decision to come back to God or a spouse.

> One miracle God will never do is to change a person's choice.

During my "Jesus Freak" days in college, I made it my habit to pray, "God, put one person in my path today that I can help." I believe that prayer opens me up to being much more mindful of those around me. God could, therefore, answer that prayer through me every day that I prayed it. I cannot begin to remember all the people that I was able to help by seeing myself as the hands and feet of Jesus. I will share two memorable experiences later in this chapter. I believe there are many righteous (in Jesus) people who make themselves available for God to use, and, since it is their free choice, God can work through them. This is how God can also answer a prayer for a son, daughter, or spouse. This is where the power lies. God can still honor the law of love and freedom in this manner.

When God does act by miraculously intervening in nature, such as the biblical flood, he is taking the risk of being misunderstood. This is the reason people built the tower of Babel. They were afraid of God and did not trust him. I believe that's why God is hesitant to work miracles like the flood. God seems only to do these kinds of things when the circumstances warrant a drastic intervention. These kinds of miracles are not an everyday occurrence. Sometimes a parent needs to take an extraordinary action to keep a child from significant harm, even though it may not be the parent's preferred method of discipline.

Suppose someone shows up at church and says, "The devil caused me to be late for church. He placed a board with a nail in it to give me a flat tire when I backed out of my driveway."

The next week, the same person comes to church and says, "I was wrong, God placed the board with the nail in my driveway because if I had been on time, I would have been in a thirty-car pileup on the freeway."

There is a third option. Perhaps the neighbor kid dropped the board with a nail in it on the driveway. Miracle? If so, was it the devil or God? Was it science? Nails sticking out of a board can cause a flat tire. Was it a coincidence? Somebody dropped the board in the driveway.

We are encouraged to pray for the sick. "Are any of you sick? You should call for the elders of the church to come and pray over you, anointing you with oil in the name of the Lord" (James 5:14). These kinds of prayers also require an attitude of, "Thy will be done." If a person dies because God chooses not to perform a miracle, we must not conclude that the death was God's will. It is God's will that freedom reigns in the universe, unless he has a particular reason for intervening.

Juanita pointed something out to me one day. We hear stories of people being cured of cancer and other similar diseases. There seems to be no record of someone being cured of a mental illness such as the one her adopted son has, global delayed development.

265

His body is thirty years old, but his mind is about ten years old. Why might this be so?

I believe that God can cure cancer, but most of the stories of miracles may actually be science or coincidence. Science can do a lot of good when it comes to diseases like cancer. Still, there's no scientific solution for global delayed development. To heal it, God would have to miraculously rearrange a lot of brain molecules, perhaps making the person someone different in character and personality.

My Miraculous Experiences

Someone once told me that when we get to heaven, our guardian angel will reveal all the miracles that happened to us that we were unaware of. Perhaps this is true. I'll have to wait and see. The following are what I believe could have been miracles in my personal life. I won't repeat the stories I've already shared of what seemed to me like miracles. Then again, who really knows but God.

Construction Accident

The first time I thought that I'd experienced a miracle was in college (in fact, most of the miracles that I experienced were in my college years). I was working in construction during the summer between school years. We were framing houses. I was working alone because the other workers had left to go to another building site. I'd been given a task to complete in the meantime. I was walking on the ceiling joists, nailing straps across to keep them stable. There was a gust of wind, and I stepped back in order to get my balance. I looked behind me and saw a piece of

2 x 10. I thought it was a long board, but it was too short to hold any weight, so I fell between two joists towards the floor below. Miraculously, or perhaps coincidentally, there was a power cord from the skill saw lying across the joists. My body landed on the cord perfectly, so that it broke my fall. I gently came to a stop before touching the floor. I had to explain to my boss why the cord had been stretched and torn. He was glad that it was just a cord and not my body that he would have to deal with. Miracle, science, or coincidence?

Praying for People

I was in my second year of college and had become perplexed about my personal salvation. I was uncertain about how a person was saved. I was hanging out with people who were teaching that unless we are perfect before we die or Jesus comes, we won't be saved. They seemed like spiritual people, and they showed me some convincing Scriptures. My girlfriend was trying to help me, but it wasn't working. Then one day, I saw a brochure advertising a Bible conference. I didn't know what a Bible conference was, but I bought a new Bible and signed up.

The Bible conference was held in a huge lodge just outside of Portland, Oregon. There was a big meeting room on the main floor and rooms with bunk beds on the top floor. The first night, I woke up suddenly in the middle of the night. I couldn't get back to sleep, so I went downstairs.

I was surprised to see a small group of students in a circle, talking. They called me over and asked me why I'd come down. I explained that I had no idea. They told me that they'd been praying for God to wake someone up who needed to know him as Savior and bring that person downstairs. I started to cry and told them about my perplexing questions. They explained to me in no time that when we accept Jesus as our personal savior, he justifies us (treats me just as if I'd never sinned). I was declared perfect in God's sight, and if I should die or if Christ should return, I would be saved. I felt like a huge weight had come off my back. What a relief! Later, I identified with the experience of the pilgrim in the book *Pilgrim's Progress* when he came to the foot of the cross—his heavy backpack fell off, rolled down the hill, and into a grave.

The group continued to pray. This time, someone suggested that we pray for a friend of his to wake up and come down. His friend was being very resistant to accepting Jesus. We prayed for a short time, and down this person came. They told him what they'd prayed for him, and then talked to him about Jesus. He gave his life to God just like I had.

We repeated this, naming people that someone in the group knew needed Jesus. It happened a few more times that night before we all decided that we'd better get some sleep. The Bible conference was the most profound turning point in my life. Miracle, science, or coincidence?

A Stranger in the Bakery

Following the Bible conference, I was sharing Jesus with anyone who would listen. I would get bored studying, take my Bible, walk across the street from the men's dormitory, and knock on doors. There were people living right across the street from the college who hadn't known it was a Christian college!

I worked part-time in the college cafeteria. As I mentioned earlier, I started the day asking God to send someone in my path who needed help. One day, my manager sent me to the bakery section because someone hadn't shown up for their shift. I'd never met the man whom I was sent to help make cookies. We struck up a conversation, and I began to share my experience at the Bible conference and how I became a Christian. Near the end of our shift, he said, "This was going to be my last shift at the bakery. My car is packed and ready to move out of town. I was leaving my wife, but because of what you've shared with me, I've changed my mind. I am going home to make things right with her." Miracle, science, or coincidence?

Summer Student Task Force

The summer following the Bible conference, I chose to apply for a position on a student task force instead of working construction. We were sent to a city in Canada, to work for a few churches. We'd be given a scholarship towards our tuition for this work. The unique thing about this task force was that we were dependent on the churches to provide our living expenses for the summer months. We knew that we were going to be living by faith, but I was excited about the experience.

During that summer, there were days when we had little food to eat. One week, we had only two things to eat for a few days in a row—green beans and cantaloupe. These were my two least favorite foods. Who says God doesn't have a sense of humor? Just kidding. Unlike I believed at the time, I don't believe God arranged that menu to teach me to like green beans and cantaloupe. Anyway, I actually love both those foods today!

There were days when we didn't know if we were going to end up sleeping in a car. Someone from one of the churches, however, would come in the "nick of time" and offer us accommodations for a short time. When we didn't even have green beans and cantaloupe, someone would donate some money through a church offering, and we were able to purchase food. It was an experience of living by faith that I will never forget. Miracle, science, or coincidence?

Funding for College Tuition

Recall the story of my five friends who were killed in a tragic car accident. Here is the rest of the story. Before this accident, I'd received a letter from the Canadian government, denying my requested grant for college tuition because I was in the United States. I wrote a long letter explaining why I had chosen this Christian college in the US, and asked them to reconsider. My friends were praying for me to get the grant. The day following the car accident, I was at my lowest point ever. I'd even started to doubt that God really cared at all because he had let my friends die so tragically. I reasoned this way before I discovered the law of love and freedom.

The day after my friends were killed, I did my daily check for mail. In my mailbox was a reply from the government with an affirmative answer. I was getting the grant, and I could stay in school for the balance of the year! Then, for some reason, I checked the postmark on the envelope. It was postmarked two weeks before it had arrived in my box. That was more than twice the usual time for a letter to get from Canada to the US. I interpreted it as a miracle from God, reminding me that he cares. I needed to be cheered up and encouraged on that day more than any other. Miracle, science, or coincidence?

Another Postal Miracle

I had such a great experience working on the student task force that summer, I signed up for another one the next summer in a different city. There I met three people who were from other colleges and places. One of them was Nellie, who'd come from the eastern states to the task force by "coincidence." She'd just broken off an engagement with someone that was not right for her. She had to give back all the shower gifts. Then Nellie happened to walk into a bookstore where she met a woman. The woman asked her what she was doing, and Nellie explained what had happened, and that she had no idea what to do now. The woman told her that her brother was putting together a task force in Canada that summer, and they could use another person. Nellie looked into it, and ended up in a place she had never heard of before (Nellie had grown up in Alaska). I was engaged to another girl that summer, so I had no romantic attraction to Nellie at the time. She became a really good sister to me.

Upon returning to school at the end of the summer, my fiancée broke up with me. I began dating other women, but no one seemed right for me. Then, out of the blue, I thought of Nellie. She had an outstanding character and loved God more than anything in the world. I wrote her a letter, asking her if she would consider being more than a sister to me. As I placed it in the mailbox, I prayed, "God, if Nellie is meant to be with me, please bring a reply back within four days." Considering that this meant two days there and an instant reply, and two days back, that was a crazy request.

On the fourth day, I got a letter back from Nellie. Before I opened the letter, I knew that it was a "yes." But her letter informed me that, although she was honored by my request, she was already going with someone else. Nevertheless, I knew that it was a "yes." I just had to wait. Nellie sent another letter a couple of months later. She explained that she had broken off the relationship with this other man. She wanted to know if she could come down and see me for a weekend. She had an aunt living there by the college. The rest is history. We were married after my graduation from college. Miracle, science, or coincidence?

Stranded in the Mountains

On another workday in the cafeteria, I was peeling potatoes with two women I'd never met before. I began to share my story of conversion with them, and they began to mock me. They claimed that God was not real, and that I was just telling cute stories. I began to pray for them while I continued peeling. I prayed that God would reveal to them that he was real.

The next day, I was placed in a different area of the cafeteria. I was helping my best friend wash pots and pans. Suddenly, along came one of the two women with whom I'd peeled potatoes the day before. My friend asked her out on a date. He asked her if she would go with him for a drive in the mountains on Saturday. I almost fell over. My friend hadn't dated anyone as long as I had known him.

Then he turned to me and told me that I had to ask a woman out on a double date because he was not going to go alone with her. I was now stuck with the problem of who to ask. Then the other woman who was peeling potatoes came in with some more dirty pots. I have no idea why, but I blurted out an invitation to accompany me and the other two on the trip into the mountains. She agreed to come.

My friend and I picked the two women up in his Volkswagen Beetle, and then we headed out of town. We had no idea where we were going. We followed a road that led up a mountain. Then it seemed that we hadn't seen any buildings for more than an hour. The weather had been quite moderate so we weren't wearing any sweaters or coats. The snow on the road was continuing to build up. We stopped once in a while and threw snowballs at each other. Then it was starting to get near sundown, so we decided to turn around to go home.

In attempting to turn around on such a narrow road, the Beetle's back wheels sunk into a ditch next to the mountain. The car was now perpendicular to the road. The front of the car was about four feet from the cliff on the other side of the road. No matter how hard we pushed while one of us sat ready to steer, we could not get out. Eventually, the car battery went dead. It was now almost dark, and we were freezing.

As we all sat in the car shivering, I cautiously suggested that we pray for help. I remembered how the women had scoffed at me a few days before. Everyone went silent. One of the women asked, "How can God get us out of this jam anyway?" So we brainstormed some ideas, coming up with only two. First, God could charge the car battery, and we could then push ourselves out if we tried even harder. Second, God could lift the car up off the ground, turn it around, and push us downhill until we could start the engine using the clutch. We did decide that the second suggestion was highly unlikely to happen.

Everyone agreed to pray. We got out of the car and knelt down in a circle in front of the vehicle. After we'd prayed, we scrambled back into the car because we were freezing by then. I don't remember how long we sat there in the dark, but after quite a while, we saw the single headlight of a snowmobile coming up the road. We were so excited. The snowmobile drove right past the front of the car and on up the mountain. We just about fainted. "Why didn't he stop?" we cried!

Then we saw the light coming back down the road, so we quickly formed a barrier with our bodies so he couldn't drive by again! He had gone farther up the mountain in order to find a place where he could turn around.

"Who are you?" I asked.

"I'm the abominable snowman," he answered.

"No, you're not. You're an answer to prayer!"

"You're right. As a matter of fact, I am!"

Then he proceeded to tell us that he and his buddies had been partying at the base of the mountain. We could smell the alcohol on his breath, and he was swearing (I left those words out of the above dialogue).

I said, "Hey! I am serious! See, these are our knee marks in the snow where we prayed for help."

He replied, "I know. I was playing cards with my buddies when I heard a voice that said, 'Get on your snowmobile and head up the mountain.' I didn't know why, but I did it anyway. And where I go, my buddies will follow."

We heard some motors humming in the distance. When we looked over the edge of the cliff, we could see a chain of seven lights winding their way up the mountain. Soon, seven snowmobiles, each carrying two men, drove by us and up the road, and then turned around to come back.

Some of them began to curse and swear at us for being so foolish. The first man ordered them to stop swearing because "we're an answer to their prayer!" Before we knew what was happening, fifteen men surrounded the Beetle, picked it up, and slid it around, pointing it down the hill. My friend hopped in, and they pushed it until it started. While this was happening, the two women were jumping up and down, yelling, "God is real! God is real!"

After we drove awhile down the mountain, we all got out and prayed a prayer of thanks. What a night to remember. Miracle, science, or coincidence?

African Snakes

Snakes are plentiful in Africa. I killed a couple of green mambas and a black mamba on my property where my kids played. I once saw a long spitting cobra on the path between my house and the school. It raised itself up to the height of my head. I discovered that the local people had no name for most snakes. To them, any snake caused fear, whether they were poisonous or not.

One night, Nellie got up to comfort one of the kids in the dark. It was too much work to light the kerosene lantern. She yelled from the kids' room, "Don, one of those crabs from the river just bit my toe!" I got up, lit the lantern, and set it on the floor in order to look under the bed. Staring at me was a large snake.

First, Nellie checked her toe in the light. There were four fang punctures. I ran for a machete and a broom. I carefully pulled the bed away from the wall. Keeping the snake at bay with the broom, I brought the machete down hard enough to cut the snake in two pieces and chip the cement floor. Then I got a dustpan, put the head end on it, and rushed out to wake up another faculty member and show him the snake. He lost it and started screaming. He gathered up a few more teachers, and they came up right away to pray for Nellie.

In America, our first response would be first aid and a trip to the hospital. With no hospital anywhere close, their first response was prayer. Her toe did not swell, and she never got sick. After that, people would stop by to see the woman who had been bitten by a snake but didn't die because God healed her.

Months later, when we were in Nairobi, Kenya, we went to the reptile museum. We always wondered what kind of snake it had been and whether it was venomous. We identified it as a house snake, and found out that it was poisonous. Miracle, science, or coincidence?

Later, after Nellie died of hepatitis A, I questioned God on why he would work a miracle about the snake but not one for hepatitis A. At the time, I didn't understand the law of love of freedom. If I had, I would not have struggled with the "why" questions. Maybe one day I'll find out, but for now all I have is faith. It is the faith that says, "God, I have faith that you can heal. If you choose to heal, then thank you. If you choose not to heal, I will love and trust you anyway."

Paris, France

In 1996, I teamed up with the youth pastor to start a mime ministry for the youth of our church. We would go to public parks and do mime to songs that presented positive lifestyle choices. Our team was invited to Ukraine to teach youth how to do mime outreach on the streets.

After we completed our three-week mission trip in Ukraine, I took off on my own to explore some other countries for a couple of more weeks. I was a bit worried about traveling alone in eastern Europe because I'd read some frightening stories. In that part of Europe, you have no idea who will be your roommates in a train cabin. As I boarded the train in Kyiv, I saw what looked like some tough male characters, and my heart began to beat a little faster. As it turned out, I ended up in a room with three young women. It felt awkward because, in that culture, walking around the cabin in your underwear was normal. But I at least felt safe. During the day, the women would giggle and practice their English on me.

I visited Auschwitz, Poland, where the infamous Nazi prison camp was located. I cried my way through the tour. I cried at the piles and piles of combs, brushes, shoes, and more. I cried at the gas chambers and ovens that cremated the bodies. It was a sorrowful time in history. Around then, I was beginning to understand the law of love and freedom. I could have some peace about why these catastrophes occurred, and the assurance they were not God's will.

From there I boarded another train, but only had a third-class seat this time. I was going to have to try to sleep sitting up all night. But I ended up in the wrong car, with a Swiss grandfather and his teenage granddaughter, who could translate Swiss to English. They persuaded the conductor to allow me to stay with them in second class. They had a bed for two by laying the opposite seats down, but they insisted that I stay and squeeze in with them. The grandpa snored all night, but it was sure good to lie down to sleep.

I traveled through East Germany, exploring the former wall between what had been East and West Berlin. I took a full day cruise down the Danube River. Next, I went to visit a former exchange student that I'd taught in high school. Her family royally welcomed me, and I stayed for a couple of days. Across the street from their house was the border with France. From there I took a train through Switzerland, where I visited my favorite mountain, the Matterhorn. Then, I went to Venice, Italy for a gondola ride, visited Rome, and the French Riviera. I ended the trip with a high-speed train up to Paris, from where I was going to fly home.

I got off that train in downtown Paris, and began looking at a subway map in order to find a train to Notre Dame. It was the next station up the track from where I was. I was standing, ready to board the next train, when I suddenly got the impression that this was not the right train. I went up to the top level and jumped onto a different train. Just as the doors closed, it dawned on me that the other train was actually the right one. I never had a problem understanding train directions in several different languages until Paris. Even though French was the language I was most familiar with, I could not figure out the routes for these trains.

I got off at the first station, and then went back to the former station. By the time I did that, there was no way that I could catch the train I had planned to take. I would have to wait for the next one. But when I arrived at the platform, there was yellow tape and police everywhere. I asked someone who spoke English about what was happening. I was informed that the train was closed down, and I would have to walk to Notre Dame.

I walked along the river all the way to Notre Dame Cathedral. When I arrived, I couldn't go into the Cathedral because there was more yellow tape, police, the military, helicopters, and ambulances. I found someone who explained that a bomb had gone off in the train between where I was supposed to get on and Notre Dame.

My legs felt like jelly. Now I knew the reason why I hadn't gotten on the correct train! I had to keep walking all the way to the Eiffel Tower. Then I walked up the stairs to save the price of an elevator. I was physically and emotionally exhausted by then. I later found another train to the central train station, where I'd planned to sleep on the floor like I usually did. But they kicked everyone out of the train station at midnight because of another bomb threat, so I walked the streets, wondering what to do. All the bars and cafés began to close around three in the morning, so I broke down and rented the first hotel room on my two-week journey. The next morning, I saw the reports on CNN. Over two hundred people were injured or killed in that bomb attack. Miracle, science, or coincidence?

An Undeniable Miracle

There was one miracle I witnessed in my college years that could never be explained by science or coincidence.

I had just arrived back from that trip to a college in Canada I wrote about in the first chapter. The weekend following the all-night drive back, I joined a van load of students heading to Idaho for another Bible conference. I was so tired that I found a way to lie down on the floor, stretching out underneath the seats between the feet of others. I found a small plastic bottle that just fit under my neck for a pillow.

I suddenly awoke because it was too quiet. Everyone was outside, standing around the open hood of an old station wagon. A mother and her daughter were stranded in the middle of nowhere because their car radiator had boiled dry. There was no water anywhere. I remembered that there was some in the bottle that I'd been using for a pillow. I went and retrieved the bottle from the van, but discovered that it was almost empty. There was about an inch of water in it, with some grass floating on it. It was practically nothing.

Someone suggested that we pray because there's a story in the Bible about a widow who had only a little oil. After Elijah prayed, the oil never ran out while he stayed with her and her son. So, we prayed, asking God to remember the widow's oil. One of the guys volunteered his shirt to cover the radiator opening to screen out the grass. Someone began to pour the water into the radiator. While they poured the water from the bottle, everyone was watching and chanting prayerfully, "Widow's oil. Widow's oil."

The water kept pouring and pouring for a long time. It was more than several bottles of water that came out of that one bottle. The radiator filled to overflowing. The woman and her daughter were wide-eyed and spellbound. They asked who in the world we were. Someone gave them a Christian tract and wished them well as we left. Miracle, science, or coincidence? Miracle!

Conclusion

We may always have questions regarding miracles. Why does God work a miracle for one person but not another person? We may never be able to determine if an event is a miracle, science, or coincidence in some circumstances. The only solution to these perplexing questions is faith. We don't have to figure it out. We don't have to have all the answers. I always go back to the law of love and freedom. God is good all the time, miracle, or no miracle. There is no love if there is no freedom, which is why God values freedom. It is only occasionally that God works a miracle. Faith is saying, "God, I don't have to know the answer to why (or why not) certain things happen, but I will continue to love and trust you anyway."

Faith is a bridge to freedom. Be free!

Recommended Reading
to Go Deeper

Abuse

The Emotionally Abusive Relationship
by Beverly Engel

Hurt People Hurt People
by Sandra D. Wilson

Acceptance

Abba's Child
by Brennan Manning

Addiction

In the Realm of Hungry Ghosts: Close Encounters with Addiction
by Gabor Maté, M.D.

Never Good Enough
by Carol Cannon

Broken Toys Broken Dreams
by Terry Kellogg

Anxiety

The Anxiety Cure
by Archibald D. Hart

When the Body Says No
by Gabor Maté, M.D.

Anger

Anger
by William Gray DeFoore

Assertiveness

The Assertiveness Workbook
by Randy J. Paterson

Borderline Personality Disorder

Sometimes I Act Crazy
by Jerold J. Kreisman, M.D. & Hal Straus

Boundaries

Boundaries
by Dr. Henry Cloud & Dr. John Townsend

The Brain

Mindsight: The New Science of Personal Transformation
by Daniel J. Siegel, M.D.

Codependency

Love is a Choice
by Dr. Robert Hemfelt, Dr. Frank Minirth, & Dr. Paul Meier

Depression

Unmasking Male Depression
by Archibald D. Hart

Forgiveness

Forgiveness is a Choice
by Robert D. Enright

Grace

In the Hands of a Loving God
by Brian Zahnd

What's So Amazing About Grace?
by Philip Yancey

God in Pain
by David Asscherick

Psychotherapy

Telling Yourself the Truth
by William Backus & Marie Chapian

How God Changes the Brain
Andrew Newberg, M.D. & Mark Waldman

Battlefield of the Mind
by Joyce Meyers

Awaken the Giant Within
by Tony Robbins

A Resilient Life
by Gordon MacDonald

Relationships

10 Lessons to Transform Your Marriage
by John Gottman

Love & Respect
by Dr. Emerson Eggerichs

The 5 Love Languages
by Gary Chapman

Self-Esteem

Approval Addiction: Overcoming Your Need to Please Everyone
by Joyce Meyer

Spiritual Growth

What's Your God Language?
by Dr. Myra Perrine

Rhythms of Rest
by Shelly Miller

Suffering

Disappointment with God
by Philip Yancey

Reaching for the Invisible God
by Philip Yancey

God bless your search for more understanding!

Reference List

Brand, Dr. Paul and Philip Yancey. 1993. *The Gift Nobody Wants.* New York, NY: HarperCollins Publishers.

Brittle, Zach. 2014. "P is for Problems." *The Gottman Institute* (blog). August 4, 2014. http://www.Gottman.com/blog/p-is-for-problems/.

Burney, Robert. 1995. *Codependence: The Dance of the Wounded Souls; A Cosmic Perspective of Codependence and the Human Condition.* Encinitas, CA: CreateSpace.

———. 2011. *Codependency Recovery: Wounded Souls Dancing in the Light.* Encinitas, CA: CreateSpace.

Butina, Ben. 2014, June 20. "What is Mindfulness?" Middlestream Mindfulness Group. YouTube video, 4:03. https://www.youtube.com/watch?v=0-YsqdHLP5o.

Cannon, Carol A. 1993. *Never Good Enough: Growing Up Imperfect in a "Perfect" Family; How to Break the Cycle of Codependence and Addiction for the Next Generation.* Nampa, ID: Pacific Press Publishing Association.

Chen, Jennifer. 2018. "The Connection Between a Healthy Marriage and a Healthy Heart. *Yale Medicine* (Stories), February 7, 2018. https://www.yalemedicine.org /stories/healthy-marriage-healthy-heart/.

Cherry, Kendra. 2019 (updated April, 2020). "The Study of Punishment in Psychology." *Verywell Mind*: About, Inc. (Dotdash). http://www.Verywellmind.com/what-is-punishment-2795413.

Cloud, Henry and John Townsend. 1992. *Boundaries: When to Say Yes, How to Say No, To Take Control of Your Life.* Grand Rapids, MI: Zondervan Publishing House.

Colier, Nancy. 2018. "What Is Forgiveness, Really?" *Psychology Today* (blog), March 15, 2018. https://www.psychologytoday.com/ca/blog/inviting-monkey-tea/201803/what-is-forgiveness-really.

Corsini, R. J., ed. 2001. *Handbook of Innovative Therapy*, 2nd ed. New York, NK: John Wiley & Sons, Inc.

Davis, Kenneth C. 2010. "America's True History of Religious Tolerance." *Smithsonian Magazine.* https://www.smithsonian.com/history/americas-true-history of-religious-tolerance-6132684/.

Defore, William G., Ph.D. 2004. *Anger: Deal With It, Heal With It, Stop It from Killing You.* Deerfield Beach, FL: Health Communications, Inc.

Divecha, Diana, Ph.D. 2018. "Can a Pregnant Woman's Experience Influence Her Baby's Temperament?" *Developmental Science* (blog), October 8, 2018. https://www.developmentalscience.com/blog/2018/10/1/can-a-pregnant-womans-experience-influence-her-babys-temperament.

Dollard, Christopher. 2017. "Invest in Your Relationship: The Emotional Bank Account." *The Gottman Institute* (blog). September 13, 2017. http://www.gottman.com/blog/invest-relationship-emotional-bank-account/.

Eareckson Tada, Joni. 2001. *Joni: An Unforgettable Story.* Grand Rapids, MI: Zondervan Publishing House.

Engel, Beverly. 2002. *The Emotionally Abusive Relationship.* Hoboken, NJ: John Wiley & Sons, Inc.

Enright, Robert D. 2001. *Forgiveness is a Choice: A Step-by-Step Process for Resolving Anger and Restoring Hope.* Washington, DC: American Psychological Association.

Enright, Robert D. and Richard P. Fitzgibbons. 2000. *Helping Clients Forgive: An Empirical Guide for Resolving Anger and Restoring Hope.* Washington, DC: American Psychological Association.

Forsyth, John P. and Georg H. Eifert. 2007. *The Mindfulness & Acceptance Workbook for Anxiety*. Oakland, CA: New Harbinger Publications, Inc.

Frankl, Viktor E. 2006. *Man's Search for Meaning*. Boston, MA: Beacon Press.

Gottman, John M. 2006. *10 Lessons to Transform Your Marriage*. New York, NY: Three Rivers Press.

Grant, Amy. 2010. "Better Than a Hallelujah." YouTube video, 3:57. Posted by AmyGrantOfficial, July 16, 2010. https://www.youtube.com/watch?v=Rm5kx3xqmg0.

Hari, Johann. 2015. *Chasing the Scream: The First and Last Days of the War on Drugs*. New/York, NY: Bloomsbury.

Hart, Archibald D. 1999. *The Anxiety Cure: A Proven Method for Dealing with Worry, Stress, And Panic Attacks*. Nashville, TN: Thomas Nelson, Inc.

————. (2001). *Unmasking Male Depression*. Nashville, TN: Thomas Nelson, Inc.

Hemfelt, R., F. Minirth, and P. Meier. 1989. *Love is a Choice: The Definitive Book on Letting Go of Unhealthy Relationships*. Nashville, TN: Thomas Nelson, Inc.

Hick, Kev. 2018. "8 Reasons Why Guys Shut Down Emotionally and How to Save Your Relationship!" *Girl Talk with Guys* (blog), February 16, 2018. https://www.girltalkwithguys.com/8-reasons-why-guys-shut-down-emotionally-and-how-to-save-your-relationship/.

Kellogg, Terry and Marvel Harrison. 1990. *Broken Toys Broken Dreams: Understanding and Healing Codependency, Compulsive Behaviors and Family*. Amherst, MA: BRAT Publishing.

Khoddam, Rubbin. 2014. "The Psychology of Forgiveness: A how-to guide on the science behind learning to forgive." *Psychology Today* (blog), September 16, 2014. https://www.psychologytoday.com/ca/blog/the-addiction-connection/201409/the-psychology-forgiveness.

Lipton, Bruce. 2020. "The Most Eye Opening 10 Minutes Of Your Life - A MUST SEE!!!" (Part 2) YouTube video, 10:48. Posted

by Never Give Up, January 9, 2020. http://www.youtube.com/
watch?v=h-kZHcW9sfM.

Manning, Brennan. 2002. *Abba's Child: The Cry of the Heart for
Intimate Belonging*. Colorado Springs, CO: Navpress.

Marcin, Ashley. 2017. "9 Ways Crying May Benefit Your Health."
healthline (blog). April 14, 2017. https://www.healthline.com/
health/benefits-of-crying.

Maté, Dr. Gabor. 2008. *In the Realm of Hungry Ghosts: Close Encounters
with Addiction*. Toronto, ON: Random House of Canada.

———. 2009. "Brain Development and Addiction with Gabor Maté."
YouTube video, 1:04:25. Posted by heartspeak, February 23, 2009.
https://www.youtube.com/watch?v=BpHiFqXCYKc&t=12s.

———. 2012. *When Your Body Says No*. Toronto, ON: Random House
of Canada.

McGonigal, Kelly. 2013. "How to Make Stress Your Friend." YouTube
video, 14:28. Posted by TED, September 4, 2013. https://www.
youtube.com/watch?v=RcGyVTAoXEU&t=39s.

McKeenhan, Toby, Ryan Stevenson, and Jamie Moore. 2012. "Speak
Life." Brentwood, TN: Capitol CMG, Inc.

Meyer, Joyce. 2008. *Approval Addiction: Overcoming Your Need to Please
Everyone*. Nashville, TN: FaithWords.

Meyers, Laurie. 2014. "Connecting with Clients." *Counseling Today:
A Publication for the American Counseling Association*. August 18,
2014. https://ct.counseling.org/2014/08/connecting-with-clients/.

Newberg, A., M.D and M.R. Waldman. 2009. *How God Changes
Your Brain: Breakthrough Findings from a Leading Neuroscientist*.
Ballantine Books New York, KY: Trade Paperbacks.

Pearson, Catherine. 2017. "Female Hysteria: 7 Crazy Things People
Used to Believe About the Ladies' Disease." *Huffpost*, Canadian
Edition. November 21, 2013. https://www.huffingtonpost.ca/
entry/female-hysteria_n_4298060?ri18=true&guccounter=1.

Rankin, Dr. Lissa. 2013. *Mind Over Medicine: Scientific Proof That You
Can Heal Yourself*. Carlsbad, CA: Hay House, Inc.

Robbins, Tony. 1991. *Awaken the Giant Within: How to Take Immediate Control of Your Mental, Emotional, Physical and Financial Destiny!* New York, NY: Simon & Schuster, Inc.

Schwarz N. and I. Skurnik. 2003. "Feeling and thinking: implications for problem solving." *The Psychology of Problem Solving.* Edited by J.E. Davidson and R. Sternberg. Cambridge, England: Cambridge University Press.

Seligman, Martin E. P. 2011. *Flourish: A Visionary New Understanding of Happiness and Well-being.* New York, NY: Free Press.

Shapiro, Francine. 2001. *Eye Movement Desensitization and Reprocessing: Basic Principles, Protocols, and Procedures*, 2nd ed. New York, NY: The Guilford Press.

Shapiro, F. and M.S. Forrest. 1997. *EMDR: The Breakthrough Therapy for Overcoming Anxiety, Stress, and Trauma.* New York, NY: Basic Books.

Siegel, D.J. 2011. *Mindsight: The New Science of Personal Transformation.* New York, NY: Bantam Books.

Simons, Daniel J. 2010. "The Monkey Business Illusion." YouTube video, 1:41. Posted by Daniel J. Simons, April 28, 2010. https://www.youtube.com/watch?v=IGQmdoK_ZfY.

Stokes, Kevin and Tony W. Wood. 1995. "Sometimes He Calms the Storm." Brentwood, TN: Capitol CMG Inc.

Van Leeuwen, M.S. 1996. "Five uneasy questions, or will success spoil Christian psychologists?" *Journal of Psychology and Christianity.* 15: 150-60.

Venden, Morris. 1994. *Modern Parables: Stories That Make Spiritual Truth Come Alive.* Nampa, ID: Pacific Press.

Wilson, James L. 2001. *Adrenal Fatigue: The 21st Century Stress Syndrome.* Petaluma, CA: Smart Publications.

Wilson, Sandra D. 2001. *Hurt People Hurt People: Hope and Healing for Yourself and Your Relationships.* Grand Rapids, MI: Discovery House Publishers.

Yancey, Philip. 1992. *Disappointment with God.* Grand Rapids, MI: Zondervan Publishing House.

———. 2000. *Reaching for the Invisible God.* Grand Rapids, MI: Zondervan Publishing House.

Zahnd, Brian. 2017. *Sinners in the Hands of a Loving God: The Scandalous Truth of the Very Good News.* New York: Penguin Random House.

Workshops and Training Opportunities for Churches and Businesses Offered by Don Straub

Bridges to Freedom Workshop

This is not a typical workshop with workbooks, note taking, and information as provided in a book like this one. It is an **experiential** workshop using music, video clips, small groups, and exercises involving moving around the room and interacting with other participants. This is what makes the workshop so powerful, creating change quickly. It is held on a weekend, which includes Friday evening (7:00 to 9:30 p.m.) followed by a full day on Saturday (9 a.m. to 6 p.m. with a break for lunch).

To discuss the possibility of holding a "Bridges to Freedom" workshop, contact Don Straub:

Email: kelownacounsellor@gmail.com
Phone: 250-869-7137

The following are some short testimonies
of a few who have participated.

Testimonials

My husband and I took the Bridges to Freedom course with Don. Not only did the course open new doors in our relationship with each other, it gave us both freedom within ourselves so we could move forward in a more positive light. Don has changed both our lives, and we are forever grateful for his knowledge and passion for helping others.

(Preschool teacher)

Bridges to Freedom is just that, a bridge to walk away from what holds you back in life and experience freedom. Don's kind heart, experience, and working with those who have trauma are insightful, supportive, and life-changing. He is a guide and support on this spiritual journey. I highly recommend the program and him for any of his services. You and I deserve these bridges to freedom!

(female participant)

Bridges to Freedom was very helpful.

(60+ year-old female, cake decorator)

I was looking for authenticity, and I found it here at Bridges to Freedom.

(60+ year-old female business owner)

The bridges to freedom workshop was such an emotional let go for me. It helped get rid of the emotions that I didn't realize were weighing me down for my whole life. It's such a freeing feeling.

(53-year-old female)

Bridges to Freedom weekend is based on love, healing, and growth; at least that's what it was for me. The process was food for my soul, healing for my broken heart, and peace through the storm. Don and his assistants were instrumental in guiding our group to Freedom.

(50-year-old Educator)

Bridges to Freedom was the turning point in my life when the lies that I had been believing about myself were identified. It was the start of replacing the lies with truth and beginning to heal from a lifetime of pain. Don's background in science, theology, psychology, and his personal experiences allows him to facilitate individuals on their journey to living in freedom.

(47-year-old female healthcare professional)

This workshop allowed me to gain insight into self and access my intrinsic power to make forward progress.

(Clinical Counselor, 37-year-old male)

When I attended Bridges to Freedom I anticipated that I would be dealing with issues concerning bondage of my past. But God had other plans and revealed the truth to me in an intimate special way, only when I was ready to listen. It was an extremely special and enlightening experience and I received freedom of something I was unaware I had been holding onto. I am grateful and so thankful that God knows and loves me best and knew I was ready to feel the healing He always had for me. I am so blessed to have had this opportunity to be free from part of my past.

(Female from Westbank, BC)

I attended Bridges to Freedom 6 years ago after leaving a very abusive relationship. It helped me to start healing my toxic past, and it taught me to start to believe in myself and to define my true Identity through God who created me and loves me unconditionally.

(61-year-old female Social Worker/
youth addiction counselor)

Bridges to Freedom classes were safe and beneficial for me to DEEPLY get in touch with myself. I was also able to forgive myself and others in my life; transformational and FREEING.

(a retired female)

Before I took the program, I did not like me at all. I really never left my house. After I finished the program, I got a job and now I am waiting to start college next month. All due to the program and GOD.

(38-year-old female)

43-yr-old male that got a lot of stuff released due to this course. It helped me deal with the underlying problem of my dad passing away at such a young age and never let go of it till I took this course.

Bridges to a Better Marriage

This workshop can be done over four weeks (assuming it is close to Kelowna, BC, Canada) or as a weekend "intensive" course. In this workshop, I provide quite a few handouts, mainly consisting of exercises on communication skills that a couple can take home and practice. They are meant to be fun exercises so couples can begin to communicate without the negative experiences that may have developed.

Most of the participants find the material covered to be very different and helpful from other workshops on marriage.

To discuss the possibility of holding a "Bridges to a Better Marriage" workshop, contact Don Straub:

Email: kelownacounsellor@gmail.com
Phone: 250-869-7137

Comfortable in Your Own Skin – The Art of Assertiveness

Many people are familiar with the books and video workshops on the topic of boundaries by Cloud and Townsend. In this workshop, I provide a combination of theory on boundaries with practical, hands-on experience in communicating boundaries using the skills of assertiveness.

About half of the time is devoted to practicing skills by breaking out into pairs. Each person in the pair gets an opportunity to practice an example of a practical situation and receive feedback from their partner. Participants pair up with a different partner for each new example situation.

The following skills are covered in the workshop:

1. Giving positive feedback
2. Receiving positive feedback
3. Giving your opinion
4. Saying "No" to a request
5. Giving constructive feedback
6. Receiving constructive feedback
7. Making a request

The workshop can be presented weekly (assuming it is close to Kelowna, BC, Canada) or as a "intensive" course. The number of sessions may vary according to the total time available and the desired depth of the content.

This workshop can be used in churches or corporate/business environments. The skills are useful within intimate relationships and in the workplace. It is especially useful for business owners and managers of employees.

To discuss the possibility of holding a "Comfortable in Your Own Skin" workshop, contact Don Straub:

Email: kelownacounsellor@gmail.com
Phone: 250-869-7137

Index

B

baggage, 155, 192, 235
barriers, 223, 224, 260, 273
beliefs
    feeling, 46, 47, 48, 51, 102, 117,
      122, 127, 129, 255
    negative, 9, 37, 125, 254, 255,
      256, 257
    positive, 256, 257
BFT sandwich, 194
brain
    autonomic, 42
    conscious, 42, 43, 44, 49, 259
    left and right, 132, 259
    logical, 42, 48, 147, 195, 218,
      255, 259
    middle, 42, 44
    unconscious, 111, 256, 259
    waves, 47
breath, 10, 42, 84, 85, 175, 249,
    250, 274
burn out, 115, 116
butterfly hug, 249, 250, 259

C

calm place, 249
catharsis, 144
CBT, 194, 244, 253, 258, 259
choice, 42, 44, 45, 60, 75, 76, 78,
    92, 94, 100, 113, 146, 152,
    163, 182, 189, 211, 227, 230,
    233, 234, 238, 252, 263, 264
codependent, 138, 139
commitment, 148
common sense, 149
community, 94, 113, 178, 223,
    224

concentration, 44, 247
condemnation, 18, 19, 20, 21,
    227
confession, 9, 14-16, 28-30, 168,
    188
consequences, 27, 29, 56, 77, 83,
    102, 120, 214, 215, 217, 227,
    262
control, 43, 72, 73, 92, 120, 134,
    147, 149, 150, 151, 153, 202,
    204, 205, 207, 208, 211, 212,
    218, 220, 228, 239, 247, 259,
    262
coping, 81, 111, 113
courage, 95, 148, 152, 188
crisis, 93, 94, 179
criticism, 119, 127, 210
cross, 4, 29, 30, 76, 88, 96, 137,
    172, 198, 221, 227, 268
crying, 3, 16, 46, 72, 79, 80, 91,
    98, 102, 129, 137, 142, 144,
    145, 155, 156, 173, 198, 212,
    237, 267

D

death, 5, 18, 29, 35, 59, 61, 68,
    69, 71, 72, 73, 74, 75, 77, 80,
    81, 84, 85, 86, 92, 94, 96, 97,
    105, 118, 121, 126, 143, 163,
    164, 189, 190, 231, 232, 246,
    265, 273
defensiveness, 125, 150
dependent, 139, 215, 269
depression, 63, 79, 102, 103,
    208, 228, 241, 242, 243, 244,
    245, 254
desensitization, 60, 254, 257

mindfulness, 44, 48, 53, 54, 93, 143, 144, 146, 147, 153, 195, 206, 218, 243, 247, 248-250, 252, 264

mirror neurons, 220

N

neglect, 117, 118, 253
neuro-connections, 110
neurofeedback, 43
nonverbal communication, 212

P

pain, 13, 35, 50, 51, 53, 56, 59, 60, 65, 72, 73, 76, 77, 79-88, 90, 93, 97, 111, 113, 114, 121, 122, 123, 145, 160, 161, 189, 191, 198, 216, 223, 228, 234, 235, 237, 246, 253, 255, 256, 257

parasympathetic system, 145, 251
passive, 192, 203, 205, 208, 209, 217, 218, 219
passive-aggressive, 205, 209, 217, 218
people pleaser, 8, 124, 134, 137
perspective, 26, 38, 39, 40, 72, 82, 117, 125, 182, 232, 260
placebo effect, 55
praise, 105, 115, 175, 178, 179, 181, 195, 203
prayer, 6, 9, 11, 15, 19, 27, 28, 65, 68, 72, 107, 128, 133, 137, 174, 188, 189, 194, 212, 227, 243, 244, 246, 260-265, 268, 272-275, 279

psychotherapy, 43, 50, 60, 112, 226, 239, 240, 259, 260
PTSD, 49, 64, 252
punishment, 19, 20, 21, 61, 83, 214, 216, 217, 219

Q

questions, 3, 14, 19, 74, 164, 190, 233, 240, 241, 255, 256, 262, 267, 276, 280

R

Rat Park, 113
reaction, 10, 45, 48, 49, 54, 59, 60, 87, 146, 147, 149, 193, 218, 226, 259
reconcile, 231
reconciliation, 221, 228, 231
recovery, 112, 114, 116, 124, 125, 126, 132
rejection, 8, 9, 10, 18, 102, 113, 124, 187, 206, 208, 223, 225, 256
relaxation, 123, 133, 145, 243, 251, 257
repentance, 3, 16, 18, 19, 21, 22, 28, 29, 30, 188
respect, 12, 32, 33, 152, 189, 206, 208, 210, 212
reticular formation, 36
revival, 3, 4, 5, 67
Robbins, Tony, 144, 190
roles, 33, 74, 75, 83, 156, 197, 198, 201, 208, 223, 224, 231, 234, 236, 258, 264
rumination, 7, 259

CPSIA information can be obtained
at www.ICGtesting.com
Printed in the USA
BVHW071446100820
585984BV00001B/16